THE LONG EXILE

THE
LONG EXILE

*A Tale of Inuit Betrayal and
Survival in the High Arctic*

MELANIE McGRATH

ALFRED A. KNOPF · NEW YORK · 2007

THIS IS A BORZOI BOOK
PUBLISHED BY ALFRED A. KNOPF

Originally published in Great Britain by Fourth Estate, an imprint
of HarperCollins Publishers, London, in 2006.

Knopf, Borzoi Books, and colophon are
registered trademarks of Random House, Inc.

Library of Congress Cataloging-in-Publication Data
McGrath, Melanie [date]
The long exile : a tale of Inuit betrayal and survival
in the high Arctic / Melanie McGrath.
p.   cm.
Includes bibliographical references.
ISBN 978-1-4000-4047-6 (hardcover)
1. Inuit—Relocation—Arctic regions. 2. Inuit—Government policy.
3. Indians, Treatment of—Arctic regions. 4. Wilderness survival—Arctic regions.
5. Racism—Political aspects—Canada. 6. Canada—Race relations.
7. Flaherty, Josephie. l. Title
E99.E7M473 2007
305.897'12—dc22   2006046852

Manufactured in the United States of America

First American Edition

An Eskimo lives with menace, it is always ahead of him, over the next white ridge.

—ROBERT FLAHERTY

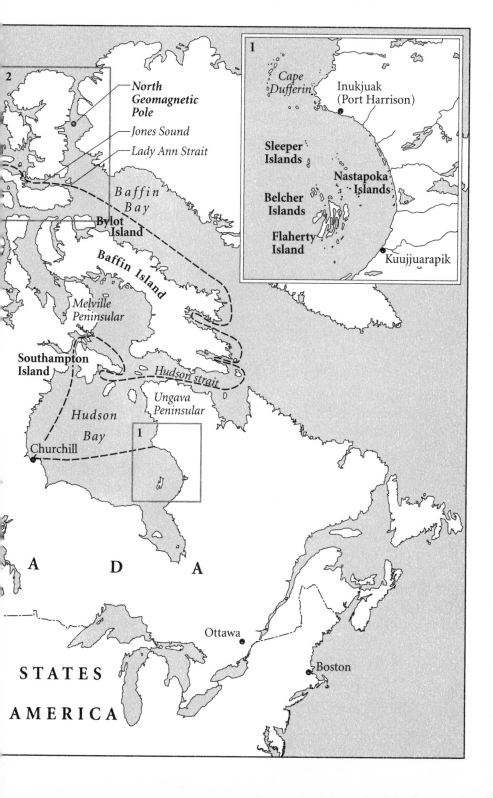

THERE HAVE BEEN many books written about the Arctic, mostly tales of explorers and derring-do. This book isn't one of those. It is rather the story of a movie and the legacy left behind by its maker. The film is *Nanook of the North,* which has been described by filmmakers as diverse as Orson Welles and John Huston as one of the greatest pictures ever made. Its Irish-American director, Robert Flaherty, arrived in the small settlement of Inukjuak on the east coast of the Hudson Bay in 1920 to make it. He filmed it in a year, but was haunted by it for the rest of his life. The movie's success helped colour the Western view of Inuit life in the Arctic for generations. It does so today. Flaherty never returned to the Arctic, but he left a son there, who grew up Inuit. More than thirty years later, a group of Inuit men and women were removed from Inukjuak by the Canadian government and taken hundreds of miles north to the uninhabited High Arctic. Among them was Robert Flaherty's son. This book is as much about Josephie Flaherty and his family as it is about his father's movie.

It is often said that the Inuit have dozens of words for snow. While this is true it doesn't tell the whole story. The Inuit *do* have many words to describe snow, but they also differentiate between various kinds of snow those of us who don't live in the Arctic would see as being essentially the same. It's not so much that the Inuit have dozens of *words* for snow, as that, in the Inuit world, there are dozens of different kinds of snow.

There are also emotional differences in the way Westerners and Inuit view the world. Until very recently, emotions like envy or sexual possessiveness were so perilous to the equilibrium of the Inuit—living as they did in family groups, often separated from each other by thousands of square miles of ice and tundra—that they were vigorously discouraged. There was a time when expressing rage, lust or ambition was considered so threatening to the group's survival that persistent offenders were ostracised from the community and sent to their deaths on the tundra; some were even killed outright, often by their own families. For thousands of years, these threatening emotional traits were suppressed to such a degree that they were rarely felt among the majority. Other, more helpful traits crept in to take their place: modesty, patience, acceptance of group decisions and a sense of being not just bound to the group, but being an integral part of it, a vital organ in the family body. These are more common and more valued character traits among Inuit even today than they are among people living in large cities in the West.

Although it regularly occurs, we are not necessarily aware of a similar process of emotional editing taking place in our own lives. It's not hard to recall feelings those of us living urban lives have allowed to wither: a wonder and respect for nature, a feeling of being at one with the land, an inexorable identification with home and family, a sense of belonging. We may regret the passing of these feelings; indeed, if our appetites for nostalgia are anything to go by, we certainly do, but few of us would want to go back and live as our great-great grandfathers and grandmothers lived; nor must we in order to feel respect, even awe, for what our ancestors endured and the kind of people they were.

It is easy to feel disconnected from human beings to whom we are neither related by blood nor fate and with whom we share few cultural connections; people whose range of emotional expression and personalities may feel very different from our own or from anyone we know.

And so, when you read this story, bear this in mind: however many kinds of snow there are and however many words for them, they all, in the end, melt down to water.

THE LONG EXILE

CHAPTER ONE

IN THE EARLY AUTUMN of 1920, Maggie Nujarluktuk became a woman with another name. It happened something like this. Maggie was sitting on a pile of caribou skins. She had a borrowed baby in her *amiut,* the fur hood of her parka. A man was filming the scene. His name was Robert Flaherty. Maggie was about to pull the baby out of the *amiut* and set him to play beside a group of puppies as Flaherty had instructed, when looking up from his camera, he said, "Smile," grinning to show Maggie what he was getting at and told her, through an interpreter, that he had decided to change her name. She laughed a little, perhaps conscious of his eyes, blue as icebergs, then lifted the baby into her arms, placed him beside her and pulled the puppies closer to keep him warm.

"Well, now, Maggie," Robert said. He winked at her, wound the camera and lingered on her face. She watched his breath pluming in the chill Arctic air.

"How's about Nyla?" He allowed the name to roll around his mouth. "Yes, from now on you are Nyla."

If Maggie minded this, she didn't say. She already knew she had no choice in the matter anyway.

Maggie Nujarluktuk was very young back then (how young she didn't know exactly), and very lovely, with a broad, heart-shaped face, unblemished by sunburn or frostbite or by the whiskery tattoos still common among Ungava Inuit women. Her thick hair lay in lush coils around her shoulders and her skin and eyes were as yet unclouded by years of lamp smoke or by endless sewing in poor light. Her lips were bowed, plump but fragile-seeming, and it was impossible to tell whether her smile was an invitation or a warning. Beneath the lips lay even teeth that were white and strong, not yet worn to brown stumps from chewing boots to make them soft. And Robert Flaherty had just renamed her Nyla, which means the Smiling One.

Robert Flaherty's movie had begun in something of a rush. Only three weeks earlier, on 15 August, the schooner, *Annie*, had dropped anchor at the remote Arctic fur post of Inukjuak, on the Ungava Peninsula on the east coast of Hudson Bay, and a tall, white man with a thin nose and craggy features had come ashore with his half-breed interpreter, introduced himself to the local Inuit as Robert Flaherty, and announced his intention to stay in the area long enough to make a motion picture there. The film, he said, was to be about daily life in the Barrenlands.

The stranger moved into the fur post manager's old cabin, a peeling white clapboard building on the south bank of the Innuksuak River and hired a few hands to help him shift his things from the shoreline where the *Annie's* crew had left them. Among the expected baggage of coal-oil lamps, tents and skins were the unfamiliar accoutrements of film-making, lights, tripods, cameras and film cans, plus a few personal belongings: a violin and a wind-up gramophone with a set of wax discs and three framed pictures, one a photograph of Arnold Bennett, another of Flaherty's wife, Frances, the third a little reproduction of Frans Hals' *Young Man with a Mandolin*. The number of possessions suggested that Robert Flaherty was settling down for a long stay. Within a day or two of his arrival, he had hung his pictures above the desk in his cabin, lined up his books along a home-made shelf, rigged up a darkroom, setting several old coal-oil barrels outside the door to serve as water tanks for washing film, and found three young men he could pay to haul his water and supply him with fresh meat and fish. By the time a week was up, the cabin looked as though it had always been his home and Flaherty was busy assembling his lights and cameras and running tests. In the evenings, he could be heard humming along with his gramophone (he was particularly fond of Harry Lauder singing "Stop Your Ticklin' Jock") or playing Irish jigs on his fiddle.

The local Inuit were not much used to white visitors, and the new arrival turned the little settlement of Inukjuak upside down. No one knew quite how to place Robert Flaherty. His particular brand of whirlwind energy was new to them. Nor had they ever come across a *qalunaat,* a white man, with such sturdy warmth and rushing good humour. The fur traders they had encountered were glum and troubled and fond friends of the whisky bottle. News of the stranger spread, and the Inukjuamiut, as the people living around Inukjuak are called, began coming in from outlying camps to inspect this new addition to their world. Flaherty greeted them all with smiles and gifts of ship's biscuits and this, too, felt out of the ordinary. A few wondered, darkly, what the strange *qalunaat* wanted from them and drifted back out to their camps, but more stayed on, intrigued by the stranger and eager to audition for a part in the movie he said he was about to make.

Flaherty was soon holding try-outs on the river bank in front of the fur post manager's cabin. To play his leading man he picked a strong, good-natured fellow in his thirties called Alakariallak, who was renowned throughout Cape Dufferin for his hunting prowess. Flaherty renamed him Nanook, meaning "bear." To play one of Nanook's wives Flaherty chose a local woman called Cunayou, to play the other, Maggie Nujarluktuk.

This was not Robert Flaherty's first attempt at making an Arctic film, but it *was* almost certainly his last chance to get it right. A few years later, when he had become famous, a journalist asked him why he had persisted back then, after so many setbacks and difficulties, and he replied, as he often did, with an aphorism, saying that "every man is strong enough for the work on which his life depends." In 1920 Robert Flaherty believed his life depended on this movie. And, as it turned out, he was right.

Flaherty had first pitched up in the Canadian Arctic ten years previously, looking for iron ore, in the employ of Sir William Mackenzie, a Canadian mine owner and railroad baron whom Flaherty had met through his father. Mackenzie had invested considerable capital in a transcontinental railway across Canada and he was planning to lay track as far north as Churchill, Manitoba, a bleak Barrenlands settlement on the west coast of Hudson Bay. Mackenzie's goal was to link the railway with a new shipping route across the bay and thereby create the shortest navigation between the wheat plains of Manitoba and the flour mills of Europe, which were then connected overland and by sea through the St. Lawrence River to the Atlantic. There were additional benefits, which Mackenzie, being a good businessman, had not ignored. It was well known that Hudson Bay's seabed was rich in iron ore—for centuries whalers had reported compass interference whenever they sailed there—and some enormous iron ore lodes had been discovered on the east coast of the Bay in the Ungava Peninsula just north of Labrador. Mackenzie reckoned there might be money to be made extracting the ore and shipping it to Europe.

His geologic interest focused on the Nastapoka Islands, a cluster of granite nubs lying just off the east coast of Hudson Bay at 57° North. The Nastapokas had figured in some prospectors' logs as being worthy of exploration. Inuit had been living in the area for thousands of years but the place was only scantily mapped and virtually unknown to white men. Mackenzie needed someone young and ambitious with courage and flair, even a little recklessness, to blaze a route through. In 1910 he chose Robert Flaherty. The railroad baron had employed Flaherty's father, Robert Flaherty Sr., and knew the family from the old days, when the American frontier was still open and the Flaherty family had helped to settle it. At twenty-six, Robert Jr. already had a reputation for adventurous prospecting in the northern forests of Canada and although he had had no direct experience of the Barrenlands, Mackenzie felt inclined to take the risk on him.

The Flahertys had come over from Ireland sometime during or just after the potato famine and, travelling south from Quebec, they had settled in the tough mining country of Michigan. There Robert Jr.'s father, Robert Henry Flaherty, had met and married Susan Klöckner, the daughter of Catholics from Koblenz. Robert Henry had done well for himself, buying up a modest little mine at the foot of Iron Mountain, Michigan, where Robert Joseph was born, on 16 February 1884, the first of seven children.

The family lived a comfortable upper-middle-class life. Robert Jr. grew up with a love for the outdoors and a disdain for civilisation which was remarkable even among boys living in the wilds of Michigan. This untroubled existence came to a sudden end, though, in 1893, when the price of iron ore slumped and Robert Sr. was forced to lock out the miners at his Iron Mountain operation and later, when things did not improve, to close the mine down altogether. Of necessity, he took up a position as a mining engineer in the tiny backwater of Lake of the Woods in upper Ontario, leaving his wife to bring up their children alone.

Susan Klöckner was a loving, devout and uneducated woman and she did her best to raise Robert Joseph in the fear of God, but none of her sermonising appeared to have the slightest effect on her eldest son. If there was a god in Robert Flaherty's life he was to be found in the woods with the bears.

So the boy grew up wild, and when Robert Henry returned to Michigan his son begged to go with him on his next posting to a remote outpost, the Golden Star Mine in Rainy Lake, Ontario. It was a Huckleberry Finn kind of a life and Robert Jr. took to it like a trout to tickling. For two years father and son camped out in the woods, hunting rabbits, tracking bear and learning woodcraft from the local Ojibwa Indians. During the long winter nights, the boy lost himself in the adventure stories of James Fenimore Cooper and

R. M. Ballantyne and in the long summer evenings Robert Sr. taught his son to play the Irish fiddle. Robert Jr. learned some sharper lessons from the Ojibwa too. Years before, miners and fur trappers had brought booze and misery into the lives of the Indians living in northern Ontario. The sight of strong, capable men staggering around begging moonshine off the miners crept across the young Robert's tender heart like a shadow. If this was what men called civilisation, then he wanted no part of it.

When Robert Sr.'s two years in Rainy Lake were up, the Flaherty family moved on again, to the Burleigh Mine back near Lake of the Woods. Deciding their son needed some formal education, Susan and Robert Henry dispatched Robert Jr. to Upper Canada College in Toronto. The college was run with the rigid discipline of an English public school. It was intended to whip the boy into shape, but only made a square hole for a round peg. Robert Jr. soon contrived to get himself expelled, returning to Port Arthur (now Thunder Bay) on Lake Superior, where the Flaherty family were then living and enrolling in the local school. Even there Robert Jr. chafed against any kind of formal instruction, preferring instead to spend most of his time with the English mining engineer and adventurer, H. E. Knobel, who encouraged the boy's fiddle playing as well as his fantasies.

It was through Knobel that Flaherty first heard tell of Hudson Bay, a remote seaway bitten out of the eastern Canadian mainland. Knobel had been canoeing there and had stories to tell of the rapids he had paddled, the portages he had passed and the Indians and Inuit he had met on the way. The young Robert was so taken with Knobel's stories of adventure in remote places that, after a final and brief flirtation with book learning at Michigan College of Mines, he gave up formal education altogether and went north, into the woods to prospect for ore, hoping, one day, to travel as far as Hudson Bay. When, in 1910, Sir William Mackenzie asked him to lead an expedition to the Nastapokas, Robert Jr. felt his destiny calling. He did not hesitate.

Taking his tent, his rockhound kit, canoes and an Indian guide, the twenty-six-year-old Flaherty paddled along the Mattagami River north, across some of Canada's toughest portages, then followed the Moose River as far as the Hudson Bay trading post at Moose Factory in James Bay, a broad finger off the southernmost curve of Hudson Bay. At the factory, he stopped briefly to resupply, then took a boat to Chariton Island and hitched a ride on a schooner going north to Fort George. There he came upon an encampment of Inuit who guided him to the Hudson Bay post at Great Whale, otherwise known as Kuujjuarapik, a tiny settlement on the tree line, at the edge of the Barrenlands.

Flaherty was used to wilderness, but no wilderness he had ever experienced matched this. The Barrenlands made the deep, silent forests and rugged hills of his childhood seem as safe as apple orchards. He felt the flinty, lichen-painted sweep of the tundra and the great expanses of sea and ice and sky as a swelling in his chest. The starkness of the place enthralled him. It was as though every step farther north was a footfall on a new discovery. The tundra rolled out, empty and uncompromised, all around him. If any land could be said to be the antidote to the diseased, corrupted, famine-ridden Ireland of his ancestors, it was here, where there were none of the tired overlays of human history, only the shallow sun and the shadows of low clouds chasing along the rock. Nowhere, not even in northern Ontario, had Flaherty felt more free.

He took on some Inuit guides at Kuujjuarapik and was soon as captivated by them as he had been by their land. These men understood the Barrens in a way Flaherty had never understood Michigan or lower Canada. Only now, in all this emptiness, did he begin fully to comprehend the fullness around him. He watched these men pull their living from it. He saw them moving over the fearsome weft of ice and stone as if it were a carpet and across the sea as if it were a lawn. He had grown up a witness to the demoralisation of the Indians who lived to the south. But these Barrenlanders were different. They still seemed in possession of a raw, unquestioning confidence, a strong, visceral simplicity which had long been lost at the tree line and, further south, in the hubbub of the cities. This huge, open terrain lived in them. You could not separate them from the environment, as the Indians had been separated from theirs. Without the Barrens, they would cease to exist. It dawned on Flaherty that he was witnessing something unique and precious, a window into an older and, perhaps, a better world.

The Inuit were not the first people to visit the Arctic. That accolade belongs to the Indians. As early as 5500 B.C.E., Indians had been moving from the forest on to the tundra in summer, following the migration routes of caribou, and they continued to move seasonally on to the Barrenlands for the next two thousand or three thousand years, until a change in the climate drove them back down south. It was not until some time between 3000 B.C.E. and 2200 B.C.E. that the Inuit crossed the Bering Strait, which was then a land bridge, into what is now North America, and spread eastwards until, by 1000 B.C.E., they had reached Labrador. The Inuit were the first people to occupy the Arctic permanently and they brought with them two technologies essential to their survival there, the bow and arrow and the *kayak*. From time to time they encountered Indians and when they did there were skirmishes, but for the most part they lived, untroubled, for two thousand years or more until around 1000 A.D. when they had contact first with Vikings then with European adventurers, the best known of whom was Martin Frobisher, who arrived on Baffin Island in 1576 looking for gold. By the seventeenth century whaling ships from Scotland and North America were making regular forays into Arctic waters and overwintering in Hudson Bay. There they set up whaling camps to which the Inuit were drawn by the promise of paid work and by metal knives and, later, by rifles.

The Inuit were friendly towards Robert Flaherty, perhaps because they sensed his admiration for them. He was genial and gave off an air of integrity without ever being stiff or formal. Unlike most *qalunaat* he seemed genuinely keen to learn Inuktitut and the Inuit at Kuujjuarapik quickly got the sense that he saw them as equals and understood that, in the Barrenlands, it was they and not white men who were kings. His good manners, amiability and his fiddle-playing all helped endear him to them, as did his willingness to pay for the guiding and hunting they did for him. In the long history of contact between whites and Inuit, he was, they could see, someone quite rare. White men like Flaherty were hard to find in Inuit country.

From Kuujjuarapik, Flaherty continued north, and, after four months of travelling, he finally reached the Nastapoka Islands in January 1911. He and his guides set up camp and he began immediately to explore, digging through the hard-packed snow for rock samples and documenting everything he saw with photographs. He also took pictures of the men and women he encountered along the way. In their company, he began to feel both recognised and exposed. Their resilience, their competence and their good humour touched him. More than that, he felt drawn to their wildness and after only a few days in the Nastapokas he began to sense his destiny lay not in the rock but in these people and the way they made him feel.

After returning to Toronto to report his findings, Flaherty almost immediately found an excuse to go back up north. This time his aim was the Belcher Islands, an obscure cluster of rocks off the coast of Cape Dufferin, just south of the Nastapokas. The cape occupied an area the size of England and had a population of two hundred Inuit, some of whom hunted walrus out on the Belchers. On the Nastapoka trip he had been told of the existence of a large island in the Belcher group whose tall blue cliffs bled when scraped and this suggested to Flaherty the presence of high-grade iron ore there. The island did not appear on any of the maps and there was no mention of it in any navigation charts, but Flaherty had witnessed the precision with which the Barrenlanders memorised their landscape and were able to recall its contours. He decided not to believe the maps but to put his trust in the Inuit instead.

The following year, he set out in the sixty-three-foot sloop,

Nastapoka, but was forced back to Kuujjuarapik by bad weather. Running low on supplies, he sailed south to Fort George to restock and when the sea froze over some months later he took off once again, this time by dog sled, intending to cross the Ungava Peninsula to Cape Dufferin, then complete the remainder of the journey to the Belchers on the sea ice. That far north, he figured, the ice would be stable. He was wrong. The ice proved so turbulent that year that Flaherty had to abandon his original plan. Instead, he decided to cross the Ungava Peninsula and try to reach Fort Chimo, or Kuujuak, on the eastern side. It was a crazy plan. Ungava was an unmapped, treeless tundra the size of Norway. No white man had yet crossed it from one side to the other, partly because travelling in the interior was exceedingly dangerous. Away from the coast, the only available food, aside from the odd Arctic hare, lemming or fox, was caribou and the caribou populations had been radically reduced since the introduction of rifles to the region. The adventurer Albert Peter Low had recently been forced to turn back from the Ungava interior to the coast on the point of starvation and Flaherty had none of Low's experience.

Undaunted, Flaherty hired three Inuit guides, "Little" Tommy, Tookalok and Wetallok, and the four men took off on three dog sleds. For several days they followed Wetallok until the guide finally admitted that he had no idea where they were but had been too proud to say. Poor weather set in and the men, weary and hollow with hunger, had no choice but to stop and dig in. Over the next few days, frostbite got to them, snow blindness followed close behind, but they could do nothing except sit inside their snowhouse waiting for the storms to clear, making mental lists of the dogs they would eat and in what order. Flaherty wrote in his diary that the temperature fell so low the dogs vomited from the cold. The four men survived, but did not reach the Belchers.

Flaherty set out again to go north the following year, 1913. In St. John's, Newfoundland, he bought a seventy-five-foot topsail sloop, *Laddie,* and had her rerigged and belted with greenheart to withstand ice. He loaded up his rock hammers, his acids, litmus and sampling bottles and this time he took along a Bell and Howell movie camera, portable lights, film stock and a developer and printer. His photographs had generated some interest in the south and he wanted to capitalise on that. By now, Flaherty was a good deal less interested in iron ore than he was in the ordinary life of the Barrenlanders. Wherever he went, he sensed that Inuit culture had already been compromised by contact with whaling crews and white explorers and he was desperate to film a way of life whose existence was fragile. He begged to be taken along on *kayak* trips and to be taught how to flense seals and sew clothes from caribou skins. At every opportunity he got out his camera and filmed. On one of his filming expeditions to the interior of Baffin, Flaherty's *komatik,* dog sled, broke through some rotten ice and his film fell into the water and was ruined but with his characteristic aplomb Flaherty took this setback in his stride. When Christmas came that year, he threw a party and Inuit sledged in from camps two days away at Fair Ness and the Isle of God's Mercy and Markham Bay to see what the *qalunaat* had to offer. Flaherty treated them all to "varicoloured paper hats" and to tinned sardines. He was delighted by his new friends and, by and large, they returned the compliment.

On 14 August the following year, *Laddie* sailed into Hudson Bay on a course for the Belchers. A week later the islands hoved into view, exactly as the Inuit had described them: a hand of long, icy fingers the chief of which bore blue spiny cliffs. The *Laddie* moved towards this largest island but as she did so, a terrific gust of wind roared out of nowhere, blew her on to a reef and tore a hole in her hull. The crew piled into the whaleboat and made for the shore. Flaherty decided there was nothing to be done but to get on with what he had come here to do. Once the prospecting was finished, they would have to rely on the little whaleboat to get them across the notorious waters of Hudson Bay back to the safety of Moose Factory. Over the weeks that followed, Flaherty collected samples, labelled and weighed, took pictures and sketched plans of the location and distribution of the iron ore. Then he and his men clambered into the whaleboat, said a quick prayer, and turned south.

Late August/early September is storm season in the eastern Arctic and the little whaleboat was buffeted around like a twig in a stream. It took them ten days to travel the eight hundred miles south. Several times they considered themselves as near to dead as made no difference. Eventually, the outline of the Moose Factory post came into view and they raced towards it, feeling they were finally safe. When they got close they noticed that the post flag was at half-mast and assumed some dreadful calamity had befallen the post. They disembarked with caution and were greeted by Monsieur Duval, the post factor, dressed in linens and a straw hat, who explained that he had set the flag at half-mast because he missed his beloved Normandy and longed for a little Camembert and a glass of apple brandy and sensed that France and all her loveliness was for ever lost to him.

Before leaving on the Belcher expedition, Flaherty had used his time in the south to court Frances Hubbard, the daughter of eminent geologist Lucius L. Hubbard. Now he returned to her and, despite rumours that Flaherty's affections were not confined to Frances alone, the couple were married in New York City on 12 November 1914, with Frances buying the ring. A friend of theirs later noted that Robert "was like a light and [Frances] was like a sensitive photographic plate." The couple passed their first winter together editing what remained of Flaherty's film of Inuit life and the following spring they showed a rough cut at the Convocation Hall in the University of Toronto, where the picture was met with a wall of polite incomprehension.

By the autumn of 1915, Robert and Frances were apart once more. Robert spent that Christmas back at the Belchers, feasting on pea soup and currant buns and whiling away the time it took for the sea ice to freeze solid teaching the Inuit how to sing "London Bridge Is Falling Down." Between times he set his camera rolling. The following September he headed south, with thirty thousand feet of exposed film.

The Flahertys worked through the early winter of 1916 and by Christmas they had a rough cut of the new film prepared and printed. This they sent off to Harvard in the hope that the university might screen it and Robert set himself to the business of refining the edit. As he was sitting over the negative one day, concentrating on the frames, a cigarette dropped from his fingers on to the film can, and the film flared, and burst into twists of flame before finally slumping to the floor in a heap of blackened celluloid. It was a bad film, Flaherty said later. He would just have to go back out to the Arctic and make a better one.

But not on Sir William Mackenzie's time. Flaherty's old benefactor had long since turned his real attentions away from Arctic ore to the war in Europe. There was no money to be had for Flaherty's adventures from that quarter and Flaherty had none himself. For a while, he ploughed his energies into the lecture circuit and making babies. Frances gave birth to three girls in close succession: Barbara, Frances and Monica. The new family moved to Houghton, Michigan, to stay with Frances' parents, then found a house of their own in New Canaan, Connecticut. But the empty spaces of the Arctic tapped on Flaherty's heart and he longed to return.

In the early spring of 1920, he saw his chance. At a particularly dreary cocktail party in New York he was introduced to Captain Thierry Mallet of the Révillon Frères trading company. Flaherty was a warm, convivial man, and he was used to people gravitating towards him, rewarding them for their attention with his rough-tough tales of the kind of pioneer life which already seemed to belong to another, more fascinating, age. Thierry Mallet was no exception. Mallet knew the settings of Flaherty's tales. Révillon Frères had recently opened posts in the Ungava Peninsula to capitalise on the Arctic fox populations there. The fur trade was picking up after a long wartime stagnation. As Mallet told Flaherty, a good white Arctic fox pelt was now selling at the wholesale fur market in Montreal for C$25 and Mallet's company was feeling buoyant. Its great rivals still needled it, though. The Hudson Bay Company was celebrating its 350th anniversary that year and Révillon Frères was hoping to outdo its rivals when it came to celebrating its own 200th anniversary in three years' time. Did Flaherty have any good ideas, Captain Mallet wondered.

As it happened, Flaherty did. His idea, he told Mallet, was to make an adventure film about an astonishing group of people living in a world of unimaginable harshness, a world in which Révillon Frères also operated. It would be the first film of its kind, a genuine trailblazer and he, Flaherty, would be willing to sell Révillon Frères the rights to it. Flaherty saw Mallet's eyes take on a new intensity. He was in.

A few weeks later, the venerable Révillon Frères company signed a contract promising Flaherty C$11,000 in exchange for the rights to his as yet unmade Arctic adventure film and on 18 June 1920 Flaherty found himself at the railhead in northern Ontario with some new camping equipment, a canoe, a Haulberg electric-light plant and projector and two movie cameras. Just about two months after that, on board the schooner *Annie,* Flaherty "let go anchor at the mouth of the Innuksuak River and the five gaunt and melancholy-looking buildings" of the post "stood out on a boulder-ridden slope less than half a mile away," as he wrote in his diaries.

By the time he reached Inukjuak in 1920, Robert Flaherty had a good sense of what he needed to do and how to do it. Before he left New York he had paid a visit to the Craftsman Laboratories to get advice from Terry Ramsaye and Martin Johnson, who were trying to put together an adventure film from Johnson's various travels in the tropics. Film-making was new and, in spite of his experience filming on Baffin Island, Flaherty was unsure about the grammar of film sequences and shots. He had also updated his equipment. The Akeleys he had bought to replace the earlier Bell and Howell used graphite for lubrication rather than oil so they were less likely to freeze. They were also the first cameras to be fitted with gyroscopic tripod heads allowing the camera to be tilted and panned by a single movement without too much jerking. Eastman Kodak had provided an old English Williamson printing machine, which Flaherty screwed to the wall of his cabin beside his Frans Hals print. He had also brought developing fluid and a small battery of lightweight lights and a Graflex stills camera, and soon after his arrival in Inukjuak he fixed up a rudimentary darkroom with a drying annex, heated by a coal-burning stove, in which to dry the developed film.

So Flaherty finds himself in this tiny, remote settlement, with nothing but his equipment, a few pictures, his gramophone and a tremendous sense of his own destiny. He is keen to begin filming before the weather closes in and ice creeps across the sea so he takes Alakariallak, Maggie and Cunayou out along the coast and he films his first sequence, of hunter, wives, children and dogs all emerging, one by one, and as if by magic, from the one-man *kayak* seat. It's a bit of a joke, a moment of comedy in what will, he hopes, be a tense and dramatic tale of survival against the odds. He films Maggie pulling the baby from her *amiut* and setting him down among the husky pups. He watches her smile through the Akeley. He says, "Smile!"

A few days later, Flaherty sets up the projector in his cabin and invites his cast in for a viewing. He offers round hot tea and sea biscuits and quickly discovers that Maggie, Alakariallak and the rest have no idea what a film is or, for that matter, what the images represent. When he shows them stills of themselves, they hold them upside down and he has to take them to a mirror before they are able to understand what it is they are looking at. Finally, when everyone is crammed in and settled and seems to have at least some idea of why they are there, he runs the rushes, noting with satisfaction, later in his diary, the gasps and giggles of his cast as they recognise themselves in black and white and two dimensions.

Summer is short in the Arctic and this one is quickly done. By mid-September the summer birds are gone and the long winter is once more closing in like a fist around Inukjuak and the business of making a movie suddenly becomes a good deal more complicated. Inukjuak lies south of the Arctic Circle but by October the light is already limited to six hours a day and by November there is only sufficient daylight for three hours' filming. The water for washing the film begins to ice up and, as winter grips, Flaherty's helpers are forced to cut a hole through six feet of ice, pull water up in buckets, pour it into barrels and load it on to a fourteen-foot-long sled hauled by a ten-dog sled team to the little cabin. A constant wind sends smoking whorls of dry snow blasting into the camera lens, blizzards break open and in a matter of minutes the cast are unable to see as far as their own hands. As temperatures drop, film shatters inside the cameras from the cold and the men are forced to stash the retorts and sometimes even the cameras inside their parkas to keep them warm enough to work. The moment the cameras are brought into the relative warmth of the cabin, they frost up and have to be taken apart and dried piece by piece. One time the Graflex is so badly affected by condensation that Flaherty has to dismantle it completely only to discover that he cannot recall how to put it back again and one of his Inuk helpers has to sit down at his table and gradually, by candlelight, put it back together.

Flaherty constantly finds himself having to charge after hunters too excited by the prospect of a kill to stop and remember to pose for the camera. He spends a good deal of time trying to persuade the Inuit to repeat their actions or simply stand where they are told. Maggie and Cunayou fall out. There are disputes over pay.

But none of these setbacks seems to discourage the film-maker for long. He bounces from day to day in a kind of ecstatic trance. In his spare time he fiddles for the locals, or sets up impromptu screenings of his rushes. In all the excitement, the contradictions of his ambition pass him by. Here he is, a white man banked by a fur trader, making a film about an idealised kind of Inuit life which, if it ever existed, has long since been turned upside down by, among others, white men and fur traders.

By November the sea around Inukjuak is frozen firm and by December it is stable enough to travel on long distance. At Christmas, Flaherty throws his customary party for the Inuit, serving up sardines and sweet tea, and making a space in the fur store to dance square reels and Irish jigs. When the New Year arrives he decides that what his film needs is a polar bear hunt. The bears are rarely seen around Inukjuak but Alakariallak says that female bears often pass the winter with their cubs in dens at Cape Sir Thomas Smith, two hundred miles north along the Ungava coastline, and so, on 17 January 1921, Flaherty sets off with Alakariallak and another man he has nicknamed Harry Lauder after the singer and the party turns north. They reckon on being away a month, allowing ten days each for the journey there and back and another ten for bad weather, stopping to film wherever they find polar bear. But the going proves difficult, the ice near to the coast pushed into mountainous pressure ridges and the dogs hard-pressed to pull the sleds over broken ice fields and knife-sharp candle ice, and when eventually they reach Cape Sir Thomas Smith there are no polar bears. For a few days they meander across the cape, one time travelling all day and night only to find themselves within two miles of their starting point. No bears. The dogs become more and more desperate from cold and hunger until they eventually stage a rebellion, making a dash for the shelter of the hunters' snowhouse and refusing to allow themselves to be harnessed, and Alakariallak has to carry the lead dog to the sled whimpering with misery and cold. Still, they see no bears. One by one the dogs begin to starve. The men are so cold now and so low on fuel, they are reduced one night to burning the cross bars from the *komatik* to keep them warm. The following night they have nothing left for a fire but film. Four two-hundred-foot rolls are sacrificed to boil water for their tea. They lose two dogs to starvation before Flaherty finally makes the decision to turn back for home. In eight weeks away they have not run into a single bear. They begin the return journey by day, travelling in small bursts, walking beside the sleds whose dogs are by now too weak to pull them. The sea ice pours on either side, as flat and formless as a newly ironed sheet. As they walk, Alakariallak keeps them cheerful with stories of the bears he has killed the year before. At night they build a makeshift snow-house and he sings them versions of the songs he has heard on Flaherty's gramophone. The following day they stumble into Inukjuak, dark with snow blindness, their hearts like old stones, their noses half eaten by frostbite, their feet frozen into their boots, hardly able to believe they are alive still.

The Révillon Frères post manager, Stewart, comes out to meet them, brings them back to the cabin, unwraps their feet and sets them up with mugs of hot, sweet tea. Only the week before, he reports, two huskies dug a female bear and her two cubs from their den a couple of hours' travel away from the settlement. The bear and her cubs battled it out against the dogs and sent them spinning into the air and sliding back on their bellies. There was no need to have gone all the way to Cape Sir Thomas Smith. For a moment silence falls. Then Alakariallak grabs his sides with both hands and laughs and laughs so hard that tears leak from his eyes.

Perhaps it is this brush with mortality which draws Robert Flaherty closer to Maggie Nujarluktuk. In any case, he begins to spend more time with her. Everything about Maggie must seem so fresh, so unpolished and innocent, as different from the huddle of sophisticates Flaherty knows in New York as snow is from Shinola. Of course, he knows nothing about what she is thinking or feeling; neither, really, can he imagine it. She is unexplorable, a terrain that even he cannot reach nor will ever fully know. This, precisely, is her charm. Who knows why she goes to him? Ambition, curiosity, love even? He cannot tell, and it does not matter.

As winter deepens, Robert Flaherty and Maggie Nujarluktuk become lovers. They conduct their affair in the clapboard cabin, overlooked by Frances Flaherty and the boy with the mandolin and a pile of cameras. After a while she moves from her family snowhouse to live with him. No one expects it to last and this, too, is part of the beauty of it.

All through the winter, Robert Flaherty continues filming, developing the film as he goes along and staging little shows of the rushes in his cabin with hot tea and sea biscuits and, often, music and even dancing. As winter gives way to the spring, bringing long, clear days of brilliant sunshine, Flaherty films Alakariallak cutting snowblocks with a walrus tusk snowknife, heaving them one on top of another to form a dome, while Maggie goes in after to caulk the joints between the blocks with dry snow, packing the surface smooth, the baby tucked safely in her *amiut*. When it proves too dark to film inside the snowhouse, Flaherty has Alakariallak and his friends build a half-dome exposed to the daylight as a prop. For two days they labour but each time the structure proves unstable and collapses and Flaherty stands by while the Inuit laugh out loud at their mistake and set themselves to the task once more. At the end of the second day, a stable half-dome stands on the sea ice. They build a sleeping platform of snow inside and line it with skins and Maggie sets a *qulliq*, or blubber stove, burning with seal fat. While Robert Flaherty winds his camera this made-up family goes through the routine of turning in for the night, Alakariallak sliding under the sleeping skins while Maggie and Cunayou undress the children and slot them in their places, before pulling off their own sealskin parkas and slipping naked between the children and their man.

Spring gives way eventually to summer and finds Robert and Maggie still together, communicating, now, in a mix of Inuktitut, English and sign language. The tundra, too, ends its silence. By late June, the snow is melting on the tops of eskers and hills, then later on the lower ground. The sun warms the black soil and speeds up the process. Where the tuff gives out to lake water or streams, seams of ice-free water appear. The night shrinks into a thin, blue glimmer. Heather begins to uncurl and grow buds. Summer birds appear from the south, rustling among the willow collecting twigs for their nests and, later, insects for their young. The air whines with bees and mosquitoes, pink saxifrage bursts from the willow bed, the grasses grow cotton tops and, when the *Annie* drops anchor at the mouth of the Innuksuak River in August 1921, the lovers already know that Robert Flaherty will be heading south alone. He will leave Maggie Nujarluktuk there, on the shores of Hudson Bay, with their baby swelling in her belly.

CHAPTER TWO

THE INUIT SETTLED BACK into their habitual routines and the events of the previous year faded to the stuff of campfire stories. In New York City, Robert and Frances Flaherty shut themselves in a room in a walk-up apartment and edited seventy-five thousand feet of film. By November they had a rough cut and were touting around town looking for a distributor. Just before Christmas, the Flahertys managed to persuade Charlie Gelb at Paramount to screen a version of the movie, now being called *Nanook of the North*, before an invited audience at Paramount's screening rooms. It had taken Flaherty a decade to get this far and he knew that *Nanook* was his last chance. If it failed, he would have a hard time finding another backer. But his movie-making career was not the only thing on the line. Flaherty had poured his passion into *Nanook*. For ten years, he had brooded over the Arctic and its people. Up in Inukjuak, he felt he had witnessed something great and timeless about the human spirit which it was his duty, even his destiny, to pass on. At the time, he had written in his diary that he wanted to capture "the former majesty and character of these people, while it is still possible, before the white man has destroyed not only their character but the people as well." He still felt that way. He had documented a disappearing world. He had to hope that *Nanook* would go down better in New York than his first effort in Toronto. If it did not, it would be too late to make another.

The hour or so that followed would be one of the most agonising, and most important, of Robert Flaherty's life. As the opening image of ice and rock and dark water flooded the room, Flaherty felt the audience tense. The intertitle appeared. "No other race could survive," it read, "yet here live the most cheerful people in all the world—the fearless, loveable, happy-go-lucky Eskimos." Alakariallak's image faded up and cut, eventually, to Maggie pulling the baby from her *amiut*, the faces so familiar to Flaherty but so distant now. The audience went quiet. He saw one or two of them straining for a better look at the screen. Maggie and the rest spilled from the *kayak*. A few people laughed. The film segued from one sequence to another until, in the final moments, they were witnessing Alakariallak and his family going to bed in anticipation of another day. The end credits appeared, the lights went up and the audience began streaming out but Robert Flaherty was left with no clue. Some were smiling, others looking dazed, even grim, a few wearing no expression at all. He waited with Frances. When the room had finally been cleared, the screening room manager sidled over to him. Well, he said, *Nanook of the North* was a brave film all right, and he could see that Flaherty had put a great deal of time and effort into making it. The manager knew what he was about to say would not sit easily but the plain fact of the matter was that the movie was unwatchable. A bunch of strange-looking people dressed like animals eating walrus meat. Who in their right mind would pay to see such a thing?

Robert and Frances Flaherty spent the holiday season licking their wounds. Twelve hundred and fifty miles away in Inukjuak, the Révillon Frères factor gave a Christmas party for the Inuit, with ship's biscuit, tinned sardines and bannock bread. People sledged in from all over Cape Dufferin, danced a few Scots reels and some American square dances and staged sled races. When the light failed they bundled inside the fur post, drank sweet tea and sang songs about the old ways.

One of the few who did not join in the festivities that year was

Maggie Nujarluktuk, who spent Christmas Day in her family's snow-house, giving birth to a baby boy, Robert Flaherty's son.

Early in the New Year, Robert and Frances began once more to look for a distributor for *Nanook of the North*. Flaherty showed the picture to First-National, who turned it down, then to Pathé in New York, who agreed in principle to distribute it. Some time in early spring, Pathé struck a deal with the owner of the Capitol Theatre in New York City to show the picture on condition that Pathé package it with something more commercial. Pathé had just taken on a distribution contract for Harold Lloyd's first big feature, *Grandma's Boy*, and this they decided would be just the thing to tin can with *Nanook*: Capitol okayed the package, sight unseen. When the manager of the Capitol Theatre actually *saw* the Arctic picture he tried desperately to backpedal, but by then he was locked in, and so, on 11 June 1922, Alakariallak and Harold Lloyd burst on to the New York scene together. Even by New York standards, it was an eccentric coupling. About the only thing Alakariallak and Harold Lloyd had in common was that they both smiled a lot. *Grandma's Boy* went down tremendously well, but not half as well as Nanook. The audience took to the Inuk man in an instant. Here he was, a decent, hard-working, good-natured individual, hemmed in on all sides by natural terrors, cheerfully carving out a life for himself, for Nyla, his sweet-faced wife, and their romping children, with no sense of how much easier and more comfortable were other lives being lived by men and women only a few hundred miles to the south. Sure, the movie was disjointed and rough in places, but it was filled with bright, unforgettable moments; Nanook struggling to extract a seal from its breathing hole, Nyla pulling a boy from her *amiut*, the family diving under their sleeping skins at the end of another frozen day. To this audience, still reeling from the trenches and the mustard gas of the First World War, Nanook and Nyla were innocent wanderers in an as-yet unblemished world. They saw in *Nanook of the North* a story of love and through love, survival. What they were watching was not simply some performance put on for their entertainment. At some level, at least, it was the truth. *Grandma's Boy* could wait. What New Yorkers wanted was *Nanook*.

Word spread and soon people from all over the city were flocking to the Capitol Theatre. Pathé hastily expanded its distribution and, before long, *Nanook* was playing in theatres as far away as Tennessee and Nebraska. By September 1922, three months after its first release, Flaherty's "adventure picture" had crossed the Pond and was playing to sellout audiences at the new Gallery Kinema in London and at the Gaumont Theatre in Paris. From there it went on to Bangkok, Peking and Moscow, picking up ecstatic audiences everywhere. *Nanook* was fast becoming a huge, global hit. Confectionery manufacturers began turning out ice creams with Alakariallak's face printed on the wrappers and, before long, he was unwittingly advertising everything from chocolate bars to cleaning fluid. In Los Angeles, a three-man team of songwriters whipped up a popular song about him, with a chorus which began "Ever-loving Nanook/Though you don't read a book/But oh, how you can love/And thrill me like the twinkling northern lights above . . ." Thousands of miles away, in Malaysia, Nanook entered the language. Even now *nanuk* in Malayan means a strong man.

And so Alakariallak and Maggie gradually became famous. But it was an odd kind of fame because neither Alakariallak nor Maggie knew anything about it. What little mail reached Inukjuak came once a year on the annual visit of the Hudson Bay Company supply ship and almost all of that was for the post trader. The Inukjuamiut rarely received any news from outside Cape Dufferin, and when they did, it was often so garbled that it made little sense to them. Eventually they heard that *Nanook of the North* had opened in New York City and that it had gone on to England, France, Malaya, Russia, Siam and China, but all these were places they knew nothing about and had a hard time imagining. Even their own country, Canada, seemed so remote to them as to be the stuff of dreams, or, rather, of nightmares, since they knew it principally as the place in the south to where Inuit people were sometimes transported when they were ill and from where, generally speaking, they never returned.

Four years after the film's first showing, Robert Flaherty's charming, violent depiction of the lives of Alakariallak and Maggie Nujarluktuk in the Barrenlands had grossed US$251,000, five times its initial cost, and Robert Flaherty had become a household name. He was taken out to fancy dinners and asked to speak at meetings and conventions. Louis B. Mayer called, as did Irving Thalberg and an assortment of other producers, agents and managers. Everyone wanted the same thing. Another *Nanook*.

Flaherty took his new-found fame in his stride. He was already thirty-eight years old and from a very early age he had marked himself out as having some special place in the world. Now others were simply confirming his opinion. After ten years in the Arctic he felt he had earned his reputation.

Of the legacy he had left there, he knew very little. News of Inukjuak reached him only rarely. When he left, Maggie Nujarluktuk had been five months pregnant so Robert could not have been in any doubt about her condition, but sex was different up on Cape Dufferin and it was custom, sometimes, for a woman to sleep with more than one man. Flaherty may well have told himself that the child was not his. And if it was his, well, then, he may have thought that his wilderness baby was best left up in the Barrenlands.

If he did think of his bright-eyed, smiling Inuit girl from time to time, if his heart occasionally hollowed for her, then he kept the feeling to himself. In any case, he was not given to introspection. The plain fact of the matter was that he already had a wife and daughters back home and they were where his heart ultimately lay.

Alakariallak continued to hunt and Maggie Nujarluktuk took care of her baby. The winter of 1923 was brutal. Sea currents broke the ice into floes and the prevailing westerlies turned to the north, roaring across Hudson Bay and pushing the floes together into monstrous pressure ridges which rose like great walls from the sea.

For a time, hunting seals became impossible and Alakariallak was forced to take his dog team inland in the hope of finding caribou, but after days of sledging he failed to come across a single animal. He turned back west towards the coast and began to make his way home but he and his dog team were caught in a blizzard. They carried on as best they could but at some point the dogs must have grown hungry and exhausted. Although they were now only a few days' travel from the coast, they stumbled and began to die, until there were no longer enough dogs left alive to pull the sled. Alakariallak, too, was spent. As the blizzards blew up again, the great hunter and—though he didn't know it—international movie star set about making himself a snowhouse for a shelter, then spreading his sleeping skins inside he lay down to die.

A few miles to the southwest of Alakariallak's lonely grave, on the coast at Inukjuak, Maggie Nujarluktuk pulled a little half-breed boy from her *amiut* and set him down on a pile of caribou skins beside her.

CHAPTER THREE

In 1902 the geologist A. P. Low had wintered at the mouth of the Innuksuak River and named his campsite Port Harrison after the director of the mining company he was working for at the time. To the Inuit the place had always been Inukjuak, which means "many people" or "great people" or, sometimes, "giant." The elders could remember a time before the whalers came when beluga whales had congregated in the little bays around the river estuary to breed and Inuit had come in from their camps all along the eastern shoreline of Hudson Bay to hunt them. They still spoke of that time with a longing and sometimes with a dread born of the memories, which had never quite left them, of bad seasons which had pushed their families so near starvation they had had no choice but to brick their babies into tiny snowhouses and leave them there to die.

No one knows exactly when the first Inuit arrived on Cape Dufferin. The earliest occupation is marked by rock circles and, here and there, by the crumbling remnants of ancient huts. The men and women who built them, people the anthropologists now call the Dorset Culture, arrived from the northwest some two or three thousand years ago, having made the long, bleak trek across the Canadian Barrenlands from Asia by foot and by sled. The Dorset people were nomadic hunters, moving with the herds of caribou which then populated the tundra. They lived in small houses half buried in the shale and kept no dogs and although they spread through the

Arctic their culture was, relatively speaking, short-lived. When the climate began cooling, around 500 B.C.E., their populations dwindled. They were followed, or pushed out, no one knows which, by the Thule people, named after the site in northern Greenland where, in the early 1920s, Therkel Mathiassen first unearthed their remains. The Thule arrived from the west around 400 C.E., when the Arctic climate became drier. They lived semi-nomadically, settling for short periods near the coast, erecting huts from mud or slabs of sod and living off the great whales they hunted from their *kayaks*. A single forty-ton bowhead whale could feed five families, between twenty-five and fifty individuals, for a year. The Thule were one of the great early human cultures, as wondrous in their way as the Aztecs or the Babylonians, their technologies so beautifully adapted to the terrain that they were able to survive and to prosper in a place no other people had been able to settle. Where they encountered Dorset people, there were sometimes skirmishes, which the Thule, with their superior technologies of tailored skin clothing and bow and arrow, the metal arrowheads fashioned from scavenged meteorites, usually won. In the eastern Arctic, the Thule reached as far north as Ellesmere Island at the 80th parallel and as far south as Labrador at the 50th, a distance of some 1,800 miles. The Inukjuamiut are their descendants. They were, and remain, the Arctic's most successful colonisers.

At the southern fringes of their world, where the Barrens met the ragged northern tree line of white spruce and alder, the Thule clashed ferociously with Indians, who had taken occupation of the northern boreal forests many thousands of years before, venturing out on to the Barrens only during the short Arctic summers. Eventually, the forest dwellers and the Barrenlanders reached a kind of uneasy truce, the Indians remaining in the forest, the Inuit in the tundra, their mutual hostility confined to a band of stunted conifers where one world met another. On the eastern shoreline of Hudson Bay, the line is drawn at Kuujjuarapik, or Great Whale, at 56° North. South of there, the world belongs to the Cree. Maggie's ancestors (and Maggie herself) knew them as "head lice." The disregard was mutual. Everything above Kuujjuarapik was Inuit land. The Inuit became, almost by definition, people of the tundra. Even today, they cannot be understood in any other context. They have lived successfully on the Barrens all these years because the Barrens have lived in them.

The Ungava Peninsula, of which Cape Dufferin and Inukjuak are a part, is a diverse region and, around the time of the birth of Maggie's son, Josephie Flaherty, it had a population of around 1,500 souls, almost entirely Inuit and Indian. In the north, the land is a high relief of acid granite and gneiss, pitted with volcanic rocks, among them the vivid green soapstone the Inuit use for carving. It slopes southwards until, just south of Inukjuak, it stoops and embraces the sea. Everything to the north of Inukjuak as far as Cape Jones is high coast, everything to the south, low, horizontally orientated and blessed with coves and wide beaches. Though Inukjuak lies at approximately the same latitude as, say, Inverness, Scotland, it is, all the same, resolutely Arctic, thanks in part to the uncompromising winter ice which stills the waters of Hudson Bay for eight or nine months of the year. The interior is a plateau of granite overlaid with glacier-scoured limestone which the Inuit call *sekovjak,* a word meaning "resembles landfast sea ice." What constitutes the Arctic is often disputed, though never by the Inuit, for whom it is simply home. Some non-Inuit commentators define it as the area north of the Arctic Circle at 66° 33', but this merely marks the point where there is midnight sun at summer equinox and no sun at all at winter equinox. Others claim it is most easily characterised by the presence of permafrost, but that, too, is a problematic definition, because at lower latitudes the permafrost is patchy and often incomplete in places which seem to be, in every other way, part of the Arctic region. Surprisingly for a region so often characterised by its coldness, winter temperature is a bad indicator of where the Arctic might begin and end. Nowhere in the Canadian Arctic does the winter temperature routinely fall below −46°C and, when it does, it rarely stays that way for long, while parts of Siberia regularly experience winter lows of −73°C. The Yukon and other subarctic Canadian regions can sometimes be colder in winter than parts of the country farther north. In the end, low temperature matters less than the persistence of permafrost and ice, or even aridity.

A working definition on which most people agree is to say that the Arctic begins where trees end. The tree line is not really a line at all. It is rather a zone, or an uneven strip, where candelabra spruce gradually give way to ever smaller, simplified specimens until the entire species becomes so stunted and so widely dispersed that it takes on the appearance not of a tree but of a gnarled finger. A little farther north trees of any kind give out altogether. Those trees which do persist in the northernmost reaches of the tree line "zone" are unable to produce seeds, but reproduce by layering, sending a branch to the ground where it roots and grows a clone of the parent tree. In some parts, this strip of dwarfing, scattering and layering is hundreds of miles wide, in others, it narrows to just a mile or two. Nor does it appear at any particular latitude. In the northwest of the continent, near the Mackenzie delta, there are trees as high as 66° North. The tree line drops to lower latitudes as it meanders east, largely as a result of the freezing action of Hudson Bay. The area at the tree line may well be solid permafrost or, as around Kuujjuarapik, the permafrost may appear in patches, but it will follow a single rule. Above the "line" the temperature on an average July day will remain below 10°C, the temperature necessary for tree growth. By this reckoning, the Arctic proper begins roughly at the tree line and the subarctic region lies in the northern boreal forests below. Thus the Arctic begins at latitudes as high as 60° and as low as 55° North. By this reckoning, the Arctic and subarctic regions of Canada together make up 40 per cent of the country. The region is almost mind-bendingly vast.

Barrenland tundra, the region of land above the tree line stretching across the whole of Canada, has many unique characteristics not found in any other land formation. The Arctic tundra looks the way it does first and foremost because of the action of ancient glaciers, which have for eons ground up rock and dragged it down to the sea. In Ungava, glaciers also carved out a flotilla of basin lakes and channels which now sit stranded on the plateau, giving it, at least from the air, the appearance of an old bath sponge whose pores are baggy with wear. Lakes, rivers, summer run-offs and spills are all extremely common in the Barrenlands, though many of them may either be solid with ice or dry through most of the year. There are more lakes in Arctic and subarctic Canada than in the rest of the world put together.

Glaciers are also responsible for dumping sand and gravel into ridges, or eskers. In the deep interior of the Ungava Peninsula, where Alakariallak met his end, the eskers sometimes rise a hundred feet into the air and they are broken by spillways and erosion gullies. Many are marked with *inukshuks,* the man-shaped mounds of rock built by Inuit to act as pathfinders. Arctic foxes and caribou also use eskers as lookouts, so they have historically been good places to hunt. Despite all this glacial carving and dumping, the low, scoured hills around Ungava are, relatively speaking, not deeply eroded. The tops of what were once hills have been reduced to naked rock but you find none of the horns, corries, U-shaped valleys or fiorded coasts that there are further north, on Baffin Island, say, or among the islands of the Queen Elizabeth Group. In Arctic terms at least, Ungava is a gentle, open land with less to hide than its more northerly neighbours.

Its relatively mild nature does not render Ungava any less bleak. There is plenty of naked rock. On the edges of the eskers no plant-life is able to endure the relentless, desiccating westerly winds and in the absence of any firm purchase for plant roots, these formations are usually naked. The worn slopes of the granite hills are also bare, partly for the same reason and partly because no soil is able to settle there. But the westerlies are not all bad. In the summer they bring cloud and summer fogs and so, in spite of the drying effect of the wind itself, the area is damper than much Arctic tundra, and there are grey-green lichens to be found in every sheltered spot.

Arctic soil everywhere is, unsurprisingly, poor and nitrogen deficient, but on the rocks beneath bird colonies or on perching knolls or fox lookouts, nitrates accumulate and there the tangerine splash of nitrophilous lichen, *Caloplaca elegans,* blends with the more familiar grey-greens creating points of brilliant colour. More important than the clouds and wet fog to plant growth is the permafrost which keeps the moisture brought by the westerlies in the topsoil allowing dwarf shrubs to thrive across much of the inland plateau. The areas not directly fringing the sea are covered by scrubby heathland. As in the rest of the Arctic, the growing season is too short for annuals, but on the heathland below the nubs of rock and esker, the ground is carpeted in creeping willows whose branches can reach as high as two feet in sheltered spots. By Arctic standards a willow that high is as much of a giant as a sequoia in Yosemite. In Arctic conditions a willow may take as many as four hundred years to grow as thick as a man's thumb.

Around Inukjuak itself, dwarf willows are the only tree-like shrub, but south of Inukjuak a few dwarf birches grow, though these rarely venture out more than six inches or so from the root. Among the perennials are the Arctic heathers, *Cassiope,* and Arctic cotton-heads, whose stems Maggie Nujarluktuk gathered to serve as wicks in her stone lamp. In September, the berry-bearing members of the genus *Vaccinium* growing on Ungava's southern slopes produce the tiny blueberries and lingonberries so beloved of Ungava Inuit and of their children in particular. Furry mosses grow around Ungava, too, and, in summer, Arctic poppies, rosy sedges and pretty, bobbing saxifrage poke up from the willow carpet. On alluvial flats beside the Ungava's many rivers, cotton grasses wave above the thick cushions of sphagnum moss which the frost heaves up into tussocks. Where the rivers disgorge into the bay there are white strands of sand, and in the pockets of soil trapped by boulders, sandworts and scurvy grass flourish. Sea pinks raise their heads above the rocky parapet and crowd the tops of the low cliffs where the air is warmer than at the frosty selvage of the shoreline.

In Ungava human life has always been concentrated along the coast where there are seals, walrus, beluga and, in the past, large whales. By comparison, the interior is forbidding, and in Maggie's time it had become more so, because the once dense herds of caribou had been reduced by the introduction of rifles. Before 1900, the caribou were uncounted and uncountable. Like the American buffalo, they ranged in herds with no discernable beginnings or ends. In 1900, when naturalists, sensing a sudden and dramatic drop in their numbers, began counting, there were something like 1,750,000 caribou living in the Canadian Barrens. Fifty years later this figure was 670,000, 60 per cent down on the previous half-century and in 1955, only five years after that, the herds had diminished to 277,000 individuals, 60 per cent down again. Changes in the pattern of the weather and gradual variations in the tree line have always made caribou populations vulnerable to catastrophic but temporary declines but nothing had done anything like the damage caused by the rifle. By the fifties, those quarter of a million or so surviving caribou were scattered across land far larger than western Europe and locating them had become a hunt for needles in haystacks. Between 1900 and 1950, caribou had virtually disappeared from central and northern Ungava and Inuit living around Inukjuak were forced to paddle south by *kayak* or *umiak,* often as far as Richmond Gulf, near Kuujjuarapik, a round trip of four hundred miles, to stand any hope of hunting them. And hunt them they must, not so much for the meat, nutritious though it is, but because the animals' skins were absolute necessities of Inuit life. Caribou hair is cone-shaped and hollow, making its insulating properties second only to those of musk-ox hair, while being a good deal lighter and more flexible. Without caribou pelts for clothing and sleeping bags, neither Inuit nor any other human being would ever have been able to settle in Arctic conditions.

In Maggie's time, Arctic hare and fox remained relatively plentiful in Ungava and there were trout in the lakes and Arctic char in the rivers. The waters of Hudson Bay have always been home to large numbers of sculpin, harbour, ring and bearded seals and, more rarely, beluga whales and walrus. Ravens and ptarmigan have always been permanent Ungava residents and migrating birds arrive in their millions as early as July and stay until the September snows. The islands off the coast of Cape Dufferin are so densely populated with birds during the summer months that the rocks and cliffs at the shoreline seethe and foam like pots of boiling milk. At McCormack Island, twenty miles north of Inukjuak, vast colonies of murres nest on the leeward side along the headlands and in the hollows carved by glaciers beneath them. Nourished by their guano, clumps of deep, luxuriant moss grow. Fantastic numbers of geese and ducks gather on the rocky edges of the Hopewells, the Sleepers and Nastapokas. All along the island festoons of the Belchers, one of which now bears Robert Flaherty's name, eiders, snowgeese and American pintails make their summer homes. During the annual moult, when the birds temporarily lose their flight, Inuit go out in boats and scoop them off the beach.

Autumn arrives relatively late at Inukjuak and is relatively mild. The first snows begin in September, but it does not start snowing heavily until October. By November the snow is so dry and wind-packed you can walk on it with the same ease as asphalt. The days draw in and the nights are coloured by displays of the Northern Lights. The snow continues to build up through December. In January, conditions change sharply as the sea ice in Hudson Bay thickens and stabilises. It stops snowing and temperatures plummet. The air becomes crystalline. The Arctic midwinter begins. In contrast to the summer, with its bustle of insects and yammering birds, midwinter is almost deathly silent. There is rarely a sound to be heard beyond the rush of the wind and the cracking of the ice, a terrible, raw, geologic sound. Midwinter is all about ice. A short way out to sea an ice foot forms, its base lying on the beach. Beyond it sits a rough strand of barrier ice, which takes the brunt of the tide. Farther out still, the land-fast ice stretches smooth all the way to the floe edge. The pack ice, or floe, slides over and under the land-fast ice and grinds against it, lifting pressure ridges as solid as ice walls or as jumbled as ice boulders. As the tide pulls out, a hinge appears where the barrier ice and the land-fast ice join and the floe edge separates more widely from the land-fast ice, creating a tumbled mass of ice which moves with the tide. Frost smoke, ice flowers and hoar crystals appear where the floe edge pulls away from the land-fast ice, exposing liquid sea. These movements all have their own sounds. As children, Inuit become accustomed to them and learn to distinguish between them but to any outsider it can seem as though they herald the end of the world.

In Ungava, the temperature rarely slips below −40°C in winter and in the blaring January, February and March sun it can feel much warmer. Conversely, when a northwesterly wind is blowing, the windchill can take another ten or fifteen degrees off the ambient temperature. January is often still, though, and January, February and March are all good months for hunting seals at their breathing holes and for trapping foxes. The wind is low, the snow is packed and the ice is stable. The sun shines for at least a few hours on most days and by March the days are long and almost blindingly bright. In April it snows again but this snow never really dries and hardens. By May it is beginning to soften, by June it is in full rot and ice is beginning to melt from the edges of the lakes and at the shoreline. Summer arrives in July, along with the birds.

Generations of Maggie Nujarluktuk's family had made this land their home. Ungava was all they knew and all they were. They were bound to it by blood and by the spirits of their ancestors. Their stories were all here. For centuries, Ungava Inuit had moved around the coast following the migration of whales and birds, jigging for fish in the lakes and rivers and hunting seals, walrus and whales just off the coastline in the bay. They had married and given birth and died. They had played drums and cat's cradle, staged sled races and played football using walrus skulls for balls. They had sung their songs of great hunting exploits and passed them down to younger generations. At times they had eaten well, at other times, starved.

Contact between the Ungava Inuit and white men had been infrequent and short-lived. Every so often an explorer and his crew would overwinter somewhere along the east Hudson Bay and hire a few locals to hunt or sew skin clothes for a few months. The explorers often traded metal needles, harpoon heads and blades, tobacco and cooking pots in exchange for the Inuit's skins and meat and, sometimes, for sexual favours. While they stayed, the whites seeded a few half-breed babies and passed on their diseases, but for the most part, life on the east coast of Hudson Bay went on as it had ever since the Thule had settled the place.

Then, in the mid-nineteenth century, whalers came into the bay, and although whaling along the eastern shoreline never assumed the large-scale industrialised killing that was taking place along the bay's western coast or off Baffin and Herschel Islands, the presence of the whaling ships and, in particular, of those from New England which, unlike the Scots, overwintered in the region, increased the fraternising between white men and Inuit, with mixed results for the natives. Tuberculosis, measles, diphtheria, syphilis and missionaries spread through the region with equal enthusiasm. Entire families died of TB, whole settlements were ravaged by influenza. At the beginning of the twentieth century, the population of Southampton Island, around three hundred souls, was wiped out in a measles epidemic.

The first mission was established by E. D. Peck in 1894 at Kuujjuarapik. Increasingly, the Ungava Inuit congregated around the whaling and trading posts and missions to trade pelts, meat and clothes with the whalers and receive medicines, food and benediction from the missions. They began to settle, or at least to limit their previous wanderings to within a day or two's travel from these little settlements. The more concentrated their populations, the more game they took from the surrounding areas. Before long, all the land close to those stations had been hunted out and the Inuit found themselves more and more dependent on the largesse of the whaling crews or the missionaries.

The missionaries helped bring an end to the desperate Inuit practice of infanticide by parcelling out destitution rations to starving Inuit families and by taking in babies, particularly girls, whose parents could not feed them, and bringing them up as servants in the missions. They also helped put a stop to the widespread, if last-resort, Inuit custom of leaving their elderly to die. The fact that this was most often voluntary, the elderly themselves caulking in the final snowbrick, or setting themselves adrift on the waves in a paddleless *kayak,* made it no less traumatic for the families. But God's messengers also had a sinister side. In the space of a generation they had persuaded the women of Ungava to dump their warm and very practical caribou-skin trousers for flimsy tartan skirts and Mother Hubbards. And on the subject of sex they were particularly punitive. They forbad Inuit men to take more than one wife, which sometimes left widows and their children to starve to death, and frowned on the age-old Inuit custom of wife swapping which, though it could be hard on the wives, nevertheless helped keep most camps free of the toxic intrigues of sexual jealousy. But what was more devastating to the Inuit sense of themselves was the missionaries' relentless suppression of their traditional beliefs and complex system of taboos. In most Inuit communities where missionaries held sway, shamans were banned from their customary practices and there were stories of missionaries smashing Inuit skin drums and forbidding the drum dances and songs by which Inuit passed on news from elsewhere. In the course of only a few years the doughty men of God had set the lid on a rich stew of belief which had been bubbling for a thousand years. Inuit were so cowed by what appeared to them to be Christianity's unsparing dogmatism, and so awed by the material riches it seemed to bring, that within the space of a few short years, most Ungava Inuit were refusing even to speak about the old beliefs and there were cases of families preferring to starve rather than take themselves hunting on a Sunday.

By the time Maggie was born, life in Ungava was becoming a mess of competing interests and contradictions. Whalers wanted the Inuit to be one thing, fur traders another and missionaries required something else again. None were content, it seemed, with leaving the Inuit to be Inuit. The confusion came to a head in 1906 when Thomas Watt Coslett killed the whale trade off with his invention of a means to prevent iron stays from rusting. As a result, the demand for whale bone in Europe and America ceased almost overnight. Some of the whalers packed up and headed off to the great fisheries at Grand Banks, others returned to their own countries and a few stayed in Arctic Canada and set themselves up as fur traders, or went to work for one of the established fur companies. The fur trade was nothing new and in Ungava it was centred almost exclusively on the Arctic fox. Unlike its cousins farther west, whose fur is often speckled with blue, the Ungava fox is a wonderful creamy white in winter and this made it particularly sought after. Ever since their arrival on the eastern shores of Hudson Bay, whalers had been buying and selling fox pelts as a subsidiary business to their chief interest in bone and blubber. Those from New England were particularly strong on the trade, each whaling ship regularly bringing back a thousand or more fox pelts at the end of the annual whaling season. What was different now was the scale and organisation of the enterprise.

In 1909, when Maggie was still a child, the Révillon Frères Company set up the first permanent fur post on the banks of the Innuksuak River at Inukjuak. Around the same time, the Frères' great rival, the Hudson Bay Company, began to take a serious interest in the eastern reaches of the bay. The company had long since established posts along the western coast, principally at Fort Prince of Wales, now Churchill, in 1717, but it had left the east largely unexplored. Now it had no choice but to expand. Competition between the two great fur companies had become so intense that there were tales of fur traders in remote outposts keeping sleds ready-packed so that they could rush across the tundra and claim for their employers any rival post which had temporarily shut down through the ill health or death of the former post manager. Three years after the Frères arrived at Inukjuak, the Hudson Bay Company commissioned an icebreaker, the *Nascopie,* to patrol the eastern Arctic checking on its existing posts and looking for new openings and in 1920 the Bay finally opened up its own post at Inukjuak, to rival the Frères', with another the following year in nearby Povungnituk.

By the time Josephie Flaherty was born Inukjuak was a flourishing fur post and, instead of hunting and occasionally assisting whaling ships, the Inukjuamiut were living principally on their earnings from trapping Arctic fox. The Hudson Bay Company and the Révillon Frères were encouraging this trade, handing out the new, steel-sprung traps on credit and favouring those who brought back the largest number of pelts. Competition between the rival traders kept prices high and for a few years in the 1920s the winners in this great—and as it turned out, final—battle between the two fur giants were the trappers themselves. Though life in Ungava was by no means easy, no one starved to death, except by dint of the kind of terrible accident which befell Alakariallak.

Trapping was no longer a sideshow to the main event of hunting for meat. It had become the principal reason for men to go out on the land. It was a labour-intensive business, because the traps had to be maintained, checked and rebaited continually. The fox population was subject to a seven-year cycle. In peak years, trappers could expect to trap ten times the number of fox that they could in lean years. The changing fox population coupled with fluctuations in the price per pelt at the trading stations made the business uncertain even in good years, and the focus on trapping left Inuit families more dependent on the food, traps and ammunition to be had at the store. Although they did not know it, the Inuit of Inukjuak were about to fall into a web of dependency on southern trade from which they have not to this day been able fully to extricate themselves.

CHAPTER FOUR

ALTHOUGH there are no written records of Maggie Nujarluktuk's life, it is safe to say that she would have pressed her new baby's nose to her own and given him an Eskimo kiss, which is not so much a kiss as a transfer of energies. We know she named him Josephie for his father, Robert Joseph Flaherty. Her midwife, a family member, would have picked him out an *atiq,* a soul name, to join his as yet unformed soul to all those who shared the same name. His grandmother would have found him an Inuk name, something that reflected the way he seemed to live in the world.

The little boy would have spent his first few months of life in Maggie's *amiut.* There he would have lain warm and naked, the filling in a sandwich of animal fur and human skin. His earliest view of a landscape, one whose contours he would never forget, would have been the rise and fall of his mother's strong, sealskin-scented back. When he was hungry, his mother would have lifted him from the hood and put him to her breast. When he shat, she would have cleaned his naked skin with her hair. For months he would have slept, watching the Arctic world go by, and dreamed. By the time summer came he would probably have already been eating what would become the mainstay of his diet, seal meat, chewed and softened by Maggie. Already the breezes and the low contours of the land would have been familiar to him. He would have had a strong sense of where he was.

Each June, the Nujarluktuk family moved out to their summer camp. The muskeg was spongy with meltwater and it was too difficult to travel far on the land during July and August. For the next few weeks, the family would confine themselves to forays along the coast, the men in *kayaks* and the women in larger *umiaks* made of sealskin and driftwood, visiting other camps, hunting, fishing, or simply trading. They would not have roamed as far as they had before, when Maggie was a child. It made more sense to stay close to the trading posts with their supplies. The family would also be living in a larger grouping than had been customary a generation before, a group headed by a "camp boss," a fictional title conferred by the fur traders upon whichever man in a group spoke a little English and seemed pliable. Needless to say, these "bosses" had no particular authority among the Inuit, who made decisions collectively, but they tolerated the invention of the "camp boss" because it made little difference to everyday life in the camp, and seemed to please the trader.

Maggie's family occupied a strip of coast just north of Inukjuak. It was this broad sweep of low rock with its detail of lichen and crunchy willow which became the canvas on to which Josephie painted his childhood. He would have sat in Maggie's *amiut* while she wandered along the coast gathering the plants they call *qungik* and *airaq*, which make good tea; the grasses she would use as wicks in her *qulliq*, and the willow twigs she needed to weave into mats. As she went, she would have checked the willow bed for ptarmigan eggs and chicks and then inspected the willow branches for willow worm cocoons which she could dip into seal fat and put out for supper.

By early September Maggie would have been picking the tiny Arctic cranberries, cloudberries and lingonberries that ripen on the south-facing slopes and scouring the heath for newly shed caribou antlers, which she could peel and boil into a rich and bloody soup. Soon the winter would be down on them again and they would be building snowhouses and there would be nothing visible along the coast but mile after mile of ice and snow. The young Josephie Flaherty would have watched ptarmigan pluming from their nests in the willow, seen lemmings mustering and followed fox tracks and the remains of ancient caribou paths and thought about the seasons. This would have been his education. He would get no other. The first school did not arrive in Inukjuak until 1949, by which time Josephie was twenty-eight.

The fact that Josephie Flaherty survived into his second year was something of a miracle, since babies born in Inukjuak in the first half of the twentieth century had about the same chance of seeing their third birthdays as those, say, born in medieval Europe. Malnutrition and hypothermia were common, and there were the usual round of childhood perils, including those diseases visited on the Inuit by whalers and fur traders and, later, by the annual arrival of the supply ship and to which the Inuit had no immunity. The average life expectancy among the Inuit in Arctic Canada in 1923 was about twenty-eight years and falling, considerably less than half that of southern Canadians.

Inuit bring up their offspring in a particular way. In the Inuit world, babies are born without *ihuma*, the part of the mind that has ideas, constructs order from impressions and experiences, solves problems and remembers their solutions. *Ihuma* develops with experience and the only way to get that is to live. So, like all Inuit children, Josephie would have been allowed to make his own mistakes, even when they were alarming and potentially dangerous ones, like putting his fingers in the *qulliq,* or teasing the sled dogs. He wouldn't have been scolded. Whenever he had temper tantrums or expressed childish frustration his family would simply have laughed them off until he had grown out of them. This he would have been encouraged and expected to do. Inuit value serenity and self-possession. To them explosions of rage or pique are childish characteristics.

Arctic explorers of the early twentieth century like Robert Peary and even Roald Amundsen often made note in their diaries and other writings of the impassivity or inscrutability of Inuit, little understanding that without great emotional self-restraint, life in Arctic conditions would, for human beings of any kind, be impossible. To be inscrutable, which is to say, restrained and self-contained, is a good thing in the Inuit world. More than that, it is a tool for survival. Almost by definition, the Arctic's white explorers failed to understand this. For the most part they were vainglorious, self-serving men. The Arctic was a very expensive place to explore. Funds would not have flowed to wallflowers. But they were not the kind of men who would readily have understood the Inuit.

In Robert Flaherty's day Inuit beleived that the only fixed part of a person's personality was their *atiq,* or soul. All the rest was *ihuma,* the gradual deposition of experience. Even now a bad-tempered or hysterical person is said to be *nutaraqpaluktuq* or childish, and his *ihuma* stunted, making him ebullient and oversensitive. A person with too much *ihuma,* on the other hand, is said to be narrow-minded, overdemanding and analytical. In the Arctic, each condition is a liability. The man with too much *ihuma* will allow his brooding to take him away from the real world, until he falls through the ice one day, or stumbles into a crevasse. A person with too little is bound, sooner or later, to go crazy. The ideal Inuit type, a man or woman with just enough *ihuma,* is cheerful, calm and patient in adversity, immune to irritation, sulking or to the hostility of others. He takes his life as it comes, recognises its limits and accepts its various outcomes. The most important words in his vocabulary are *immaga,* perhaps, and *ayunqnaq,* it can't be helped.

Which is not to say the Inuit value dourness or solemnity. On the contrary, Inuit children are brought up to be happy, or, leastwise, to look it. When a person feels happy, or *quiva,* people are drawn to him. In this respect we are not so different. As much as life in the temperate zones, or in the tropics, leading a successful life in the Arctic is all about having people on your side.

Displays of rage, frustration or depression are so disapproved of among the Inuit that many grow up without any conscious sense of having these feelings. In every community, of course, there are misfits, men and women whose inner selves grind against their outward expression, men and women, in other words, who live a gentle, or not so gentle, lie. In the past, these more tortured souls might find outlets as shamans or *anatoq,* and their internal ruffles might become a sign of peculiar power. Unable to find their place in conventional life, they would be honoured and respected as exceptions. This had always been the way Inuit managed the unconventional, the eccentric and the mentally ill, and it remained so until missionaries stamped out shamanism in the late nineteenth century. By the time Josephie was born, the old ways had become shameful and the people who practised them were neither spoken about nor publicly acknowledged. This was no longer a world with any place in it for misfits.

So far as anyone can tell, or cares to recall, Josephie Flaherty was a balanced child with neither excess nor deficit of *ihuma.* In retrospect, some who knew him talk of having detected a hint of oversensitivity, some nub of excess, but most speak of him as a loving boy, helpful, loyal and a good son to Maggie. He was, they say, self-reliant, quiet, even brooding, someone who got on with what he had to do without a fuss, and with no particular consciousness, at least in his early life, that his mixed blood marked him out as different. He felt himself to be Inuit, with all that being Inuit means. The ties that bound him were the ties of his Arctic family and for the remainder of his life they would be indissoluble.

There was no getting away from the fact that Josephie *was* different, though. He grew up tall with gangly limbs and softer, less ruly hair than that of full-blood Inuit boys. His lips were fuller, the face longer, his eyelids adopting a compromise position, halfway between Asia and Ireland. His arms were unusually long and his paddle hands lent him a seal-like air, an impression only strengthened as he headed into puberty and sprouted whiskery facial hair.

Josephie Flaherty's early life was measured out in ship years, by the annual arrival and departure of the supply ship, *Nascopie.*

There was a saying in Inukjuak that the second best day of the year was the day the *Nascopie* arrived and the best day was the day it left. No one disputed which of these days was the more exciting. The moment news of the ship's imminent arrival reached them from the north, men all along the coast would fire their rifles. The members of the Nujarluktuk family would quickly change into their smart clothes, rush down to the shore and paddle out to meet the ship, moving alongside it for a while to exchange smiles and waves with the crew, the Hudson Bay trader, the policemen moving between posts, the missionary, the medic, the civil servant and the occasional geologist or researcher on board. If young Josephie ever looked for his father's face among the passengers, he would not have found it, but it is perfectly possible that he would not have looked.

The family would make their way south along the coast to the mouth of the river, where the high-summer water, free now from ice, rushed to meet the sea, and they would tie up their boats at the "pier," a strip of sand lined with rocks at the water's edge. By the time the *Nascopie* was at anchor, the family's tent would be up, its guys secured to rocks, and the women would be arranging skins at the sleeping end and stoking a willow-twig fire on which to make tea. A while later, the ship's whaleboat would begin chugging towards the shore, and the Hudson Bay Company post's boat would head out to meet it. From 1935, when the first police post arrived in Inukjuak, an RCMP Peterhead joined the little flotilla. The police were not a welcome arrival. The Inukjuamiut could not see the point of them, since no one ever broke the law. Their chief role, so far as the Inuit were concerned, seemed to be to busy the settlement flagpole with its Union Jack and Maple Leaf every ship time. The routine was always the same. Shortly after the flags began to billow a priest of some sort would be dropped off at the detachment, along with another man in police uniform and an assortment of other *qalunaat,* the flags would flutter upwards and the assembled would sing "O Canada" to a circling audience of mildly puzzled loons. From the vantage of their tents the Inuit would shrug and mutter *ayunqnaq,* it can't be helped.

For the next three days they would all be treated to the bounty of the Hudson Bay Company and the government of Canada combined, which is to say that once the ship was unloaded, the bill of lading checked, the cargo neatly stacked in the Hudson Bay Company store, there would be a "mug-up" and all the sugared tea the Inuit could drink accompanied, perhaps, by some hardtack biscuits and a sardine or two. The mug-up would give way to races, a cat's cradle competition and, perhaps, a football game, the prize for which might be a can of sardines or, perhaps, a tin of hardtack. The following day there would be more tea, a solemn sermon from the visiting priest (Anglican), followed by a photography session during which various *qalunaat* would snap Inuit stiffly sporting their best ceremonial parkas. These same *qalunaat* might then buy a few souvenirs, sealskin clothing, ceremonial drums, soapstone carvings and the like, before boarding the ship once more. After that, the Inuit would be sent to the *Nascopie's* medical rooms for a cursory checkup and a reward of a box lunch of hardtack biscuits and sardines. Finally, there would be a showing in the Hudson Bay Company store of a movie, often something with a sea or sailing theme. Though you might think it an obvious choice, so far as we know, *Nanook of the North* was never shown.

The *Nascopie* also brought the annual mail. For the first thirty-three years of his life there was never anything for Josephie, which was okay since he could not read.

The day after the screening, at some point during the night, the *Nascopie* would weigh anchor and begin its four-hundred-mile journey west to Churchill, Manitoba, on the other side of Hudson Bay. Some of the Inuit would paddle with the ship for a while, others would watch from the shore, then they would change back into their workaday clothes and would begin to gather their belongings for the journey back to their camps. Those who had credit at the store would stock up on ammunition, flour, lard, tobacco and tea before they went. The remainder would have to make do until the winter trapping season began once more. Within a week, most of them would already have left the settlement. Another year would go by before they would hear again from the other world to the south.

And so the years floated inescapably by. Josephie grew taller, angular, nervous and quick to smile. His contemporaries had him down as a watcher, one of those people who are forever to be found on the edges of things, looking in. In January 1929, when Josephie was just seven, Thomas Mayne "Pat" Reid piloted the first plane across Ungava. It was a fine, sun-dazzled winter day, the sky vivid, cloudless, the air crystalline and smelling of electricity. The first hint that this day was likely to be any different from the last was when the dogs started to become restless and shift about. A long while later, an unfamiliar whirr was carried in on the wind. People emerged from their snowhouses, tied their snowgoggles to their faces, gazed up at the sky. The noise did not go away. Instead, it devolved into a tremulous buzz. Children clamped their hands to their ears. Their mothers gathered them up, shooing them back into the snowhouses, whilst the men grabbed their guns and stared at the clouds, waiting, until the throb accreted into a whine and the whine slid into a sound something, but not quite, like the clash between two bull walruses, and a giant mechanical mosquito suddenly appeared, dipping dementedly through the sky towards the settlement. The machine continued along the shoreline, swooped down momentarily, then passed by, gradually diminishing until it disappeared in a band of coastal fog, the final remnant of its existence an almost imperceptible shivering in the air, an electric smell not unlike the Northern Lights and a distant sound like the burr of bees.

For weeks after this event, no one could speak of anything else. Inuit families sledged between camps and into the settlement, trying to glean more information. The Inuit rapidly found in it a rich vein of humour. A giant mosquito with a man inside! The post manager's explanation seemed just as unlikely as the creature itself. Why would anyone have wanted to cross so much land when there was already so much nearby?

As for Josephie, he just watched.

Pat Reid's remarkable flight came to be seen as the last good thing to happen in Ungava for a very long time and it marked the end of Josephie's untroubled early life. Later that year, the price of fox fur plummeted. A creamy, unblemished pelt which, the preceding winter, would have sold for C$7 or C$8 fetched only C$1.50, not much more than whalers would have paid for it a quarter-century before. To add to the problem, the Hudson Bay Company acquired a controlling stake in Révillon Frères and had taken out the competition. As prices slipped further, trappers were soon forced to go out to their trap lines every day, extending them beyond their usual confines into unfamiliar terrain. But foxes were scarce that year and no rise in the numbers could in any case make up for the fall in the price of a pelt. The Inuit held on, expecting things to change. Within weeks, they had eaten all their credit at the store and by 1930 the situation was becoming desperate, as the principal markets for Arctic fur sank further into the slump. For the first time in a decade, the hunger the Inukjuamiut had so happily forgotten roamed around the camps once more.

Though Josephie was unable to comprehend the vagaries of the Montreal fur market or, on a larger scale, the fragilities of economic cycles and stock markets, he was as well able to feel his empty stomach as anyone. In Arctic conditions, a human being requires three times the number of calories that he might in temperate zones. From time to time and for short periods during Josephie's early life the Nujarluktuk family had gone hungry, but this new hunger had certain novel qualities. First, it seemed unrelated to any physical conditions. The weather had not changed, the fox cycle was unaltered. The abstract nature of this famine made it peculiarly frightening. Added to that was the fact that the concentration on trapping had left many families more dependent on store-bought food. Had the starvation hit a decade before, many families would have had dried meat and fish and meat cheese cached away, but they had grown used to buying flour and sugar, and their meat and fish caches had dwindled. Last, no one travelled as far and as often as they once had done, so the camps were closer together and the population less widely scattered. Each family's hunting grounds now overlapped more widely with those of its neighbours. Hunting and trapping trips began to take on a relentless, desperate quality.

About that time, so the story goes, Maggie Nujarluktuk's husband's sled was found out on the sea ice and, beside it, a neat, man-shaped hole. Of the truth of this, there is still no knowing. Of the man himself, there remains no trace. An accident would have made sense but whether it was an accident or not, the timing of the death of Maggie's husband could not have been worse. For a while Maggie and Josephie got by on soup boiled from the stomach contents of seals and walrus given them by their relatives, but with no hunter in the family, it was not long before they were forced to move in with the dead husband's brother, Paddy Aqiatusuk. From then on, they were Paddy's charges, their survival in his hands.

Luckily for Maggie and her children, Aqiatusuk was no ordinary Inuk. People went to Paddy when they had family disputes, or decisions to make. They went to him with their sick children or their hungry dogs. They sought his advice on camp politics, on alliance-making and settling scores. If they had a disagreement with the fur post manager they would ask Paddy to act as advocate. He was the nearest thing the Inukjuamiut had to a marriage broker, psychologist, politician, sage and benign patriarch.

Paddy Aqiatusuk was also an artist. In his spare time he took pieces of green soapstone and walrus ivory and carved. And what carvings! Bears, walrus, hunters, seals, that would make you forget everything except their cool, seductive contours and graceful lines. In time, Paddy's carvings would grace museum collections across North America and Europe.

And so it is easy to imagine Josephie, shy, self-effacing and at an awkward, in-between sort of age, advancing towards his new step-father with trepidation and a kind of puppyish awe, and his mother, amused and a little embarrassed by her son's zeal, scolding the boy, with something like, "Don't tail after the man, you'll bother him."

But Josephie Flaherty did not bother Paddy Aqiatusuk. Between the growing boy and the sculptor a firm friendship began. No Inuk boy could have wanted a better teacher, no Inuk man a keener student. True, Aqiatusuk was demanding and often grumpy (too little *ihuma*, undoubtedly), but it was through being in his salty, bear-like presence that Josephie began to leave behind his childish sense of the world and find his way as a hunter and a man. All through the early 1930s, Josephie and Aqiatusuk were companions on the land. During the soft summers, they paddled their *kayaks* across the swell of Hudson Bay while the sculptor pointed out the unexpected currents, odd tides and anomalies of beach and shore and the boy noted the bays and inlets, taking in the contours of the coast. For days they paddled along the Hopewell Islands, out west to Farmer Island, as far as Kogaluc Bay in the north, to the Nastapokas, the Marcopeet Islands and the Sleepers in the south. From these expeditions, Josephie learned to predict the tides, the effect of the winds and the rain and the sun on the sea. He became familiar with the ice and the currents. He discovered where to look for bearded, harp and ringed seal, walrus and beluga whale.

His education continued through the hard winters. From Aqiatusuk he learned how to harness dogs and ice the runners of the *komatik* and to pack a sled so that it did not topple when the going was rough. Together they drove out across the land-fast ice, through pressure ridges, to the pack ice beyond. They ranged way beyond the low hills, where Josephie and Maggie had stopped to pick willow, to the huge, empty spaces of the interior. Aqiatusuk showed Josephie how to lead the dogs, reading their mood, sensing when it was best to run alongside, when more prudent to ride on the *komatik* with the whip, when to discipline the team and when to give them their freedom, when to offer them meat and when to let them go hungry. Gradually, young Josephie distinguished the different and subtle ways in which dogs use their intelligence. By his mid-teens the son of Robert Flaherty was an expert in dogcraft.

Those trips were Josephie's introduction to the tumultuous

churn of ice. Slowly, he learned how to recognise the thin sheet ice which formed from freezing rain and could cover the lichen and starve the caribou. He learned how to spot the thick layer of frozen melted snow which could conceal deadly melt holes below. He sensed when the *sikuaq* or ice soup, which began to form in the sea at the end of August, had become thick enough to bear weight and, later in the year, he recognised when the ice was likely to candle, throwing up the sharp spines that sliced sled dog paws. He learned to watch for ice rising up at the hinges between the ice foot and the shore-fast ice and to predict where it would rear up to form the turbulent, slabby ice ranges the Inuit called *tuniq*. He observed the shadows on the sea left by black ice, and those accompanied by frost smoke which marked open water. He discovered where treacherous ice skins were most likely to be lying across leads and where tiny tremors and a blanching of the air signalled there was land ahead.

Under Aqiatusuk's guidance, he acquainted himself with the habits of Arctic animals, where each preferred to live and how and what it ate, where it travelled, how it paired and bred, for how long the young remained close to their mothers, where they were at their most vulnerable. He learned how to stalk caribou on the flat, windblown tundra, and how to use a white fur baffle to outfox seal. He came to a precise understanding of where and when to fling the harpoon or release the bullet that would make a creature his. He discovered the arts of flensing and butchering meat and where to store it so that wolves, foxes and dogs could not take it. When Aqiatusuk had fox pelts to trade, he took his stepson with him. The boy learned how to talk to white men and how much not to say.

Another winter approached and Maggie Nujarluktuk took sick and, within a few weeks, she died. Her body, wrapped in skins and buried beneath the rocks, joined the company of silent souls out on the tundra, their skeletons kept from the prying paws of wolves and foxes, their stories meshed into the tangle of willow. The exact cause of her death remains unknown. In the 1930s, 740 of every 100,000 deaths among Inuit were unexplained, twenty times the rate among the population of Lower Canada. The family said a prayer, burned Maggie's clothes and returned to their lives. Josephie was not encouraged to cry, nor to vent his rage. No one thought to write to Robert Flaherty with the news, nor did they look for explanations. Death was the well-worn path, too familiar to be mapped.

Josephie found himself alone in the world. Alone, that was, but for Paddy Aqiatusuk, from whom this shy, sensitive, loyal boy began the slow process of learning, as he was never able to learn from his real father, how to become the son to a man. Maggie's death brought them closer. They would not realise quite how far each depended on the other until they were forced apart. But for now, all that lay ahead in a distant future neither could predict and to which, in the Inuit way of things, neither gave much thought.

Josephie Flaherty's knowledge of the world beyond the limits of Ungava remained as thin as summer ice. He got a taste of it in 1934, when the governor of the Hudson Bay Company, Sir Patrick Ashley Cooper, arrived in Inukjuak on the *Nascopie* and was borne ashore to the accompaniment of a personal piper. An inspection of the newly painted clapboard Hudson Bay post followed, and Sir Patrick distributed a few cans of sardines, the odd tin of hardtacks and a good deal of ill-conceived advice. After his inspection, he emerged to address the assembled Inuit in English.

"Now that we have seen you," declaimed Sir Patrick, "we are happy and will leave you with the confidence that you will work with our post manager as one large happy family, you following his advice as if he were your father, for he does the things which I tell him and I want you to do the things which he tells you."

The speech was later published in a book and distributed around the Hudson Bay posts of the eastern Arctic. Josephie never saw this book. Nor did he or any of the other Inukjuamiut ever master what it was that Sir Patrick wanted or why the piper had piped him in. Around Inukjuak, the incident became an old itch or, rather, the memory of an itch. From time to time someone or other scratched it. Between times, it was forgotten along with the world below the tree line that it represented.

From Inukjuak, the *Nascopie* travelled on that year to Cape Dorset, Pangnirtung and to Pond Inlet at the northern tip of Baffin Island, picking up fifty-two Inuit, one Hudson Bay Company post manager, 109 dogs and various possessions and transferring them all to new fox-trapping grounds at Dundas Harbour. When hunting was hampered by rough ice, the manager sent half the party to Crocker Bay, thirty miles west, where they proceeded to starve. The whole party was then transferred back on to the *Nascopie*, the Cape Dorset and Pangnirtung Inuit were returned home while the Pond Inlet Inuit were taken to Arctic Bay. When Arctic Bay proved uninhabitable the *Nascopie* transferred the Inuit once more, to Fort Ross near the entrance to Bellot Strait, where they passed the next ten years scraping out a meagre living from a landscape of rock and gravel. When the Hudson Bay Company post at Fort Ross was closed in the summer of 1947, the survivors from this company experiment were again moved, west this time, to Spence Bay. They were never returned to their homeland.

In 1939, five years after the visit of Sir Patrick Ashley Cooper, an ex–Hudson Bay Company fur trader called James Cantley arrived in Inukjuak and set up a rival trading post a little farther upriver, calling his new enterprise the Baffin Trading Company. The Inuit found him abrasive and mean. He did not rate them either. For a while, the price of fox fur rose steadily, the competition between the Baffin Trading Company and the Hudson Bay post keeping the price paid for pelts in line with the growing demand for Arctic fox in the southern fur markets. The Inuit of Inukjuak did their best to shrug off the horrors of the past years and settled back to their customary lives.

Far away, a war began in Europe.

CHAPTER FIVE

SUPPOSING the bad times to be over, at least for a while, Paddy Aqiatusuk married a widow. Mary brought four children with her, all a little younger than Josephie: two boys, Elijah and Samwillie, Anna, a delicate little girl left crippled at the age of two by an outbreak of polio, and a baby, Minnie. There were now five more mouths to feed in Aqiatusuk's camp and among them no adult hunters.

During the winter of 1939 snow crept across Ungava from the east, melted in a brief, warm spell, then froze hard over the tundra. Unable to scrape through the ice to feed on lichen clinging to the rocks, what few caribou remained on the peninsula began slowly to starve, their living bodies nipped at by wolves until they were little more than walking skeletons, flesh trailing in ribbons behind them as they stumbled to their deaths. There was no point in hunting them, so little nourishment remained on their bones.

By Christmas the meat caches in Aqiatusuk's camp were empty. There were seal, still, and some walrus, but they had to be hunted ever farther from the settlement, either at the floe edge or out on the islands. Paddy Aqiatusuk and Josephie Flaherty were often away for days at a time, moving their trap lines farther and farther out along the coast, camping at the floe edge where the seals swam.

Whenever they were sure they would not be going too far from camp, Josephie and Paddy would take Paddy's stepson Elijah along to hold the dogs and act as lookout. The trips exhausted the boy, just as they had exhausted Josephie before him, and before Josephie, Aqiatusuk and Aqiatusuk's father, in a continuum of extreme physical endeavour stretching back into the dimmest reaches of the past. It was a brutal regime and by the time the three of them reached the home camp they were so grim from the day's exertions that it was all they could do to sit, mug of tea in hand, sucking in the smoke from their cigarettes and staring at the icy floor. Within minutes the boy would be fast asleep, in place, chin folded on to chest. The two men would sit awhile, saying nothing. Paddy Aqiatusuk suffered from back pain and odd, inexplicable twinges which kept him from sleep. He often passed the night hours carving hunters and polar bears, building living armies of greenstone and ivory, against the time when he might have to call upon them.

The early years of the war passed Ungava by. Then, in 1941, the U.S. air force began to build a wartime air base at Fort Chimo, or Kuujuak, in eastern Ungava and American troops poured in to staff it. Inuit employed at the Fort Chimo base passed through Inukjuak on their way to other bases in the eastern Arctic, bringing with them stories of the war, but no one in Inukjuak, least of all Paddy Aqiatusuk and Josephie Flaherty, could quite believe them. There had been skirmishes between Inuit and Indians at the tree line for three thousand years, but the Inuit had lived all this time in the Arctic without an all-out war. Of the First World War, which had ended only shortly before Robert Flaherty had arrived in the settlement with his cameras, they knew nothing.

For now though, Josephie had more important concerns. A tiny, fresh-faced girl called Rynee had entered his life and become the woman he was to marry. The love he felt for Rynee was something new. The Inuktitut word for love means "to care for" or "to look after" and all Josephie knew was that he wanted to care for Rynee, that he wanted to look after each delicate little part of her. Where had they met? All these years later Rynee finds it difficult to remember the exact moment, the one precise and telling detail. Perhaps it was at a drum dance, or on a camp visit or at the trading post in Inukjuak, their mutual attraction revealed in stolen glances and open, toothy smiles. Perhaps there was some slow simmer, a layering of casual meetings over days or weeks or months, culminating in an accretion of feeling, a bubble suddenly bursting at the surface. However it came about, this miniature woman was everything Josephie wanted in a wife, beautiful and healthy, with seaweedy hair and berry lips that spoke to Josephie of quick and happy Arctic summers. It was easy to imagine her frying him bannock bread and sewing him a pair of *kamiks,* the bread soft and as fat as summer bees, the *kamiks* tough and more waterproof than ducks' wings. Before long, family alliances were hinted at, gifts promised. Until they married, the couple would live apart, and see each other when Josephie sledged past Rynee's camp or, in the summer, when he borrowed his stepfather's *kayak* and paddled up the coast.

Out on the sea ice, one spring day, Josephie Flaherty and Paddy Aqiatusuk found themselves beside the Belchers, those islands whose bleeding cliffs Robert Flaherty had once explored and the largest of which now bears his name on maps, though the Inuit have long had their own name for the place. The hunters had been sledging out for the bearded seal which sometimes basked on the shore-fast ice and, finding none, decided to make for their usual landfall. Though there were fishing nets still littering the beach and other evidence of recent occupation the island seemed on this occasion emptied out, as though a great gust of wind had come down and swept away its heart. Usually someone would come down to greet them, but today no one appeared. The reason emerged later. A man called Charlie Oujerack had been given a Bible in Inuktitut and taught how to read it by the mission at Inukjuak. After shutting himself away to study the book further he had formulated the view that he was Jesus Christ come to save the world, and that he would start with the Belchers. His first apostle was his sister, Minnie, who succeeded in making a few other converts among the tiny population and in silencing everyone else. The fantasy was harmless enough until Charlie Oujerack landed on the idea that true believers must prove their faith by walking out across the sea ice naked, as a result of which the lives of three adults and six children were lost and the remaining islanders plunged into despair.

Among the Inuit, the event was seen as the sign of a bad spirit abroad, some malcontented ancestor or river soul out to trip up the unwary. Christianity had never wholly won them over. To the missionary and the RCMP constable at Inukjuak, it was just one further piece of evidence that Inuit were best treated not as the adults they thought they were, but as the children that they had, by this small piece of lunacy and in a million other ways, proved themselves to be.

For a while, the incident became the chief topic of conversation enlivening the *qalunaat*'s otherwise humdrum weekly bridge and poker parties. In Robert Flaherty's time the sole white occupant of Inukjuak had been the Révillon Frères trader but by the mid-1940s, and partly as a result of the war, more and more *qalunaat* had begun to arrive. In 1945, the *qalunaat* population consisted of the Hudson Bay post manager, a Mr. Trafford and his wife; Trafford's rival at the Baffin Trading Company, James Cantley; his assistant, a Swede by the name of "Slim" Carlson; the missionary, the Reverend Whitehead; and a Mr. Doubleday who ran the radio station and his wife. They were joined in summer by the odd geologist, naturalist or geographer working for the Canadian Geodetic Service. Living on the opposite bank of the river were the detachment policemen, generally a corporal and a constable, and from 1943 onwards, the chief operator of the new Radiosonde station.

Before the war, most ordinary Canadians rarely thought about the great lands lying to the north. Robert Flaherty's film had left them with a strong sense of the dignity and courage of the Inuit way of life, but then it had allowed them as quickly to forget it. The Inuit were not much more than colourful characters in the press reports and in the movies, and, as Flaherty had said, "happy-go-lucky." To all but a few, the 200,000 square miles of its northern territories were not in any real sense Canada.

The eastern Arctic archipelago and its inhabitants were particularly obscure. The islands had officially become part of Canada after they were transferred by Great Britain in 1870, but for the next seventy or eighty years the question remained as to whether or not Great Britain had the right to title in the first place. In 1904 the Canadian cabinet asked Dr. William King, the Chief Astronomer of Canada, to report on Canada's Arctic possessions on the grounds that "Canada's title to some at least of the North Islands is imperfect." On maps of the time, Ellesmere Island, the largest in the High Arctic Queen Elizabeth Group, was represented as a U.S. possession or as unclaimed. Three years later, on 20 February 1907, Canadian Senator Pascal Poirier tried to clarify the issue by presenting a motion to the Senate formally claiming all the territory between two lines drawn from the North Pole to Canada. The Russians refused to acknowledge this "sector principle," as did the Americans. All through the twenties, as Josephie Flaherty was learning about ice, the Norwegians and the Danes were making tentative claims to those parts of the archipelago which had first been mapped by Norwegian and Danish explorers. These claims were gradually shrugged off and by the time Josephie reached eighteen and the Second World War began, Canada's legal right to the eastern Arctic archipelago was no longer hotly in dispute, though a question mark did still hang over whether the seas around the islands belonged to Canada or were international waters, an issue so complex that it remains a matter of contention today. The issue of sovereignty in the eastern Arctic archipelago did not entirely go away, though. The region was now shown as part of Canada on maps but as part of the war effort, the United States had constructed five airfields in Canada's Arctic zone and even though Canada officially bought these after the war for US$78.8m, they often remained staffed, at least in part, by American personnel, and the American military and some of its various satellite departments often acted as though the territory was still open. In 1946 some U.S. newspapers carried recruiting advertisements for young men to work at a series of new weather stations in the Canadian Arctic which Canada knew nothing about. After some frosty enquiries by the Canadian government, Senator Owen Brewster of Maine hastily introduced a bill into the U.S. Senate to establish these proposed stations as joint U.S.–Canadian operations. All through the forties the stations continued to be supplied and serviced by U.S. planes and ships and it was only in 1954 that the Canadian Department of Transport was able to take over sea supply.

By then, the Arctic had been drawn into the Cold War, and the Americans were announcing plans to build airstrips capable of landing heavy jets and cargo planes at the remote northern Ellesmere Island weather stations of Alert and Eureka, points on the North American continent only 1,200 miles across the Arctic Ocean from the plains of Siberia. A Canadian Department of External Affairs memorandum of 1952 drew anxious attention to the U.S. presence and predicted that the number of U.S. citizens in the Arctic District of Franklin, encompassing the eastern Arctic islands, would soon outstrip the population of "white Canadians" living there. In the same vein, a Privy Council memorandum predicted that the airstrips "would probably assume the character of small U.S. bases and Canadian control might well be lost." The memorandum continued, "Our experiences since 1943, have indicated the extreme care which we must exercise to preserve Canadian sovereignty where Canadians are outnumbered and outranked." In January 1953 Canadian Prime Minister Louis St. Laurent went so far as to say that "US developments might be just about the only form of human activity in the vast wastelands of the Canadian Arctic."

To counteract this new American occupation, and to provide more support for the Canadian Inuit, a string of Royal Canadian Mounted Police detachments was quickly opened across the Canadian Arctic. The joint U.S.–Canadian Arctic weather stations were built and the Canadian government set up Radiosonde posts to collect meteorological data for the newly opened transpolar aviation route between North America and Europe. All of this, it was hoped, would provide jobs in Arctic settlements and put the Canadian Arctic once and for all in Canada's hands.

The RCMP arrived in Inukjuak in 1935, the Radiosonde post was built in 1943 and a joint U.S.–Canadian weather station opened there in 1946. *Qalunaat* moved up to staff them.

One of the side effects of the war was that it gave thousands of American soldiers their first experience of Arctic conditions and their first real sense of Inuit lives. While the war was on, attention was focused elsewhere, but once it ended, stories began leaking out from the American service personnel of the terrible conditions they had witnessed during their Arctic tours of duty. Many Inuit living around the American airfields, among them Fort Chimo on Ungava, appeared to be poorly clothed and thin and under constant siege from white men's diseases. They noted the Inuit's cruel and arbitrary dependence on fox fur prices which meant that any surplus a family was able to accumulate during a good season was immediately wiped out the moment fox prices fell. They saw how, if an Inuk man got ill, then his family often went hungry because the extended family, though anxious to help out, had nothing to give. If the illness was protracted, the entire family would wind up dependent on the goodwill of the local Hudson Bay factor, or they would starve. The RCMP detachments were too widely spaced to be of much use. In extreme cases, whole families died together. These were tough men and women, living in the most extreme conditions, hard-working and uncomplaining, Canadian citizens whom Canada seemed to have forgotten. The stories coming from the Arctic were a far cry from the cheery, upbeat world of *Nanook,* and the American press jumped on them. The *Boston Globe* was among the first to run scandalised reports. Other newspapers followed.

As southern Canadians and Americans were beginning to learn the truth about life for many Inuit, Josephie Flaherty's fortunes were changing for the better.

Out of the blue, the Radiosonde manager offered Robert Flaherty's son the job of station *piliriji* or choreboy. Why he picked Josephie out is not clear, but it may have had something to do with the fact that Josephie was a half-breed and as such was considered, somehow, more suited to the job. It may simply have been that Josephie was strong-looking with competent hands and a diligent manner and that he smiled a good deal.

Accepting the job meant, for Josephie, having to leave Aqiatusuk's camp and going to live in the choreboy's hut beside the station. This Josephie was at first reluctant to do, feeling pushed and pulled by the competing claims of his stepfather and the Radiosonde manager, but he soon saw that by this one small sacrifice, his family could be relieved of some of their insecurity. With the meagre allowance from the choreboy's job he could at least look after himself and help them out and in some way help pay back the family for the years of care they had given him, even though he was only partly theirs. Accepting the job also meant being able to marry the woman he wanted. Finally, and this is not a trivial point, saying yes meant that Josephie would not have to say no to a white man. And so for the first time in his life the young Josephie moved far from his family camp into a hut on the south shore of the Innuksuak River in the settlement of Inukjuak and became a wage earner.

The job, as he discovered early on, was exhausting rather than challenging. He kept the floors well swept and the station cleaned, burned the rubbish, checked the station's weather balloons and parachutes for holes and tears. In the summer he maintained the station's Peterhead boat and caulked the station building with rope and tar. When the snow arrived in September, he boarded up the windows, shovelled snow against the exterior walls, fixed the insulation around the pipes and valves and made sure the chimney remained open, primed the stoves with coal and topped off the lamps with coal oil. When there were errands to be run, dog pemmican to be made, messages to be taken to the RCMP and so forth, it was Josephie's job to do them and not to question why.

In return, he received a small weekly wage. The new choreboy's remuneration was barely sufficient for a few bags of flour and sugar, a little lard and tobacco. His idea of being able to keep his family turned out to have been misplaced. When it was parcelled out around camp, there was hardly enough to make much of a difference to anyone.

The hut was a bonus, though. It had an enclosed snowporch peppered with hooks and, on the bare board floor, a boot rack and a large, flat stone to serve as a makeshift meat store. Beyond the porch and through another door lay a single room, about twelve feet square, marked off with a piece of caribou skin into two areas, respectively for sleeping and living. On one side, farthest from the door, were a couple of shelves, below which there would be room for a Coleman stove, should Josephie ever be able to afford one. The walls were lined with newspapers scavenged from the Radiosonde station, which served as insulation, as well as to lend the hut a cheerful air. True, the place was small, so small that four adults could fit in the living area only by sitting shoulder to shoulder, true also that the rough board floor was so musty and damp in the summer and the ceiling so foggy with smuts and animal fat, that Josephie preferred to live in a tent beside it, and true that in winter, icicles hung from the rafters, but there was something about this hut which nonetheless brought with it a promise of safety, even advancement. It was more *qalunaat* to live in this hut than it was to live in a snowhouse.

It also provided Josephie and Rynee with their first home. She moved in and set herself to sewing a pair of new summer *kamiks* and a winter outfit of caribou skin for her man.

Whenever Paddy Aqiatusuk came into Inukjuak to trade he dropped by the young couple's hut for a mug-up and a place to stay. Josephie's life, now suddenly abstracted by his humdrum job with its unnatural *qalunaat* timetable, was rooted by these visits; by the man himself, his presence, his strong, true sense of being Inuk. During the short weeks of summer, the two men would sit outside on the banks of the river, stirring a driftwood fire beside which Rynee dried sealskins and loops of seal gut, and talk about the land, Aqiatusuk's hunting trips, where his trap lines lay. In the winter they chatted inside the hut, on caribou skins. When they had drunk tea and eaten, Aqiatusuk would light a cigarette and set himself to his carvings, while the night passed and the two men relived past hunting trips, the dogs they had had, the winters that had come and gone. Sooner or later, always too soon for Josephie, someone from the detachment would come round to remind Aqiatusuk to leave the settlement once his business there was done and, griping like a wounded walrus, the sculptor would pack his gear and head back out to camp, leaving something of the old days hanging in the air.

The seasons turned, and at the Radiosonde station the manager was replaced by another then another still and over the months and years the Flahertys began to accustom themselves to the life that seemed to have come their way. Needless to say, Josephie and Rynee Flaherty had no idea of the incidental part they were playing in the "Canadianisation" of the Arctic. Nor did they know that a much bigger part lay waiting around the corner. To Josephie, the *qalunaat* were the strangers on their doorstep. He understood less about them than he did about the ptarmigan living in the willow. This half-breed son of Robert Flaherty carried the burden of his odd, alien, blood lightly. He had no means of connecting that part of his own heart in which the spirit of his father lay. The Hudson Bay Company, the government administrators, the RCMP, the missionaries, his own father, were all of a piece to him, a mysterious club whose rules he would never fully comprehend and to which he would never be invited to belong.

There was another half-breed living in the settlement. Tommy Pallisser worked at the Hudson Bay store and doubled as an interpreter whenever a southern scientist arrived in the settlement. Originally from Labrador, he had almost become a white person, in part because he spoke English and in part because, being from elsewhere, he was as much an outsider as the *qalunaat*. The *qalunaat* invited him to their dinner parties and to their endless games of bridge and poker and they talked to him almost, but not quite, as if he were an equal. But Tommy Pallisser knew he was not and he kept his Inuit wife from learning English lest she got ideas. The Inuit in the settlement avoided him for the most part. For all his special knowledge and privileges, he was a man caught between two worlds, belonging nowhere, with no particular affinities, a man not entirely to be trusted.

Josephie Flaherty had no desire to be white. What Josephie wanted was simple. He wanted his children to grow up strong, and to go out on the land and to catch seals and caribou and walrus as his stepfather and his grandfather and his grandfather's grandfather before him had done. He wanted his family to have enough to eat and to be able to support his stepfather when he got too old to hunt. And if all that had been straightforwardly, simply possible, then Josephie Flaherty would have been a happy man.

He rarely went out on the land now. For the most part his life was restricted to that small strip on the north bank of the Innuksuak River where the Radiosonde station stood. Without wishing to be, or even fully intending it, he and Rynee had become settlement Inuit, that small group of Inuit residents about whom the police and other *qalunaat* were forever complaining and describing in reports as "scroungers" or "slum-dwellers." Not that Josephie Flaherty had any time for scrounging. The Radiosonde station kept him fully occupied. Nor did he ever ask for anything more of his bosses than what little he was given, except, every now and then, a day or two to go out with Paddy Aqiatusuk hunting for seal, when the two men could feel the wind against their skin and the smell of the dogs in their nostrils and things were something like the old days. And it would have been quite unfair to describe his and Rynee's hut as a slum. True, it was stained with smuts and seal grease, true it smelled of uncured sealskin and fat, but every day Rynee took a goosewing and swept the place until it shined.

Very occasionally, Josephie was asked to act as guide on some Radiosonde expedition. One bright summer day finds him heading out to the quay with the radio operator, Freddy Woodrow, Tom

Manning from the Geodetic Service and two fellow Inuit, an oddity by the name of Noah, who wears an old top hat and has a reputation as a wifebeater, and Soralee, in whose Peterhead the group will travel. There are women washing sealskins down at the quay on that particular day, leaving pools of soap and milky water in the rockpools beside the shore. The men pass them by, stopping to remark on the weather, the state of the char run, then clambering aboard Soralee's Peterhead, they stow the tents, the Coleman stove, the primus and the *qalunaat* paraphernalia on board and settle in for the journey. The going is good and by early afternoon they are tying up at the Hopewells, where Manning has some surveying to do. Having the remains of the day to themselves, the Inuit men take the Peterhead out char fishing, catch thirteen and get three seal into the bargain. Pitching camp at a respectful distance from the *qalunaat*, beside a tidal lake filled with foul-smelling seaweed on a rocky platform covered in saxifrage, they put out the fish to dry and dine on barbecued seal.

The following morning they head north, past patches of ice blink and water sky, where the drifts of pack ice still remain out in the channel. A sun dog throws a halo of yellow light across the clouds and a tribe of Ungava Canada geese fly by, honking. Soon the low coast of southern Ungava has risen into the grey cliffs of the northern peninsula, a landscape Josephie recalls from his youth but now seldom visits. They stop in the middle of the day on a lonely outcrop of rock, so that Manning can find eider eggs, and by early afternoon they are at sea once again, pressing north towards Cape Smith. There they are slowed by low-hanging cloud and cobwebs of rain-filled mist and decide to put in at the Cape Smith Hudson Bay Company detachment, a neat, white clapboard building in the shadow of a wall of barren pillow lava, where Noah proceeds to mug-up while Josephie and Soralee see to the boat and unpack the *qalunaat*'s things. They stay up late that night, sitting on packing boxes, chewing over the old times, long gone and only sometimes missed, but missed sorely when they are. During the return journey on the following day, the coastal cloud momentarily lifts and Josephie finds himself sailing past land which was once, not very long ago, so familiar he would have been hard-pressed to consider it as anything other than an element of himself, the rock skeleton on which his life's body is hung. But he is slipping up now, remembering inlets where there are none, imagining around the next headland some strong feature of his childhood which no longer exists, the landscape requiring a conscious calling to mind where there was once a simple sense of knowing.

As southern Canada wakes up to her northlands so Josephie Flaherty begins, slowly, to forget them.

CHAPTER SIX

IT IS AUTUMN 1952 and Constable Ross Gibson, Royal Canadian Mounted Police number 16593, is stepping off the ski-plane at Inukjuak and taking in the scene. This is his first Arctic posting. He smells the air, so frail it is almost as if the world into which he has landed is an alternate universe perched above the clouds. Still, he is here, and determined to make the most of it. The Arctic detachments, "G" Division, are a proving ground. They possess a certain cachet back at RCMP headquarters in Ottawa, where it is said that if you can survive in "G," surrounded by thousands of miles of lonely tundra, with Inuit and no one else for company, then you can survive pretty much anywhere.

Ross Gibson was born in Gibsons, British Columbia, of Irish immigrant parents in the year before Josephie Flaherty, the great-grandchild of Irish immigrants. As a young boy, Ross Gibson passed his first years uneventfully enough. The tiny town gave out pretty quickly into deep country and there Ross learned the rudiments of bushcraft. When he was eleven or twelve, the family moved east to southwestern Ontario, where Ross Gibson grew into a loyal, straightforward, unsophisticated young man, not handsome exactly—livid skin and thick facial features perched like sausages on mashed beets put paid to that—but pleasingly tall and as strong and as solid as a tree trunk. Even then, people who met him could see that, while not all that bright, he was an honest kind of a fellow, with a certain bluff integrity.

The Gibsons did not stay long in Ontario. At the age of fourteen, Ross moved back to British Columbia with his family and it was here, while passing his free hours crashing through the nearest patch of birded forest with a sharp dog and a loaded rifle, that Ross began to think about what he might want to do with his life. Clearly he was not cut out for a desk job, but neither was he sufficiently unconventional to be able to set out on his own, as Robert Flaherty had. He needed something that would earn him a steady income and keep him out of doors.

His decision was deferred by the onset of the Second World War. Ross Gibson signed on for duty with the Canadian navy. The navy took him as far as South America and it was here that he found himself face to face for the first time with "natives," Ross Gibson's word for anyone who was not white. The "natives" made a great impact on the young Gibson. He was struck by how cheerful they seemed, in spite of their piteous living conditions. Their smiles and nods and handshakes he took at face value. He assumed they were smiling simply because they were happy and, if they were happy in the dismal situations in which they found themselves, then it was because they were admirably simple. Though he would never have admitted it to himself, the simplicity Ross Gibson thought he saw in "natives" chimed very much with his own. In admiring them, he was cheering on some aspect of himself.

By the time the war ended, Gibson knew what he wanted to be. He signed on to the Hudson Bay Company as a fur trader and post manager and was assigned initially to a trading post at Telegraph Creek, British Columbia, then to Fort St. James in the heart of beaver country. His job was to negotiate with the local trappers, most of them Indian, who brought muskrat, wolverine, wolf, rabbit and, of course, beaver pelts to the trading post. Once the furs had been inspected and a price agreed, it was Gibson's job to bundle them up, label each bundle and sort them for dispatch to the great fur depots in Winnipeg and Montreal. The work was lonely and modestly paid, but Gibson did not mind all that. There was one problem with the job, however; it was a big one, and it would not go away. It turned out that Ross Gibson was allergic to fur. The stacked bales of uncured pelts in the Bay storeroom left him so swollen-eyed and sniffly his life became impossible. Sensing the limits of his fur-trading career, Gibson eventually felt he had no choice but to quit the Bay and, shortly after, he applied to take the entrance examinations for the British Columbia Police. The force appealed to his blokeish sense of loyalty, as well as his fondness for authority. The B.C. Police accepted him and he entered the service as a constable. Two years later, when the regional force was taken over by the Royal Canadian Mounted Police, Ross Gibson put in for an Arctic attachment and in 1952 he was dispatched on a two-year posting to Inukjuak.

By that time, Inukjuak had seen more two-year men than there were ticks in a clock. Twenty-four months of frostbitten toes, seal-head stews and pitch-black winter days were enough to see off most, and those who did stay longer were usually on the run from something in the south, or else so permanently soused as to have lost all sense of time. Ross Gibson's new boss, Corporal Fred Webster, was one of these semi-permanent Arctic fellows and a hopeless dipso-maniac. He had been stumbling around the north for a number of years in the hope, perhaps, that his drinking would go unnoticed back in Ottawa and he would reach pensionable age without getting fired.

Nineteen fifty-two is a bad year to pitch up in Inukjuak. After all the strictures of the war, most Westerners have grown used to dressing modestly, and the pre-war fashion for fox-fur muffs and trims has all but evaporated. In 1950 the price of Arctic fox pelts goes into freefall. Only seven years before, when Josephie Flaherty was first settling into his *piliriji*'s hut, an Ungava trapper could expect to sell a good fox pelt for C$35. By the beginning of the 1950s, the same pelt is worth C$3.50. To make matters worse, the collapse in the price coincides with the cyclical downturn in the fox population so trappers cannot make up for the fall in the price per pelt by trapping more fox. At the same time the price of flour, lard, tea and other trade goods in the north doubles, leaving the Inukjuamiut in an impossible situation. Most have no savings. The Hudson Bay store pays them for their pelts in store credits, and those who have any surplus credits see them quickly gobbled up by rising prices on ammunition and fishing line. The Hudson Bay Company policy is to advance credit only on future earnings from fox pelts. Families, like the Aqiatusuks, who have previously been encouraged to give up their hunting in favour of trapping, have to return to hunting for their food, but with no credit at the store, they cannot buy ammunition and other hunting supplies. The concentration of camps around the fur post makes the situation trickier still. Many of the areas close by have already been heavily hunted, so the hunters have to travel long distances, taking their families with them. Some Inuit are moving inland to trap otter, whose pelts now fetch more than fox. Everyone is hoping that the situation is temporary. A report by Alex Stevenson, head of the Eastern Arctic Patrol, in the summer of 1953 notes an increase in the population of snowy owls and lemmings that year, signalling that the fox is likely to be plentiful in the year to follow. But the Inuit cannot eat reports and for now, the situation is tough. Ninety-five families, consisting of 124 men, 122 women and 218 children, are living in and close by to Inukjuak. Those with heavily pregnant wives, elderly parents, new babies or sick children who cannot make the long trips begin showing up at the settlement, hoping the police will issue them with destitution rations: a few pounds of rolled oats, a block of lard, some flour and several pounds of useless beans. (The beans take up too much precious cooking fuel and, in any case, the Inuit find them indigestible.) For months at a time, whole families survive on a daily diet of gruel supplemented by the odd piece of seal fat or walrus skin offered up by a neighbour. The more needy they become, the less willing Corporal Webster, who is now responsible for deciding who gets destitution rations, seems to be to help them. His instructions are to discourage requests for welfare and disperse Inuit who come into the settlement looking for it, so as not to encourage what HQ in Ottawa describes as "vagrancy."

The moment Constable Gibson steps down from the ski-plane he is entering a world of trouble, though he does not know it. Webster is not the end of it. By 1952, Inukjuak has gathered to it a tribe of well-meaning bossyboots each of whom has their solution to the problem. First is Margery Hinds, the welfare teacher, a woman of stout morals and stouter methods. Since September 1951, Hinds has run Inukjuak's first school, teaching English, arithmetic, natural science, social studies, singing, hygiene and handicrafts. She has drafted a report to the Department of Northern Affairs protesting the policy of sending Inuit out of the settlement. Among those being sent away are fourteen children who are regularly attending the school. Once they are out of the settlement it will be impossible to educate them. "Two of the families who have been told to go have, I understand, never asked for relief and they resent being told to go as their families have always lived here," she writes. "Probably the reason the Eskimos made this place a camping place, is because it is about the same distance from the floe edge in winter and from the ptarmigan hunting region in the opposite direction. In the fall and early winter many Eskimos fish in the lakes back beyond the hills in the opposite direction to the floe edge." Then there is the community nurse, Margaret Reynolds, who is all for sending the Inuit packing with a bottle of kaolin and a few senna pods. The Hudson Bay Company factor, Rueben Ploughman, is anxious that the best trappers be encouraged back out on the land to trap. The Radiosonde manager has another view, the visiting missionary another still. No one thinks to ask the Inuit for theirs.

From his choreboy's hut, Josephie Flaherty can see Gibson unpacking his things, folding them, perhaps, and putting them away. In the early days, Gibson seems content just to stand by the detachment building sorting his equipment and watching settlement life go by, not so much finding himself in the north as the north finding itself in him. He sees Inuit men oiling their dog harnesses, mending nets, icing the runners of their *komatiks,* Inuit women chipping chunks of freshwater ice, scraping sealskins and jigging for char through the ice down by the pier. Over those first few months, he observes, gains confidence, begins hatching his plans.

By spring, Ross Gibson's self-appointed mission is to restore some discipline and dignity to the Inukjuak police detachment, which is to say, to find whatever means necessary to subvert the louche decrepitude of Corporal Webster. He begins to make himself more visible. In the mornings, he patrols the settlement, casts an eye over the activities of the Inuit, drops in for a chat of sorts with Rueben Ploughman, the fellows at the Radiosonde, the missionary and, less comfortable with women, gives a quick nod to Miss Hinds and Mrs. Reynolds. In the afternoons, if he can think of nothing else to do, he returns to the detachment and settles to his paperwork. Administrative afternoons are his bane. He is a lousy record-keeper, at sea with the reports and forms and bureaucratic paraphernalia of his posting. Sitting in front of the typewriter in his cabin, he longs to be out there, among the rocks, the great, blank skies. Not that the cabin is uncomfortable or particularly claustrophobic. On the contrary, for an Arctic lodging at the time it could almost pass as luxurious. The clapboard walls are thickly insulated, the floor raised on a gravel bed from the permafrost below, the windows bring in the daylight and can be shuttered off during the cold, dark days of winter. There is a living room made cosy by a coal stove, a kitchen with a coal-fired range, a snowporch, two good sized bedrooms, a bathroom with running water, the office with its chaotic scatter of papers, telegrams, budget sheets, outlines for reports. A wind turbine generates electricity. A radio transmitter in the office provides a connection to the outside world.

From time to time an Inuit man might knock at the door, anxious to tell of some grievance or problem, or keen to collect his family allowance payment. Gibson finds it difficult to deal with these callers patiently. After a few weeks in his post he makes up his mind that most grievances can be dealt with by repetition of the Inuktitut words for "no good" and "dog" which are the only ones he knows, accompanied, where necessary, by the appropriate hand signals and facial expressions. The Inuit give him the nickname "Big Red" from the colour of his face during these manoeuvres, though, of course, they do not let him in on this private amusement.

The great joy of Gibson's life in Inukjuak is patrolling, chiefly because it allows him to combine his two great passions, for hunting and for dogs, and also, and not incidentally, because it requires him to put a great deal of empty space between himself and Corporal Webster. The annual RCMP patrols usually begin in late winter, once the sea ice has settled in, and continue until the ice has rotted in early July. Come January, Ross Gibson is away often, sledging his way across hundreds of miles of coastal tundra in the company of the Inuit special constable and a dog team, until he grows familiar with the web of coastal paths cut by a thousand years of occupation and the tiny, willow-covered inlets and clamshell-rubbled beaches lying along Ungava's western coastline. The more he discovers about his new home, the more Inukjuak begins to seem less and less like a posting and more and more like a way of looking at the world.

Even as he accustoms himself to the land, though, Ross Gibson continues to be baffled by the men and women who live on it. He finds so many things about them to admire: their honesty, resourcefulness, courage, capacity for hard work, their cheerful demeanour. Their lives are lean and there is a particular intensity to them which draws Ross Gibson as it drew Robert Flaherty before him. Still, he can't begin to understand them. Their impassiveness, their inscrutability. He interprets what are, in fact, a series of adaptations to harsh surroundings as evasiveness and guile. Why do they refuse to catch his eye, why declare their intention of doing something he wants them to do then simply not do it? Why appear so fatalistic, so unwilling, or unable, perhaps, to plan? Why so riotous, so childlike in their gleeful dancing, their sled races, their interminable cat's cradles, then all of a sudden, so completely self-contained, so remote, so utterly impenetrable?

Of all the Inuit he encounters during the course of his patrols around the settlement and beyond, Ross Gibson finds Paddy Aqiatusuk both easiest and most challenging. The man has a certain confidence, he has opinions and seems willing to voice them. You can get your teeth into Paddy. You can push him and feel him pushing back. All the same, he can be demanding and difficult to control.

Corporal Webster says they call him Fatty. He cannot remember why, since Paddy Aqiatusuk is not actually fat. (In fact, Aqiatusuk means replete or satisfied.)

But, Fatty it is.

Paddy Aqiatusuk comes in to the settlement often to sell his carvings. In the early 1950s, a white man by the name of James Houston arrived on the *Nascopie*'s successor, the *C. D. Howe,* with a grant from the Canadian government to help promote Inuit handicraft. He returned to the south after that first visit with several thousand carvings, including many by Aqiatusuk, and sold them more or less immediately. After that he came every year, buying carvings and holding carving workshops to encourage the Inukjuamiut to carve what those in the south wanted to see: hunters, polar bears, shamans. Of all the sculptors, James Houston rates Aqiatusuk's work as among the best. You may see some of it today among the collection of the Canadian Museum of Civilisations in Ottawa.

In mid-April 1953, only six months after his posting begins, Ross Gibson picks up a telegram from Superintendent Henry Larsen, head of "G" or Arctic Division at the RCMP HQ in Ottawa. It reads as follows:

It is suggested by Director Northern Administration to move this summer on the *C. D. Howe* from Port Harrison detachment 4 Eskimo families to Craig Harbour on Ellesmere Island and 3 families to Cape Herschel on Ellesmere Island to hunt and trap for a living under the supervision of RCM Police detachments. Please ascertain whether any families are willing to go and if so their names and identification numbers and numbers of dependants and relationships of families involved . . . Conditions on Ellesmere should be carefully explained particularly the complete dark period . . . and other short days and only annual visits by supply ship . . . Families will be brought home at end of one year if they so desire.

Gibson hands the telegram to Webster, who gives it a cursory read, flips it over in his hand and offers it back. This one's for you.

A feeling of dread wells up in Ross Gibson. He understands something of what this request entails. What he does not yet know is that this telegram will colour the remainder of his life.

In 1953, the Department of Northern Affairs in Ottawa, the "Northern Administration" of Larsen's telegram, was an extraordinary place to work. Still relatively new, a creation of Canada's postwar awakening to its great northern lands, the Department was staffed almost entirely by ex–Hudson Bay Company men, most of whom had done their time in the Arctic and knew each other from past postings there. These doughty men were young boys when Roald Amundsen sailed his way through the Northwest Passage and Robert E. Peary reached the North Pole. Their heroes were men of the golden age of Arctic exploration, men like Peary and Amundsen, Otto H. Sverdrup and Vilhjalmur Stefansson. They grew up with *Nanook,* and later, when they were working for the Hudson Bay Company in its Arctic postings, they saw Nanook and Nyla reflected in the faces of the Inuit they met. They fell in love with the Arctic but it became *their* Arctic, a whole world to the north of the tree line about which their friends and colleagues in the south knew almost nothing. They remained a tiny, self-regarding confederation of amateur experts, working now within the conventions of the federal bureaucracy but always, somehow, considering themselves a tribe apart.

Of this band of fellow travellers, there was none so confident in his own mystique as James Cantley, the man who, in the 1930s, had set up the Baffin Trading Company post in Inukjuak to rival the Hudson Bay Company post there. Born in Aberdeen, Scotland, at the turn of the nineteenth century, Cantley had done what many bright, impoverished Scotsmen had done before him and immigrated to Canada as a teenager to work for the Hudson Bay Company. He had made it as far as Assistant Fur Trade Commissioner at the Bay before leaving to go it alone. When his Baffin Trading Company went bust, which it quickly did, Cantley slunk back to Ottawa and found himself a cosy niche in the newly created Department of Northern Affairs. His failure as an independent fur trader proving no bar to success in the Arctic Division of the Department, Cantley soon found himself promoted to head of the Department's Arctic Services Section. Moving the Inuit out of Inukjuak was originally Cantley's idea and it was he who had done most of the paperwork on the move.

The telegram in Ross Gibson's hands is from Henry Larsen, head of the "G" Division of the RCMP. Younger than Cantley by three years, Henry Asbjorn Larsen is already sitting at the top of a glittering northern career. Admiring voices speak of him in the same breath as Roald Amundsen, and there are undeniable similiarities. Larsen and Amundsen were both born in the same Norwegian fiord country and, like Amundsen, Larsen spent much of his childhood around boats. In 1928, when Josephie Flaherty and Ross Gibson were both boys, Henry Larsen immigrated to Canada and joined the Royal Canadian Mounted Police and was immediately assigned to the St. Roch, based out of Pauline Cove on Herschel Island, as ship's first mate. The St. Roch was a revolutionary ship. Made from Douglas fir sheathed in Australian ironbark, she had been built with special pressure beams and a rounded hull which would allow her to bob upwards under ice pressure. Her job was to police the Arctic seas and monitor game regulations while moving personnel between police posts. Sailing in her was a test of any man's sea legs, the rounded hull listed terribly in the swell, but Larsen's salty good humour, his physical courage, his navigational skills, even his penchant for singing rousing hymns up on deck when all other hands were trembling below and praying for their lives, singled him out. After he was promoted to captain he naturalised and became a Canadian citizen. In a few years he had become known throughout the Arctic as Hanorie Umiarjuaq, Henry with the Big Ship.

While Larsen was skippering the *St. Roch* around the Arctic, the RCMP was trying to extend its reach in the far northern Canadian mainland and on the eastern Arctic islands. In July 1922, the *Arctic*, led by Captain Joseph-Elzéar Bernier and expedition commander J. D. Craig, left Quebec City to set up an RCMP post close to Smith Sound to deter Inughuit Inuit living in northwestern Greenland from crossing the ice bridge across Smith Sound between Greenland and Ellesmere Island and hunting musk ox there. The ship was beaten back by heavy ice to a rocky inlet on Ellesmere's southern coast and Bernier and Craig decided to set up a detachment wherever they could land, which happened to be on a small promontory somewhat to the east of Grise Fiord, known henceforth as Craig Harbour, the place to where Henry Larsen was now planning to send Inuit families from Inukjuak. At Craig Harbour, the Mounties unloaded a prefabricated detachment hut, along with the head of the detachment, Inspector Wilcox, a regular detachment constable, Special Constable Kakto, and his wife, Ooarloo, who would act as housekeeper. Kakto and Ooarloo's two children would live with them. The Craig Harbour post soon foundered, however, jinxed, perhaps, by the knowledge of its own, accidental, birth. Only months after landing, Kakto and Ooarloo's children died of flu and their parents began demanding to go back to their home in Pond Inlet on Baffin Island. That same winter, the burlap in the inner lining of the ceiling of the detachment building caught fire, the extinguishers were frozen solid and the men had to watch while the flames ate their home. The inspector could find no willing replacement for Kakto on Baffin Island and Wilcox wrote to his superiors in Ottawa that "the climate is far more severe than Baffin Island, colder and darker in winter, making hunting conditions far different from Pond Inlet," and that it was impossible to persuade Canadian Inuit to live there. Ottawa appeared undeterred by the news. In future, RCMP headquarters decreed, the detachment would have to recruit its Inuit special constables from among the Inughuit, or polar Inuit of northwestern Greenland, who could better tolerate the conditions. Canada needed flag bearers in her northernmost reaches and, one way or another, she would have them. The detachment at Craig Harbour would remain open.

It was no secret that life at Craig Harbour was as tough as walrus leather for any white man who had the misfortune to be posted there and tougher still for the special constables. The detachment quickly became a kind of black joke in the force, the empty threat of irritated superiors or resentful subordinates. In summer, the Mounties were expected to go out after walrus and seal in order to build up a winter cache of meat for the sled dogs. As summer gave out to the short autumn, they would have to ready the detachment building for the oncoming winter, which meant making good the insulation banking, shovelling gravel into the holes in the tuff which had opened up around the detachment building during the summer months and giving the whole place a new coat of creosote and paint. When the dark period arrived in October, the Mounties would be expected to type their reports and hunker down against the weather. After the first light of the New Year arrived in February, they would set about repairing the sleds and dog harnesses and equipment then take off on the sleds to Flagler and Hayes fiords to hunt seal there. In March they would make dried pemmican for dog food to see them through the patrolling period. During the best of the High Arctic weather, in May and June, the Mounties would take turns going out on patrol. Their trips would take them as far out west as Norwegian Bay and east to Cape Isabella, just shy of the North Geomagnetic Pole. In July and August they would make preparations for the annual arrival of the supply ship.

Despite its various depredations, Craig Harbour was an exciting posting for a man who wanted to test his limits and could stomach the isolation. There was always plenty of bully beef, tobacco and booze. Annual leave was generous and the pay included a hefty hardship allowance. Though hunting musk ox and polar bear was prohibited, headquarters in Ottawa turned a blind eye to it and an active constable at Craig Harbour could make a tidy sum from dealing in pelts. In 1932, Inspector Sandys-Wunsch of the Craig Harbour detachment earned C$5,000 from pelts alone.

The detachment was ferociously expensive to maintain, though, and it was quietly abandoned in the late 1930s, only to be opened up once again in 1951, at the start of the Cold War, when it became the closest Canadian police detachment to the Soviet Union, across the North Pole.

With Craig Harbour closed, the Canadian hold on her High Arctic territories once again became tenuous. One of the thorns in the Canadian side remained Amundsen's successful navigation through the Northwest Passage. Amundsen was a Norwegian and his voyage had been followed by enquiries from the Norwegian government as to the sovereign status of those High Arctic islands first navigated and mapped by another Norwegian, Otto Sverdrup. The Canadian administration began to look for other ways to establish authority in the region. In 1940, it asked Henry Larsen to sail the *St. Roch* and a crew of eight through the Northwest Passage. Canada was keen for a Canadian to complete the navigation before an American got to it. Larsen set out by the southern route but the *St. Roch* got stuck in ice and was forced to overwinter in the Prince of Wales Strait off Banks Island. She pulled free the following summer, on 31 July 1941, and began heading north once more, only to find herself trapped by ice again in James Ross Strait. Northwesterly gales funnelled down McClintock Channel and flung floes against the ship. The ship sailed on but by 11 September she became iced in once more near the magnetic pole. Again, the crew were forced to overwinter and the following August, with the *St. Roch* still ice-bound, Larsen ordered several gunpowder charges to be set off to break the pack around her bows and reduce pressure on her hull. It was a dan-

gerous strategy—the charges could so easily have sunk the ship—
but it worked. The *St. Roch* escaped her winter prison on the summer winds. But her difficulties were not over. The onward voyage
was plagued by dreadful weather. Blizzards started up out of
nowhere only to give way to dense banks of fog. Sometimes the fog
was so bad the crew had to navigate by watching the wake of the ship
and try to keep it in a straight line. At Davis Strait they were con-
fronted with constellations of icebergs and growlers and the sea
grew so cold that the men were forced to chip ice off the propeller as
they went. On 10 August one of the ship's cylinders blew, the engine
room flooded and they narrowly avoided sinking. They put into
Pond Inlet on the northeastern coast of Baffin Island to make
repairs and on 22 September 1942, more than two years after she had
first set out, the *St. Roch* at last arrived at Bateau Harbour, Newfoundland, to a heroes' welcome. Henry Larsen and his crew had
become the first Canadians to cross the Northwest Passage, and in
1949, after nearly twenty years at the helm of the *St. Roch*, Henry
Larsen was promoted to commander of the RCMP's "G" Division.

In all his years voyaging around the Arctic, Larsen had developed a particular attachment for the Inuit. He'd seen how tough
their lives could be, and with what great stoicism they bore their
hardships. He agreed with Robert Flaherty that their contact with
white men had done them more harm than good, but it was too late
to turn back the clock. From now on white men and Inuit were in
the Arctic together. The task was to find a way they could live
together amicably and to their mutual benefit.

Three years after Larsen's promotion to commander of "G" division, in the spring of 1952, the new Northern Affairs Department of
the Canadian government organised the first ever Eskimo Affairs
Conference in Ottawa. Its mission was to find a solution to the
"Eskimo Problem," which is to say, what white men considered to be
the Eskimo Problem, the poor and uncertain living to be made trapping fox pelts. The "Problem" impacted on the Department when
the Inuit, demoralised and frustrated by the instability of the fox-fur

trade, began to look to the government for welfare payments to keep their children fed. There seemed to be no simple solution. Prior to the conference itself, the Department invited various experts, among them Henry Larsen and James Cantley, to comment on the problem and to propose their own solutions. In his briefing document, Henry Larsen wrote:

> The average Canadian citizen has no conception of how the once healthful and resourceful Eskimo has been exploited to such a degree that he now lives a life comparable to that of a dog ... The Eskimos generally have drifted into a state of lack of initiative and confusion. Never has there existed so much destitution, filth and squalor as exists today and in the opinion of some people the conditions under which some natives live are a disgrace to Canada, surpassing the worst evils of slum areas in cities. The sordid conditions existing amongst Eskimos are not known to the general public outside, whose knowledge of the Eskimos generally is that gleaned from glowing accounts which appear in the press occasionally and from romantic photographs in the magazines. The trouble goes back many years, actually, to the time that traders first went into Eskimo territory and changed the whole way of life of the Eskimos ... from primarily hunters of meat to primarily trappers of fur ... I think it is useless to talk of [the Inuit] resuming the native way of life.

Larsen went on to argue that the Inuit must be provided with the same access to schools, medical facilities and wage employment as any other Canadians, even if this meant an end to their traditional way of life. His vision was of small Inuit villages scattered around the northern fringes of the continent, not simply where fur traders wanted them to be, but where the Inuit wanted to put them. He wanted the villages equipped with municipal buildings, schools, cooperatives and small, autonomous industries. Welfare dependency, in Larsen's view, was the direct result of fluctuating fur prices.

To counteract these, he proposed the government set up a Crown Trading Company to ensure the stability of the prices of fox pelts.

James Cantley took a different view. In Cantley's mind, the problem was as simple as its solution. The Inuit had gone soft. "Goods considered luxuries less than forty years ago are now considered as necessities," he wrote. Why should the Inuit expect to be able to buy Coleman stoves or working rifles? For thousands of years they had got by on seal-oil lamps and bone harpoons. They should be forced to hunt and trap, reckoned Cantley, but that would be possible only in those settlements where the Hudson Bay Company held a monopoly on fur supply and could control not only the price of pelts but also which trappers got credit and for what. In Cantley's mind, the damage had been done by the RCMP because the Inuit had come to expect that the police would bail them out rather than see them starve. By releasing the Inuit from their historical dependence on the Hudson Bay Company the police had wiped out centuries of effective governance by the Bay in the Arctic. In Cantley's book, it was the police not the Bay who were responsible for wrecking Inuit traditions. The Barrenlanders were used to uncertainty, they were accustomed to starvation. This was their life, their culture, their whole history.

The solution, Henry Larsen and James Cantley agreed, was to move Inuit away from problem areas. The idea was not new. For many years, whalers moved the families to wherever they could be of most use to them, returning them to their homes at the end of the whaling season. In the 1930s, Inuit were moved experimentally on the *Nascopie* to Dundas Harbour. The idea of moving people as a solution to the problem of fur prices had first been mooted two years prior to the Eskimo Affairs Conference, in 1950, when Alex Stevenson, an administrator working under James Cantley, asked Henry Larsen whether some Inuit families might be moved from Baffin Island and re-established on Devon and Ellesmere islands. "It would even be possible to go up from Craig in the spring, spend the summer at Bache then return in the fall or early winter," wrote

Stevenson in a memo to Larsen. The presence of the Canadian Inuit might deter Greenlanders from crossing over into Ellesmere to hunt musk ox and polar bear and the Inuit would have the chance to hunt and trap on virgin land. Stevenson's boss, James Cantley, encouraged the idea and took it further. "There is no reason why more [Canadian] Eskimos should not be moved over to Ellesmere Island," he said. In reply, Alex Stevenson wrote, "If police detachments could be maintained at both Craig Harbour and Cape Sabine . . . ten or twelve families could be transferred to Ellesmere Island and use made of the natural resources that are undoubtedly available there. The occupation of the island by Canadian Eskimos will remove any excuse Greenlanders may presently have for crossing over and hunting there."

Henry Larsen and James Cantley repeated their ideas at the conference that spring, to an audience of northern administrators, missionaries, policemen and fur traders. The Inuit were not asked for their opinion.

And by the time Ross Gibson stepped off the ski-plane at Inukjuak a decision had already been taken. The Inukjuamiut were to be sent north.

CHAPTER SEVEN

IT IS ALREADY halfway through April 1953, and Ross Gibson is sitting in the detachment building figuring out how best to find his volunteers in time for the arrival of the *C. D. Howe* in July. Out at sea, the ice is breaking into small floes and the Inukjuamiut are widely scattered at camps up and down the coast. To scout out all the camps around the settlement in search of volunteers, he will need to travel 100 miles to the north and 70 miles to the south by dog sled, a round trip of 340 miles. The more he thinks about this the more daunting the whole thing seems. Is the Inukjuak detachment required to find the families or merely advised to do so? What if there are no "volunteers"? Does the Department plan to carry out the relocation anyway? How much pressure can he, Ross Gibson, reasonably be expected to apply to force people to go?

He has been in the Arctic long enough now to know how hard the move will be to explain. It is always said that the Inuit are nomadic but that doesn't really capture it. Rather they move around a territory and familiarity is part of their armoury of survival. In the few months Gibson has spent in the Arctic he can see how strongly they are bonded to the land they know. They rarely venture outside it, and when they do, it is always to travel with someone who has already made the journey. Without that strong sense of knowing they are vulnerable. Their only maps are the ones they carry in their memories.

Gibson studies the charts, reads up on Ellesmere Island. The

place is as far from Inukjuak as Inukjuak is from Ottawa. It is for-
biddingly remote, the ninth largest island on the planet, but for
more than ten months of every year surrounded on all sides by ice.
On 4 May he crosses the Innuksuak River and pops into Rueben
Ploughman's place, to ask if he would mind hosting a meeting to
discuss the issue later in the day. From the Hudson Bay Company
post he wanders up to the teacher's house, then to the nursing station, returning, finally, to the detachment building to make his
preparations for the meeting. He does not think to extend invita-
tions to the settlement Inuit. In the late afternoon, he returns to the
Bay post and, over tea and biscuits, relates the content of Henry
Larsen's telegram. Discussion begins convivially but soon enough
the *qalunaat* residents of Inukjuak are bickering and at odds. Margaret Reynolds wants to know what the Inuit will do for medical
facilities up on Ellesmere Island and hopes that *she* is not going to be
the one to have to give them all a medical before they leave, since she
has had no word from the Department of Health to this effect and
is, in any case, hardly qualified for such procedures. Margery Hinds
is more concerned about how the Department plans to give the children an education there. And who will ensure they will have the correct clothing and equipment? As welfare teacher the responsibility
devolves to her, but she has had no official instructions in the matter
and is unwilling to act without them. Rueben Ploughman wonders
what will happen to his fur business if all the best trappers are sent
away. He understands that it is Gibson's duty to find these volunteers; he's only hoping that Gibson will keep the interests of the
Hudson Bay Company in mind when he does so. On the other hand,
all seem agreed that this will be a fine opportunity to rid the settlement of some of its bad eggs: the gripers, the ne'er do wells, the men
whose hunting and trapping activities never seem to keep pace with
their families' stomachs, the family allowance dependents . . . and
Paddy Aqiatusuk. It will do them a world of good to have to put their
backs into hunting and trapping again. A moral wash and brush up,
a hauling of boot straps, a collective pulling-up of Inuit socks.

A message awaits Gibson back at the RCMP detachment. Henry Larsen requires the list of volunteers by the beginning of June. Gibson has less than a month to find seven families to move a vast distance to an uninhabited spot they know nothing about in the middle of the north polar desert. By now he has been in the RCMP for six months. This is the first major test of his new career.

What Ross Gibson does not know is that white men have a long history of removing Inuit people from their homelands. The trend, if that is what it can be called, began with Martin Frobisher at the end of the sixteenth century. Frobisher arrived at Hall Island in the eastern Arctic on the *Gabriel* in 1576. The Inuit living there had never seen white men or ships before and they convinced themselves that the vessel was some kind of giant sea mammal on whose backs strange, colourless creatures rode. Nine of these lowered themselves into the *Gabriel*'s skiff and made for the shore. The Inuit met them on the beach. The Englishmen handed the Inuit each a metal needle. Using sign language, the two groups agreed that one of the Inuit would board the *Gabriel* if two of Frobisher's men remained on the beach as surety. When the Inuk returned safely, the villagers grew more confident and nineteen went on board the *Gabriel*, where they exchanged sealskin and bearskin clothes for mirrors and bells. The following day, another Hall Islander went on board and was given a bell and a knife. A group of five crewmen volunteered to row this man back to shore, but instead of putting the Inuk down on the beach within sight of the *Gabriel*, as Frobisher had ordered, the men rowed towards the Inuit village, disappeared from view and did not return. For several days, Frobisher could get no word from or of them. Seriously concerned, now, for their safety, he decided to set a trap. Using bells and beads as lures, the crew of the *Gabriel* managed to entice an Inuk man to approach the ship. As the man swung alongside in his *kayak,* the *Gabriel*'s crew scooped him out of the water, and tied him fast, hoping they could use him in a prisoner exchange, but the remaining villagers refused to discuss the disappeared crewmen or the Inuit captive. Frustrated, Frobisher set sail back to England with his prisoner still on board. The unnamed Inuk survived the trip but fell ill almost the moment he stepped ashore. A coffin and a grave were purchased for him for the sum of eleven shillings and four pence and he was laid to rest in St. Olave's Church in Hart Street, London, where he remains to this day.

The kidnapping of Inuit as surety or simply for their curiosity value became so commonplace over the next 150 years that in 1720 the Netherlands adopted a resolution banning the transporting of Greenlanders to Europe and in 1732 Denmark followed suit. Neither of these well-intentioned edicts had much effect and Inuit continued to be taken from their homes and families.

In 1897, the American explorer, Admiral Robert E. Peary, shipped six Inuit from northwestern Greenland to New York for "scientific scrutiny" but within months of their arrival, four of the six were dead, leaving only a man, Uisakassak, and a boy, Minik. Uisakassak sailed back to Greenland with Peary on the *Windward* the following year, but Minik's father being among the dead, the boy remained behind in New York as the adopted son of William Wallace, the building superintendent of the American Museum of Natural History. While wandering round the museum one day, Minik came upon an Inuit skeleton, strung up in a glass case for exhibition. Drawn to the sign on the case, Minik discovered to his horror and shame that the bones were those of his father. This puzzled him particularly because he had been to his father's funeral and seen the coffin lowered into the ground, but it did not take him long to work out that the interment had been a ghastly trick to keep him from the truth. Minik begged to be allowed to give his father a proper funeral. He would take the bones back to Greenland himself and bury them under a cairn in accordance with tradition. It was not to be. The skeleton remained, in all its immodesty, hanging from a hook on display. "I felt that I must go North, back to Greenland some how, some way," Minik wrote in a letter, adding,

I have lost hope . . . And I have given up believing your Christian creed that you taught me was meant for one and all—Christian and savage alike. I gave up that finally when Professor Bumpus at the museum told me for the last time I could not have my father's bones to bury them. Where is your Christianity? My own people are kinder and better, more human, and I am going back to them. My land is frozen and desolate, but we can bury our dead here.

While Minik was trying to recover his father's bones, Uisakassak arrived back in northwestern Greenland, bringing with him stories and impressions of the places he had seen. He told his fellows that he had found it difficult to navigate "among the man-made mountains" of the city, and that it had been "too warm and there was a great lack of walrus meat and blubber." He described the trains which hurtled "like a gust of wind across the sea," and could hardly stop talking about the streetcars "big as houses with masses of glass windows as transparent as freshwater ice, racing on without dogs to haul them, without smoke and full of smiling people who had no fear of their fate." His companions were not impressed by these tales. Sorqaq, the local shaman, told him to go and tell his lies to the women, who would be more likely to believe them, and Uisakassak was officially shunned.

The Arctic trade in goods began with an equal degree of cynicism. Canada was an early European frontier long before Christopher Columbus sailed to America. The first documented visit, by Vikings, was in 982 and by the Middle Ages, traders were regularly making the journey across the Atlantic to bring back polar bear skins, narwhal tusks and live gyrfalcons, which were then traded as far east as the Arabian peninsula. By the sixteenth century there was a thriving trade in furs between the Arctic regions and Europe, pioneered by, among others, Pierre Esprit Radisson, who remarked of his travels in the Arctic, "we are caesars, there being nobody to contradict us." In 1821 Sir George Simpson, then head of the Hudson

Bay Company, wrote, "I am convinced [the Inuit] must be ruled with a rod of iron to bring and keep them in a proper state of subordination, and the most certain way to effect this is by letting them feel their dependence upon us."

The rod of iron was rifle-shaped and it was widely used to kill and maim Inuit, and to support the rape of the women and the abduction of their children. In the Arctic there was no one but the Inuit to act as witnesses. The early fur traders were, as Radisson said, "caesars."

Trade itself was often unfair. In 1923, a .30–30 Winchester rifle sold for twelve white fox pelts, though such a rifle could be purchased for a single pelt in the south. The era of bells and needles as trade goods had long since gone and seemed now to have an aura of innocence about it. For the previous half-century the rifle had been the bestseller. Inuit looked after their things and by the time Robert Flaherty arrived in Inukjuak to make *Nanook of the North* the market for rifles was reaching saturation point. The former whaling captain turned trader, Charles Klengenberg, solved this small dilemma by giving the Inuit hard steel ramrods and advising them to scrape out the insides of their rifle barrels, an action which soon ruined the rifling, as Klengenberg knew it would. The guns then failed to shoot straight and Inuit starved until they could scrape together sufficient funds in the form of fox pelts to buy another. And so the market for rifles was restored. Klengenberg wrote of a later exchange with Inuit: "They were so innocent a people … that I had not the heart to take advantage of them in trade, so all I took was most of their clothes and stone cooking pots and copper snowknives and ice picks for steel knives and frying pans and a supply of matches. They had no raw furs with them, but their garments would be useful for my family and some of my rascally crew."

By the 1950s, the Inuit were rather wary of any "offer" emanating from *qalunaat*, especially where it involved a move from their familiar hunting grounds, but they were equally afraid of what refusal might bring. To Inuit, whalers, police and representatives of the

Hudson Bay Company were all cut from the same cloth. If you could not avoid them, you had better keep watch on them. They were not the kind of people who would be denied.

A day or so after the meeting with Hinds, Ploughman and Reynolds, Constable Ross Gibson orders Tommy Pallisser, the Hudson Bay Company translator, and Special Constable Kayak to prepare the detachment *komatik* and dog team for what might well be a long trip. They will head north towards Povungnituk. The first camp they visit will be that of Paddy Aqiatusuk.

Over the following two weeks, Gibson, Kayak and Pallisser sledge to every camp lying between Inukjuak and Sugluk, sixty miles to the north, looking for volunteers for the Ellesmere Island experiment. At each camp, the routine is the same. They unharness the dogs and set about looking for suitable snow for a snowhouse. If the men of the camp are out hunting, a local boy is dispatched to fetch those within range. While the three men of the patrol wait, Kayak and Pallisser fix up two small snowhouses, one for themselves and one for Gibson, who can never bring himself to sleep beside an Inuk, and someone boils a kettle of sweet tea. Once all of those who can be assembled are gathered round, Gibson pulls out Henry Larsen's telegram and a map and proceeds to tell the Inuit what he knows, which, in all honesty, is not very much.

Had Ross Gibson known more about Ellesmere Island it would have made it more difficult for him to sell it. The place was uninhabited and had been so since the Little Ice Age thickened its ice caps and grew its glaciers about 350 years ago. There was no evidence that the island would support human habitation. No wildlife surveys had ever been conducted there and it was not known how many fish, marine mammals, birds or land mammals populated the area. What *was* known was that the polar desert conditions did not support anything like the numbers of plant and animal life which flourished around Inukjuak. The cold and the dark were known from police detachment reports, though not to Ross Gibson. Temperatures in the High Arctic are on average 15°C lower than those in

Inukjuak. In the polar north, temperatures rarely rise much above freezing, even in summer, and in winter they regularly fall below −40°C. A modern domestic freezer is usually set at about −18°C. At −40°C a cup of boiling water turns to water vapour when thrown into the air, saliva freezes and steam rises from the fingers. In humans, hypothermia can set in within two minutes of the skin's exposure to air. The winds, too, are much fiercer, becoming katabatic as they spin along the frozen flats of the Arctic Ocean. The sea around Ellesmere is never wholly free of ice and the navigation season is often as short as four weeks, making the area more or less inaccessible to anything but ski-planes for ten or eleven months of the year. On account of its position high above the Arctic Circle, the winter dark period stretches from October to February. For four months of the year it is dark twenty-four hours a day.

What Ross Gibson *does* know is that the Inuit already live in snowhouses, they already spend their summers in canvas tents, they already hunt seal. Surely, life on Ellesmere Island cannot be all that different? He makes some effort to explain the dark period and the fact that it is a little colder on Ellesmere Island, but, since his job depends on Inuit agreeing to move, he ends his pitch on an upbeat note, emphasising the tremendous quantity of game to be hunted, the piles of soft, meringue-coloured pelts to be trapped, finishing always with the trump card: the promise that anyone who does not like it can return.

Despite these inducements, no one wants to go. Even those who are having a hard time of it with the fall in fox prices say they want to remain with their families. Trappers are predicting record fox catches for the next year and the price is bound to rise sooner or later. Until then, life will be hard but not unendurable. They will do what they have always done and sit it out. And so, in camp after camp, all along the eastern coast of Hudson Bay, with much smiling and shaking of hands, the Inuit turn Ross Gibson away. He returns to Inukjuak without a single volunteer.

Back at the detachment, he rethinks his strategy, and fixes finally on the power of repetition. The only thing for it is to return to the camps and keep returning, pressing the advantages of the move until he senses the tide turning his way. Time is tight and getting tighter. Each time he goes out to the camps the ice is a little softer and the dogs are forced to strain a little more in their harnesses and Ross Gibson feels a little more frayed and desperate. On his third pass through the camps he is downright bad-tempered. Behind his back the Inuit still call him Big Red, but now they are afraid.

At the camps of the poorest hunters and trappers, or those with the largest families, people are beginning to waver. They are imagining that, if they do not go, Ross Gibson will stop their family allowance money, a dollar or two, but right now, the only dollar or two they see.

Ross Gibson decides to target Paddy Aqiatusuk. He would like the old grouch to disappear and he knows he will be likely to take a good few others with him. He is at the head of a big family. And so Gibson returns to Aqiatusuk's camp, talks up the great hunting and trapping, the proximity of police detachments in case of any emergency and the promise the family will all be returned if, after a year or two, they decide they do not like it.

Aqiatusuk sucks his teeth, shakes his head. He is contented enough where he is, on the land he knows, among his family. Gibson tries another tack, takes out a list, pretends to check it and notes, with Pallisser translating, that some of Aqiatusuk's family have already said they will go. He spots a certain tension in the sculptor's face, knows he has hit his mark. How will they hunt? Aqiatusuk asks. Where will they live? What will happen if there turns out to be no food? Gibson bluffs his way through, loses his temper a little, becomes aware that his voice is raised. He is met with a wary silence. The truth is that Aqiatusuk has no desire to leave his homeland. His back is sore and his liver gives him trouble, he is happy to live out his days making his carvings and being a help to his family. And yet, and yet. If what Gibson says is true, he can go north with Elijah and Samwillie and his family, they can trap for a while, earn enough to buy a Peterhead boat and come back down to Inukjuak. There is something else, too, something he reads in the scowls on Ross Gibson's face. If he does not agree to go, he senses that the police will never leave him alone. The Big Red policeman will harass him from the settlement, he will refuse to pay him family allowance, he will stop him selling his carvings at the Hudson Bay Company. And he will make life unbearable for his stepson, Josephie Flaherty. No Inuit says no to a white man without repercussions. Aqiatusuk senses the menace, it is what his ancestors tell him. In his bones he feels it to be true.

The old sculptor marches into Inukjuak, sits himself down in Josephie's hut, waits for his stepson to come home from work, amusing himself by playing with Josephie and Rynee's little daughter, Martha. The door opens and Josephie shakes his boots and goes to his stepfather to hug him. He already knows his family will leave, the settlement Inuit have talked of little else, and he knows, too, that he cannot go with them because he has a job and a daughter and another baby on the way. From Josephie's hut Aqiatusuk walks to the police detachment and opens the door.

Ayunqnaq, he says, it can't be helped. Reluctantly he agrees to move north to Ellesmere Island.

On the morning of 23 May 1953, Constable Ross Gibson telegraphs RCMP headquarters in Ottawa with the names of the seven "volunteer" families who will make the 1,500 mile journey to the High Arctic in July. Then he pulls on his boots and goes out into the blinding snow. Aqiatusuk is right. Some things cannot be helped.

On the morning of 25 July the *C. D. Howe* anchors off shore and sends her cargo barges out across the water to the little wooden pier at the mouth of the Innuksuak River, where Inuit are already gathered to help bring the cargo ashore. That evening there will be races and acrobatics and cat's cradle competitions. There will be a special supper of hardtacks and sardines and pieces of candy. In the morning the Inuit will be carried on board ship for their annual medical check-ups. Thirty-three of them will remain. Among them will be:

Paddy Aqiatusuk, his wife Mary, son Larry Audlaluk, stepsons Elijah and Samwillie and stepdaughters Minnie and Anna, Paddy's fifty-one-year-old brother Phillipoosie Novalinga and his family, Paddy's son Joadamie Aqiatusuk and his family, Thomasie Amagoalik, who has been living in Phillipoosie's camp, his wife Mary and sons Allie, Salluviniq and Charlie, Thomasie's brothers Simeonie and Jaybeddie Amagoalik and their families, plus Daniel Salluviniq and his family and Alex Patsauq, whose son Markoosie is coughing blood.

The arrangements for this monumental move are hasty and primitive. Margery Hinds is asked to inspect the families' clothes and equipment but nothing is done with her report stating that in most cases they are inadequate. Since the provisions and equipment supply list has been drawn up by James Cantley with no knowledge of the number of people moving, nor their ages, sex and sizes, there is nothing to be done in any case. Each migrant is supposed to be given a thorough medical examination on board before they leave, to ensure they are fit to travel, but the *C. D. Howe*'s X-ray machine has broken down and there is no time to fix it. There are problems accommodating the Inuit's dogs and equipment, much of which is left on deck, covered by a tarpaulin. A rough storm might send dogs and equipment overboard. The Inuit quarters under the foredeck are already nearly full with sick people, in particular consumptives, on their way to sanatoria in the south, so there are insufficient beds and no division at all between the sick and healthy. Cantley has signed off on the purchase of some mattresses which will be put on the floor in the Inuit quarters to supplement the bunks, where they will pick up the damp and the cold. It will all just have to do. R. A. J. Phillips of the Department is on board at the time and later writes a report on his impressions. At Inukjuak he observes "too many white people around offering confusing and conflicting directions to the Eskimo" and adds that "there is far more racial discrimination than I had realised. There was a half-concealed air of patronage which is particularly nauseating."

Ross Gibson is surprised to find himself on board, as guardian of the new migrants. His role, he discovers, is to iron out any creases in the preparations (where to begin!) and also to keep an eye on Paddy Aqiatusuk. Unexpected though this is, and not wholly welcome, it does at least get him away from Corporal Webster.

The initial plan is for the *C. D. Howe* to sail across Hudson Bay to Churchill, Manitoba, where the ship will be met by Alex Stevenson, the officer in charge of the Eastern Arctic Patrol's northern leg. Stevenson is a veteran of the annual supply and is this year under orders from his boss, James Cantley, to inspect the tents, clothing, rifles and ammunition of the émigrés. It is not clear what Stevenson is supposed to do if he finds these lacking. After Churchill, the *C. D. Howe* will make her way up to Clyde River on the east coast of Baffin Island, stopping at the usual supply drop-offs. At Clyde she will rendezvous with the icebreaker, *d'Iberville,* under the stewardship of Henry Larsen. The *d'Iberville* will carry the migrants north to Pond Inlet, or Mitimatalik, where she will pick up another three families. The Pond Inlet people, the Ingluligmiut, are more accustomed to the kind of extreme conditions in the High Arctic and Henry Larsen is hoping they will be able to assist the Inukjuamiut in settling there.

In response to uncertainties about the wildlife population on Ellesmere, Henry Larsen proposes to divide the migrants into three groups, land one group at Craig Harbour and one at Alexandra Fiord on Ellesmere Island and the third at Resolute Bay on Cornwallis Island about four hundred miles to the west. Each group of Inukjuamiut will then be allotted one Pond Inlet family to help them settle. The Inuit are not consulted, and have no idea that they are to be split into groups.

The following day, 26 July 1953, the *C. D. Howe* weighs anchor and begins to swing out into the waters of the Hudson Bay with Paddy Aqiatusuk and much of his extended family on board.

CHAPTER EIGHT

THEY HAVE BEEN steaming along for a couple of hours in deep cloud when the sun suddenly slides out from under cover and the sea spins curls of foam across the silver surface of the waves, and when the clouds finally melt away, Inukjuak and everything they knew has disappeared, replaced on all sides by a blank swell, the only sounds the ship's engine, the slap of waves and the coarse lisping of the wind. Between them and the next stop at Churchill, Manitoba, lie four hundred miles of rough water.

The Hudson Bay coastline is 7,600 miles round. The first white man to map the area, Henry Hudson, did not realise he had entered a bay at all. In 1610 he found himself in what is now the Hudson Strait and ordered his ship, the *Discovery*, to turn south. He was looking for a short cut from the Atlantic into the Pacific which would take ships from Europe on to China and India, the infamous Northwest Passage. Almost as soon as the *Discovery* entered the bay waters, she became marooned on a sandbank and was only released some hours later by a mysterious wash of water from the west. Guessing that this water must have come from an opening between the two great oceans, Hudson felt greatly encouraged. He had no way of knowing that the wash was caused by the interaction between the bay's currents and the strong western tide. Hudson believed that if he took a course to the southwest, he would be able to locate a navigable channel or navigation giving out to the Pacific,

and from there sail all the way to China. He set a course, tacking farther and farther south until, sighting land at what is now James Bay
at the southern edge of what is now Hudson Bay, he ordered his
crew to sail along the coastline and look for the channel out to the
southern sea. For days the ship zigzagged about within sight of land
but without finding the elusive channel. The navigation season was
nearing its end, Hudson's expedition was several thousand miles
from home and they were no nearer to finding the Northwest Passage. The sea was becoming slushy and food supplies were beginning to run low. There was nothing for it but to overwinter in the
ice. By the time spring arrived, the crew were at a low ebb. They had
been able to trade for meat and a few supplies with the local Indians,
but many of them had the beginnings of scurvy and they were thin
and drawn. Hudson was keen to continue his explorations but by
now the crew was desperate to return home. When Hudson insisted
they carry on, they mutinied, bundling Hudson into a lifeboat with
his small son and seven supporters and leaving them to their fate.
The remaining crew of the *Discovery* then set a course back the way
they had come, so near starvation now that they were reduced to
chewing candles and sucking on gull's bones soaked in vinegar.
Eventually, they got themselves out of the bay and within a few
weeks arrived safely back in England. Hudson and his party were
not so lucky. Exactly what became of them no one knows for sure,
but there is one clue. Years after the mutiny, a Hudson Bay Company
factor met with some Inuit in the Hudson Strait, who told him that
the first white man they had ever seen had been washed up on their '
shores in a small and battered boat. He was dead but there was a live
white boy in the boat with him. The Inuit brought the boat in and
tried to communicate with the boy, but he seemed frightened and
did not speak their language. Not knowing what else to do, they
decided to tie the boy up in a dog harness, leave him outside their
tent and let nature work on him awhile. When he died, they took his
body out to the rocks and buried it.

As late as the 1950s, many white sailors still considered it bad luck to sail in Hudson Bay and whatever their feeling for dark, inauspicious tales, no one disputes the fact that Hudson Bay provides some uniquely hazardous problems for those crossing it. The bay's enclosed waters are cut off from the ocean currents which moderate sea temperatures and the waters of the bay are often colder than those of the Arctic Ocean a thousand miles farther north. The waters keep the ambient temperature cool. Out in mid-channel, sailors have recorded air temperatures of −63°C. For all but twelve to fourteen weeks in the year, the mouth of the bay is blocked by ice. Fierce winter winds race on to the beaches and eskers, chopping the shore-fast ice into huge floes. The floating pack breaks up late and lingers in fragments, which jam into pressure ridges. Long after the spring sun has melted the snow on shore and ground willow and saxifrage are sprouting from the dark, sun-warmed earth; the ice still lies thickly across Hudson Bay itself. As summer lengthens, great leads of open water emerge, providing highways not only for ships but also for icebergs drifting down from Davis Strait. Bergs and bergy bits edge into Hudson Bay through the clearways and threaten to overturn the sturdiest icebreaker. When autumn arrives, water vapour rises from the sea and meets the land in thick curds of fog, which then lurk along the low, flat coastline waiting to punish any overconfident mariner trying to make his way to shore. As autumn turns into winter, which it does very fast, the temperature sinks and Hudson Bay stiffens and resumes its wintry solitude.

The western tides, which persuaded Henry Hudson that there was a channel out to the Pacific and, indirectly, led to his death, are notorious now for their scale. Winds are usually high and it is often difficult to navigate by compass because the area is swept by magnetic storms and the seabed is rich in iron ore. The northerly reaches are so close to the magnetic North Pole that compass needles reel around like drunken sailors. Nearly four centuries after Henry Hudson first entered it, the bay which bears his name is the same stew of ice and treachery that it always was. Four hundred years of shipwrecks line its shores now, not least of which is that of the *C. D. Howe's* predecessor, the *Nascopie*. In 1953, when the *C. D. Howe* was making her way across the bay with Paddy Aqiatusuk and his family on board, the bay waters were still for the most part uncharted.

Paddy Aqiatusuk knows enough about the bay from his trips to the Hope, Sleeper and Belcher islands to be anticipating a rough sail and so it proves. For hour after hour the ship rocks and pitches and the Inuit passengers, most of whom have never been at sea out of sight of land, cling to their bunks and mattresses and try not to look afraid. Many are taken by seasickness and stand miserably beside the washbasins with their stomachs churning. The layout of the Inuit quarters does not allow for privacy. Bunks are set out in such close rows that it is impossible to sit upright on them. The extra mattresses take up whatever floor space there might once have been in the sleeping quarters and the single common room is filled by a huge refectory table and some bolted-down chairs on which the Inuit are served inedible meals of porridge, and potatoes with gravy. On the other side of the bunks and mattresses is the sick bay, divided from the main dormitories by nothing more than a curtain, and full, on this trip, of tubercular Inuit. Between the sick bay and the dormitories is a communal washing area, shared between the sick and the healthy. The position of the quarters beneath the foredeck does not help. The heaving and the pitching of the ship is heaviest here, which is why the cabins for the ship's white passengers are at the other end of the ship, in the stern.

Hour dissolves into endless hour and Hudson Bay creeps by without their ever seeming to go anywhere. The ship rocks and moans. At the end of the first day the damp nags like an ancient toothache and the digestive whirrs and creeks of the engine make it impossible to sleep. By the evening of the second day the Inuit are divided into those who have accustomed themselves to the awful pitching and those, the majority, who are forced to pass their hours running from mattress to washbasin in order to be sick.

The following morning a crewman tells them to pack their bags and come up on deck. They stand in foggy air and watch the low buildings and fortifications of Churchill, Manitoba, coming into view. Already it is clear to Paddy Aqiatusuk that they are in another country. The land in front of them looks nothing like the Ungava tundra. The sky has grown in size so that the clouds seem not to fit it and the land, a honeycomb of polygonal granite stones, pocked by rocky pools and pieces of crumbling machinery, lies almost flush to the sea. Sitting on a promontory is an ancient-looking fort and a little way inland, a stand of stunted black spruce leans violently in the direction of the prevailing westerlies.

On 28 July, two days after setting off from Inukjuak, the *C. D. Howe* drops anchor. Someone comes up on deck and begins throwing meat into the dogs' cages and the appetising aroma of animal fat drifts towards the foredeck where Paddy Aqiatusuk stands, bringing with it a fond reminder of *muktuk*, white whale skin, and *igunaq*, fermented walrus meat. The *C. D. Howe*'s deck crane begins to swing the Inuit tents, pots and sleeping skins into a cargo barge alongside. The Inuit will be set on shore and the tubercular patients ferried to the local clinic and from there dispatched south to sanatoria. The others will set up camp for a few days while the *C. D. Howe* unloads the settlement's supplies and the medical officer conducts his annual checks of the locals. Those families travelling on to the far north will then be allowed back on board.

Aqiatusuk and his family are set down on the far bank of the Churchill River at a distance from the settlement. From this new vantage point, Churchill appears closed in and crowded. Over the other side of the river sits the old fort and along the shore beside there is a scattering of prefabs and huts. A little farther away there stands a giant cement rectangle with a series of cranes and wide-girthed chains. A few tundra swans preen themselves on its cross-beams. This is the great grain silo, the brainchild of Robert Flaherty's sponsor, Sir William Mackenzie, whose idea it had been forty years previously to ship Canadian wheat across Hudson Bay. The final section of Sir William's transcontinental railroad reached

Churchill in 1931 and more than twenty years later it is still running. The journey, through thick boreal tundra from Winnipeg, 1,100 miles to the south, takes two days and two nights and the train runs twice weekly in the summer, but the wheat route has been all but abandoned, the navigation across Hudson Bay proving too difficult and expensive, and the grain silo sits empty, a monument to another, more optimistic age.

Paddy Aqiatusuk and his stepsons set up the tents while Mary and the other women spread out their willow mats, then go down to the beach to look for driftwood to make a fire.

Over the days that follow, they watch the cargo barges moving ceaselessly between ship and shore, offloading crates and other supplies, the crew assisted by Indians and Inuit. Supply is the *C. D. Howe*'s primary function, and it is regulated by the Hudson Bay traders, policemen, missionaries and, less often, teachers and nursing staff making up the white populations of the larger settlements who fill in the supply requests. In many settlements across the eastern Arctic supplies often run out months before the next shipment is due. The problem is always most acute towards the end of the supply year in June and July, which coincides with exceptionally lean times on the land. Hungry Inuit often come in to the settlements during the early summer to spend their credits, only to discover there is no food left in the store to buy. Predicting a settlement's annual supply requirements is an inexact science, dependant on knowing fox-fur cycles and being able to predict fox prices in advance, which it is almost impossible to do. Officials are encouraged to underestimate rather than order what might turn out to be unwanted surplus. As a result of this ordering system, Departmental officials and other *qalunaat* travelling on the Eastern Arctic Patrol often get the impression that the Inuit in the places they land are half starved. If they had travelled to the Arctic at any other time, they would have understood that this was generally not the case. In general, the *qalunaat* on these trips are rather isolated from the Inuit and they like it that way. From their camp across the river, Paddy

Aqiatusuk can see white men emerging from the passenger cabins, lowering themselves into Peterheads travelling to shore and disappearing into the administrative buildings, only to reappear with other whites and make their way back to the ship for captain's supper. When darkness finally falls, the Indian and Inuit fires flare into life along the shorelines and the delectable smell of barbecuing meat drifts across the river along with the sounds of dancing and drums. First thing in the morning, lines of Inuit and Indians are already waiting on shore to be ferried out to the *C. D. Howe* for their annual medicals.

The Inuit call the *C. D. Howe* "the place where you take your clothes off." They dread their annual medical inspections and often have to be strong-armed by missionaries or policemen into attending. *Qalunaat* have brought with them a panoply of diseases to which the Inuit have virtually no immunity. Polio, tuberculosis, influenza, diphtheria, measles and whooping cough are rife among the Inuit living along Canada's Arctic coast. The medicals are designed to detect any outbreaks of disease and limit their spread. The chief medical officer on each Eastern Arctic Patrol is responsible for isolating those suffering from an infectious illness and keeping them on board ship from where they are taken to clinics and sanatoria in the south. On board, the Inuit have their tongues depressed to search for signs of diphtheria, their eyes inspected and chests X-rayed to show up the symptoms of TB and their skin, joints and muscles prodded for anything else. The children are inoculated, then checked for scabies, lice and fleas. If any are found their young hosts will be swabbed down with disinfectant and their heads shaved. If anything more serious is spotted, they are taken away, more often than not with no opportunity to say goodbye to their parents or families. The *C. D. Howe* is often carrying so many Inuit consumptives that northern administrators label her the Shakespeare ship: "TB or not TB."

The Shakespeare ship was as much a part of the problem as she was the cure. Wherever she went in the Arctic she left behind her epidemics of what the Inuit termed "ship sickness," which could be anything from flu or pneumonia to measles and polio. The ship sicknesses were by no means trivial episodes in the history of the Arctic. In the western Arctic, where infections spread more rapidly than they did in the eastern archipelago, ship sicknesses had reduced the Inuit population from around twenty thousand at the beginning of the nineteenth century to around two thousand at its end. In 1902 a visit by the Scottish whaler, *Active*, wiped out the entire population of Southampton Island. Half a century on, ship sicknesses were rarely quite so dramatic, but it was very common for every settlement on the *Howe*'s route to lose several children and elderly people every year to ship sickness, and for many more to be hauled off to the south.

Had Paddy Aqiatusuk known about the state of the *C. D. Howe* itself he might never have got back on board. The captain, Paul Fournier, was a competent seaman in ordinary conditions, but he had absolutely no experience of Arctic navigation. He was, in all senses of the phrase, completely out of his depth. His crew were mostly greenhorns, hired off the quay at Quebec. For some reason Fournier never made any ship's inspections, perhaps because he had a sense of what he would find, so drunken sailors were left to shoot craps games in the lifeboats while the watch slept in their bunks. Safety procedures were more or less ignored. In the darkroom, developing chemicals slopped around in tanks, creosote leaked from barrels in the hull and sailors used oil barrels as ash trays. None of the crew had been briefed on the itinerary or supplies, there had been no instructions on what was expected of the crew in port and no emergency drill or storm procedures were in place. Many of the *qalunaat* passengers were themselves too drunk to notice anything was wrong, but it was. The *C. D. Howe* was ill-run and its crew and captain completely green and they were about to enter some of the most dangerous waters on earth.

Her stay at Churchill over, the ship reloaded the Inuit and their belongings, weighed anchor and continued on her way. On 7 August

1953 she crossed the 60th parallel, on the western coast of Hudson Bay, at the mouth of the McConnell River, where a grizzle of dwarfed black spruce finally gave out to the Barrenland tundra. From time to time Paddy Aqiatusuk was allowed up on deck to watch the Barrens sliding by, to smell the air, already so unfamiliar, and to see the light change colour. He had never imagined anywhere so vast, so superficially familiar to his homeland but so totally strange and there was a part of him that already felt too old for such novelty. As the ship crawled north, making short scheduled stops at the tiny settlements of Rankin Inlet and Chesterfield Inlet before turning through Roes Welcome Sound, Paddy sneaked off ship to talk to the local Inuit but their dialects were difficult to decipher and he could rarely make much sense of what they said. No one seemed to know Ellesmere Island. Few had even heard of it. He took whatever small item of trade he could from among his possessions and traded it for fresh meat, for there was none on board ship and an Inuk feels the lack of meat as strongly as he feels a lack of air or water. He returned to ship no wiser about this destination but with delicious packages of whale, caribou or seal, which he shared around among his own. Others, not bold enough to slip off ship and go ashore, took to stealing the pig fat and frozen walrus meat intended for the dogs.

They sailed on north, across a hard, antique world of naked rock and shale, under a sky as soft and luminous grey as sealskin, which billowed from time to time with storm clouds. There were fewer birds now, and those there mewed and keened as though lost and looking for company. Two and a half weeks out of Inukjuak they crossed the Arctic Circle at Repulse. At Salisbury Island they were followed for a while by a group of beluga but were forbidden to hunt any from on deck so they remained in their quarters, throwing up their daily diet of potatoes and porridge, foods that neither nourished nor sustained. It was getting noticeably darker now, and the Northern Lights sprayed the twilight sky in reds and greens. Pretty soon, they would be too far north even for those.

During the third week, they entered the Hudson Strait and Paddy Aqiatusuk mounted the stairs from the Inuit quarters and went on deck to look at the land. A few glaucous gulls stirred the air above the ship, hoping to find fish in the churn. Otherwise they were completely alone. To the north lay the low hills of Baffin Island's Meta Incognita Peninsula and to the south the Ungava Peninsula and everything Paddy had ever known. To comfort himself, Paddy recalled the stories Ross Gibson had told of the endless herds of caribou and the abundant fox on Ellesmere Island and added in a few of his own. He thought about the meat they would eat, the animals they would see, the narwhals, bowhead whales and polar bears his grandparents had spoken about when he was a child but which he had never seen. He thought about his stepson Josephie, sad thoughts mostly, but also happy thoughts about the next time they would meet. Perhaps by then, Paddy would own a Peterhead and his stepson would be able to give up working for the *qalunaat* and return to his place in the family.

A day or two later, the *C. D. Howe* pulled into Frobisher Bay which Inuit call Iqaluit. From there she would continue north along the coast of Baffin Island to Cumberland Sound, where the waters once roiled with blue whales and bowheads, now all hunted out. She would then make two more scheduled stops in southern Baffin, at Pannirtuuq and Qikiqtarjuaq, before meeting the Canadian Department of Transport icebreaker, the *d'Iberville*, at Clyde River. There, the plan was to transfer all the migrants on to the *d'Iberville*. The *C. D. Howe* would then carry on its supply duties in northern Baffin before heading back down south to Quebec, while the *d'Iberville* dropped the migrants off at the two proposed Ellesmere Island camps at Craig Harbour and Alexandra Fiord and at the Resolute Bay site on Cornwallis Island.

While the *Howe* was steaming along southern Baffin, the *d'Iberville* was in Resolute Bay unloading supplies. As she was lying at anchor, Henry Larsen paid a visit to the chief of the Resolute Bay base, Air Commodore Robert Ripley. A few weeks before, Ripley had written a stern letter of complaint to the Department about its plans to move the Inuit. He did not think there was enough wildlife on Cornwallis and he was worried that the base would wind up having to bail the Inuit out or, worse still, that the Inuit might run into some kind of trouble the air base could not fix. On the same day as Larsen's visit, James Cantley was stuck in his office in Ottawa listening to an RCAF Squadron Leader repeating the air force's gripe. Larsen knew the problem would not go away until he had given some personal reassurances to Ripley. During that meeting he promised the Air Commodore that the Inuit would be camped at some distance from the base and that they would be forbidden to travel there in any circumstances. If there were any problems at the camp, Constable Ross Gibson would have full authority to deal with them. Larsen said he was confident that the air base would not even know the Inuit were there.

After his meeting at the base, Larsen had taken off along the coast to look for a good spot for the campsite. It was midsummer and most of the snow and ice had melted into the muskeg, leaving brown pools of stagnant water. Here and there a few shreds of whitlow grass clung to the rubble of rock and Arctic lichen licked along its sunnier surfaces, but in most places the rock was bare of vegetation. Farther south, there were clouds of mosquitoes rising on the winds and Arctic bumble bees busying themselves at clumps of blossoming Arctic willow, but there was none of that here. The wind was full of ice crystals.

Down near the beach, about four miles from the air base, there were the remains of a Thule settlement. It was here that Larsen wanted the Inukjuamiut to settle. For hundreds of years, the Thule people had roamed across the High Arctic, setting up camps around the coastal area where whales congregated, but when the ice returned in the Little Ice Age during the fifteenth century, they had moved south or died out (no one knew which), leaving middens of bones, broken harpoons and chipped-granite arrowheads as well as stone polar bear traps and the bleached whale-rib frames of what were once their houses. The land they lived on was covered in ice and snow for ten months of every year, they had no access to wood nor, with the exception of one or two meteorites, to metal, yet they had moved across the huge stretches of the Arctic, building villages and settling the previously uninhabited terrain. Equipped only with sealskin and bone *kayaks* and bone harpoons tipped with meteorite iron, they had hunted bowhead whales all along the northern continental coast for a thousand years before the arrival of European whalers, oblivious to the existence of other, easier lives. To Henry Larsen, even the accomplishments of the great Arctic explorers were nothing when set beside the tremendous human feat of Arctic settlement, and the policeman had not forgotten that the Inuit currently making their way to the High Arctic on the *C. D. Howe* were the Thule people's descendants. For a little while, Larsen thought, before the air base made janitors and porters of them as it would surely do, the men and women of Inukjuak would get their chance to live alone and untroubled in the footsteps of their forebears.

The following day, the *d'Iberville* weighed anchor and began heading back east into Lancaster Sound. At dawn on 12 August, she rounded Cape Parker on Devon Island and made her way through Lady Ann Strait towards Craig Harbour and Grise Fiord on Ellesmere Island. The ice here had only just melted, letting loose the flotilla of icebergs it had captured on the previous freeze-up. The ship moved through the strait slowly, through growlers and pieces of floe which drifted about in the soupy water. At the entrance to Jones Sound, the water turned noisily, then fell silent, and the ship suddenly found herself surrounded on both sides by glassy slabs and blue ice scree. There, ahead of them, lay the Craig Harbour RCMP detachment buildings, two small clapboard houses sitting on an ocean of shale. The only land lying between the *d'Iberville* and northern Siberia, 1,500 miles distant across the polar ice cap, was the mountainous ice capped terrain of Ellesmere Island. It was a forbidding place. Layers of peaks stretched back as far as the eye could see like a great army waiting the call to march. Ice mist glittered from the crags and drifted into the air and it would have been easy for anyone of a superstitious nature to suspect the island of being some kind of rocky anteroom to eternity, an in-between world where discarded spirits and the souls of never-born children curled up from the high peaks like mist and real life was just a dimming dream.

Henry Larsen spent a little while at Craig, briefing the two detachment police officers, Corporal Glenn Sargent and Constable Clay Fryer, who together would be responsible for the welfare of the group of Inuit going to Craig Harbour, just as Ross Gibson would be in charge of those at Resolute Bay. It had been almost impossible to discuss anything with the two men in detail on the radio. This far north, the signals phased in and out. One minute you could be holding a conversation and the next listening to an opera broadcast from Beijing or some fragment of Russian music. Larsen had worked with Sargent on the *St. Roch* and trusted him. The corporal was a tough man but a true northerner and could be relied upon not to shy away from difficult decisions in hard conditions.

While Larsen briefed his subordinates, the crew of the *d'Iberville* unloaded her cargo. In three weeks' time the navigation season would be over and the *d'Iberville* still had to visit the old abandoned Alexandra Fiord police detachment on the east coast of Ellesmere to make it habitable, before her rendezvous with the *C. D. Howe* far to the south at Clyde River on Baffin Island. The *d'Iberville* left Craig Harbour with haste in a thick mist. She continued on round the heel of Ellesmere Island at Cape Norton Shaw until ice began to creep in round her hull and the sounds of grinding and moaning came through the mist like the roars of disturbed animals. Before her lay Smith Sound. The American Arctic explorer, Robert E. Peary, once wrote: "There is probably no place where ice navigation is so hazardous as Smith Sound . . . The negotiation of the three hundred and fifty miles . . . presents problems and difficulties which will test the experience and nerve of the ablest navigator and the powers of the strongest vessel that man can build." They were heading directly into it.

For hours, the *d'Iberville* inched along the eastern coast of Ellesmere, past Cape Dunsterville into the dense, moving pack near Cape Isabella. A little farther ahead the captain set the ship's position. They waited for the fog to ease. After making sure its blades had not yet frozen up, Larsen scouted from here by helicopter. Up ahead lay the Bache Peninsula, with Alexandra Fiord at its tip. From the vantage of the air, they could just see the old buildings of the abandoned post shining like wet teeth but the pack had blocked off the access point from every direction and with so much ice about the waters were too turbulent to bring the *d'Iberville* close to shore. Just after midnight, the helicopter returned to ship. They would take the *d'Iberville* into the coast at Cape Isabella.

Blocked by the ice from making a direct pass to the north, the icebreaker ploughed slowly southward in loose pack ice before turning north through a promising lead towards the open water, but the crew were unable to get a cargo barge through the ice and had to ferry supplies to shore by helicopter. By evening, the *d'Iberville* had emptied its supplies and begun to turn south once more but she had lost time and there was now no prospect of her meeting the *C. D. Howe* at Clyde River as Larsen had originally planned. The policeman radioed Paul Fournier, captain of the *C. D. Howe,* and explained the situation and the two ships agreed to rendezvous at Craig Harbour. There the *C. D. Howe* would drop off Paddy, Joadamie Aqiatusuk and Phillipoosie Novalinga and their families. The *d'Iberville* would take the remaining "volunteers" along the east coast of Ellesmere Island to Alexandra Fiord, where it would drop Thomasie Amagoalik and his family along with Samwillie Aqiatusuk and a Pond Inlet family. From there the icebreaker would continue on to Resolute Bay with Simeonie Amagoalik, Daniel Salluviniq, Alex Patsauq and their families along with the last family from Pond Inlet.

Paul Fournier set the *C. D. Howe* on a course for Pond Inlet. The settlement stood at the tip of a finger inlet on the northeast coast of Baffin Island, sheltered from the driving currents in Lancaster Sound by the icy dot of Bylot Island. Opposite Bylot, on the coast of Baffin, huge glaciers begin their slow, inexorable slide into the sea, calving blue icebergs which creep south on the currents towards the coast of Labrador. The currents keep the water in the area relatively warm and Bylot is the northernmost haven for the many migratory birds which settle there in the summer. A permanent breeze blows the artichoke smell of guano across from Bylot's roosteries to Baffin Island. In late August 1953, the place was still alive with snow buntings and thick-billed murres and every kind of northern gull. Along the shoreline a few snowgeese ran with their wings set against the breeze, strengthening their muscles for the long flight south. The frail summer had already begun to sicken and the sky pressed down on the land like a dead hand.

On Henry Larsen's instructions, the Pond Inlet detachment had gone out to camps around Pond Inlet earlier in the year and persuaded three families to move north. The Pond Inlet people, or Ingluligmiut as they called themselves, had never travelled as far north as Ellesmere or Cornwallis, but Henry Larsen was right to assume that they had more of an understanding of High Arctic conditions than the Inukjuamiut. Cornwallis and Ellesmere islands lie in the great polar desert and receive very little snow and this would make it difficult for the Inukjuamiut to build snowhouses. The Pond Inlet people knew how to build winter shelters from sod bricks and turf and Larsen was hoping they would pass these skills on. They were also familiar with polar bear hunting and they trained their dogs to help them corner the bears. They regularly hunted narwhal and even bowhead whales and they knew how to catch seals with nets laid under the ice. They were familiar with the winter dark period, though at Pond Inlet it was not as severe as on Ellesmere or Cornwallis. It had been easier to recruit the Pond Inlet families than it had been to recruit those in Inukjuak, because the people from Pond Inlet knew about the High Arctic, even if they had not been there, and because they were offered better terms. Like the Inukjuamiut, the three Ingluligmiut families had been promised a good life in the far north, plus all the government help they needed, and they too had been told that they could return to Pond Inlet whenever they wanted, but they had also understood that they would be paid for their work in helping the Inukjuamiut to settle.

The three Pond Inlet families were waiting for the arrival of the *C. D. Howe* on the Baffin shore. They had balanced a primus stove on the stones and appeared to be heating water for tea. Ross Gibson later noted in his report that their caribou-skin parkas were not as ragged as those of the Inukjuamiut and he put this down to their being better hunters. In fact, there were more caribou in northern Baffin than in Ungava so the Ingluligmiut were able to renew their clothes more often. The *Howe* dropped anchor and some of the crew went below to sort the cargo tagged for Pond Inlet while Simon Akpaliapik, his wife Tatigak; Samuel Anukudluk, his wife Qaumayuk; and Jaybeddie Amagoalik (no relation to the Jaybeddie Amagoalik of Inukjuak), his wife Kanoinoo and their families, were ushered on board and taken to the Inuit quarters.

It is well known that Baffin Islanders love to travel and they have a long tradition of it. About a hundred years before, a Baffin Islander called Qillaq had led a party of Inuit from Cumberland Sound all the way to Ellesmere Island and from there on to northwestern Greenland, saying he had been told in a vision to find Inuit living there. Some said Qillaq was a brave shaman, others that he was not a visionary at all, and would not have left his home on Broughton Island if he had not had a dispute with his hunting partner during a hunting trip and crushed the man's skull with a rock. Afraid of what Ikierapring's relatives might do to revenge his death, Qillaq had decided to flee his home and find somewhere else to settle. There were other versions of the story. In 1903, one of Qillaq's friends,

Merqusaq, told the Danish Inuit explorer Knud Rasmussen that Qillaq had met with two white men many years before, probably Francis Leopold McClintock and Edward Augustus Inglefield, who were sailing around Baffin Island to look for the disappeared Arctic explorer, Sir John Franklin. The white men told Qillaq that there were Inuit living to the north of Baffin, and it was probably this information that became incorporated into Qillaq's "vision." Qillaq and his friend Oqe mustered a group of thirty-eight Inuit on ten sledges and the group began their journey north in late winter, as the light was returning. As the summer approached, the ice thinned and they were unable to sledge along the sea ice; they found themselves travelling across immense glaciers and having to harness as many as twenty dogs on each sled. They lashed thongs around the runners so that they would not take off too fast as they descended and attached sealskin ropes to the back of the sledge on which they hauled to provide a counterweight. At the northern tip of Bylot Island they found driftwood. All winter they worked to build an *umiak* and when the sea ice melted they used the boat to take them as far as the Wollaston Islands. There, it was said, the spirits led them to a cache of rum, salted meat and flour left by the *qalunaat* ship, *The North Star*, many years before. In those days, Inuit did not eat bannock bread, so they had no use for the flour. They tried the salted meat and spat it out but the rum kept them going as far as Talluritut, the island that looks like a tattooed chin and which white people called Devon. Many *tornasuit* or bad spirits lived on Talluritut and they tried to block the group's way. Oqe grew homesick and depressed and began to talk about how much he missed whale meat. He accused his friend Qillaq of making up the story of the people in the north and announced his intention to return to Baffin Island, with any of the party who were of the same mind. Qillaq said that Oqe was envious and wanted to be leader. Twenty-four people turned back and fourteen went on, including Oqe's own son, Minik.

Winter returned and Qillaq's group set up camp. This third winter was hard and there was not enough game on Talluritut. Dogs got eaten and a few families starved. When spring came, most of Qillaq's followers left and returned home, disenchanted. But Qillaq pressed on with a few of the most loyal, and the diminished group set off across Jones Sound and on to Ellesmere Island. There they passed another winter and in spring of the fourth year they found themselves near the Bache Peninsula where they saw the first signs of human life. The group set off to find the strangers, stopping only to hunt. For a number of months game had been difficult to come by, and Qillaq appealed to the spirits to tell him why all the animals had become invisible. The spirits answered that Qillaq's daughter-in-law, Ivaloq, had given birth to a stillborn baby but had kept it secret and this, said Qillaq, was the reason for the poor hunt. He ordered his son Itsukusuk to shut Ivaloq up in a snowhouse without furs so that she would either freeze to death or die of hunger and the animals would once again allow themselves to be hunted. This the son did. Immediately afterwards they came across a large herd of caribou near what is now Etah on the northwest coast of Greenland and shortly after that there was a cry of "Sleds sleds!" from a lookout in the group and they saw two *komatiks* approaching and men running beside them. The men were Arrutsak and Agina and they were living at Pitoravik, near Etah. These Inuit and their band had lived alone for many generations. They had no idea that other Inuit lived to the south of them. They were amazed and pleased to see Qillaq and his group and made them very welcome, so much so that Itsukusuk was able to sneak off in the midst of the celebrations unseen by Qillaq, and rescue Ivaloq from her snowhouse. The Greenlanders' lives were very different from that of the Baffin Islanders. They had no *kayaks* or bows and arrows, and they spoke an unfamiliar dialect. For many generations they had been so cut off that they had gradually forgotten that other, real people existed. There were about forty of them and they had always assumed they were the only human beings.

For several years, Qillaq and his family and followers tried to live among these polar Inuit. Qillaq showed them how to make *kayaks* from sealskin and bone and how to shoot caribou with bows and arrows. They swapped wives and had each other's babies, but eventually the Baffin Islanders became homesick and, after years away, they packed their things and began the long journey south.

The Ingluligmiut were imagining their own trip north would follow in similar fashion. They were looking forward to leaving Baffin Island, mostly because it gave them a reason to come back home again. They had no idea, as they boarded the *C. D. Howe*, that most were leaving their homeland for ever.

The flaw in Henry Larsen's plan to unite the two groups became immediately apparent. The Ingluligmiut and the Inukjuamiut spoke wildly different Inuktitut dialects and their communications were no better than the crude, fragmented sign language which served for dialogue between most *qalunaat* and most Inuit. For Paddy Aqiatusuk this revelation was very unsettling. All his life, he had been led to believe that Inuit were one. The idea was embedded in the word Inuit, which means "true people." Almost everyone he had ever met was related in some way to everyone else he knew. For the first time in his life, he now found himself confronting Inuit as strangers. The situation impressed on him just how far he had come but it also made him feel like going home. He had imagined life on Ellesmere would be not so different to living out at one of the more remote camps along the Ungava coast. There the camp dwellers were isolated, but they knew the land and every so often they would get visits from people they knew from other camps, or they would go out on visits themselves. It had somehow never occurred to Paddy that, not only would he be wholly unfamiliar with the land, but he would not know all the people in it either and it dawned on him just how isolated, lonely and vulnerable that would make him and his family feel.

Ross Gibson watched the Pond Inlet families board. The farther north they travelled and the tougher conditions became, the more respect he felt for the Inuit living in the settlements and camps. This was a common view among the whites stationed in the Arctic. Like them, Gibson had been raised with a pioneer's view of the land. He still thought of it as something to be ventured across and mastered. The harder you had to fight for this mastery, the more it made a man of you. The Inuit had always measured a man's worth another way, by how well he provided for his family. For the Inuit, living in the Barrenlands was less a matter of mastery than it was a question of avoiding unnecessary risk. This they did by a careful observation of nature, an acquisition of knowledge and a willingness to wait patiently until nature provided an opportunity to act. Survival had nothing to do with battling against the natural world and everything to do with understanding and respecting it.

As the *C. D. Howe* weighed anchor, the new families settled on to mattresses at one end of the Inuit quarters and warily eyed the Inukjuamiut. Aqiatusuk made some attempts to draw Akpaliapik into conversation but the differences in their language made the exchange awkward. Both groups put their efforts into preparing for their arrival. After more than a month at sea the Inukjuamiut were desperate to reach their destination and were very glad when the *C. D. Howe* finally crept through Lady Ann Strait in early September and began steaming into Jones Sound. Ahead, waiting at anchor, the *d'Iberville* sat against a backdrop of terrific, toothy mountains and raw crumbling cliffs.

The late change of plan meant that the decision to split the families into three groups had not been relayed to the families themselves. Alex Stevenson convened a meeting of the whites involved in the move and informed them of the arrangements. He read out the list of which families were to go where, intending to send Paddy and Mary Aqiatusuk to one location and Mary's seventeen-year-old son Samwillie to another, also to separate brothers Simeonie and Thomasie Amagoalik. Even to Ross Gibson, who was still so new to the Arctic, this sounded preposterous and cruel. To separate an Inuk from his family was like cutting off his leg. You could hand him a pair of crutches or fashion him a wooden substitute, but he would still wake in the night clinging to the space where the real leg had once been. Samwillie had no wife and was dependent on his mother and half-sisters to ensure he stayed warm and well fed. Without his family, he would have no one to sew his clothes or cook his food, which, in Arctic conditions, would quickly make his life unliveable. And Thomasie Amagoalik was widely known to be psychologically fragile. Without his brother, he too would struggle to survive.

When Alex Stevenson broke the news to the Inuit, Paddy Aqiatusuk went quite wild. Stevenson tried to reason with him, arguing that splitting the group would exert less pressure on the stocks of game, but nothing seemed to wash with Aqiatusuk. Had not the Inuit been promised they were going to a place where there were no limits to the game? And how were they supposed to catch it if hunters were separated from their families? He was particularly agitated about Samwillie. The possibility of a mutiny seemed likely. To avert it Samwillie's name was quietly shifted to the same list as his stepfather and the discussion was brought to a close. The families would be divided and Simeonie and Thomasie would be separated. Discussing the matter further was just putting off the inevitable. The sea was growing icier by the day and the *d'Iberville* and the *C. D. Howe* both had long voyages ahead. The logistics of the move had already been decided. It would all work out fine, Stevenson insisted. He was confident that he knew best.

A short while later, the belongings of the families of Paddy and Joadamie Aqiatusuk, Phillipoosie Novalinga and Simon Akpaliapik were lowered into the *Howe*'s cargo barge along with their sled dogs. The barge moved towards the detachment and turned westwards up the coast away from Craig Harbour police detachment where the shore-bound ice was less dense. Up on deck, the women began to cry and their children followed. Their distress set the dogs howling and, for what seemed like an eternity, the sobs of women and animals echoed across the waters of the sound until they finally found dry land and melted into the rock. The barge came back for Paddy Aqiatusuk, his wife Mary and their children Minnie, Samwillie, Anna, Elijah and Larry, along with Joadamie Aqiatusuk, his wife, Ekoomak and daughter Lizzie, Paddy's brother Phillipoosie Novalinga, his wife Annie, son Pauloosie, and daughter Elisapee, and took them ashore at a stretch of shale beach just west of the police department. Simon Akpaliapik from Pond Inlet, his wife Tatigak, daughters Ruth and Tookahsee and baby son Inutsiak were also landed on the beach. Then the cargo barge made its way back to the *C. D. Howe.*

CHAPTER NINE

THE REMAINING two groups of Inuit were bundled into a tiny, red-lit room in the *d'Iberville's* cargo hold, after which the icebreaker weighed anchor and turned east.

The *d'Iberville* ground on through the pack ice and turned north along the east coast of Ellesmere. At Smith Sound, she encountered unexpected ice conditions. An iceberg forest had blown down from the north and was sliding along with the pack ice in the currents. The floe was so tightly squeezed that no water was visible between the plates of ice and the *d'Iberville* was quickly locked in to the pack, leaving her with no choice but to go with the floe. In the cargo hold, the Inuit lay on their mattresses in the red light, listening to the dreadful squealing and booming of the ice as the icebreaker split the pack. The ship made progress in inches, pushing and grinding against the floe. Squally sleet began rapping against the *d'Iberville's* sides. To the Inuit, it sounded like the knocking hands of desperate spirits.

Henry Larsen gave instructions for the ship's helicopter to go on ahead to scout out a possible route through the pack to Alexandra Fiord, forty miles to the north. He was particularly keen to position Inuit at Alexandra or at least on the Bache Peninsula which had long been of considerable strategic importance to Canada. From the tip of the peninsula to the northwest coast of Greenland was a journey of only thirty miles. For most of the year the channel between the two countries was frozen and it acted as an ice bridge for Greenlandic Inuit wanting to hunt polar bear and musk ox on northern Ellesmere in the region of Hazen Lake. The weather conditions at Bache were so severe that a formal border post would never be established there, but Larsen felt that the presence of Canadian Inuit in the area would at least discourage the Greenlanders. Their presence would also serve as an effective rebuttal if ever Denmark, Greenland or the United States made a claim for Ellesmere. In any case, in Larsen's mind, Bache was not such a bad spot to leave a few souls. The Meares expedition of 1870 had discovered a valley between two glaciers at Bache and had reported seeing Arctic poppies and even moths there, and during the short life of the police detachment there, twenty years before, the detachment constable had once or twice reported the presence of game.

But Alexandra Fiord was completely inaccessible and the helicopter pilot returned to ship without finding any clear channel through the ice. They drifted for five hours in the driving sleet and blanket fog waiting for a lead to open up but none did. Finally, Larsen was forced to give the order to turn the *d'Iberville* south before she became dangerously iced in. The ship steamed south at three knots in visibility of less than half a mile. Larsen ordered the helicopter out again and the pilot reported that the pack looked solid all the way through Smith Sound as far as Naires Strait. There was absolutely no way they would be able to land at Alexandra Fiord, or anywhere near it. The plan to establish an Inuit camp there would have to be abandoned. Larsen radioed Glenn Sargent at the Craig Harbour police detachment and told him to expect some extra Inuit families. Later that day, the *d'Iberville* reached Jones Sound and put off Thomasie Amagoalik and his family along with the Anukudluk family from Pond Inlet. Now only one group of Inuit were left on board. By evening, the icebreaker had turned and begun to edge back out of Jones Sound, bound for Resolute Bay. The Alexandra Fiord experiment was over before it had even begun.

A few years later, a memo passed from one office to another in the Department in Ottawa, observing that the game, reported to be in the area around Alexandra Fiord by the policemen stationed at the detachment in the 1930s, had disappeared, either wiped out in a bad spell of weather or gone north to Hazen Lake. The area was completely devoid of animal life. If the ice conditions had been different on that day in September 1953, and the *d'Iberville* had been able to drop off her human cargo at Alexandra Fiord, the families of Thomasie Amagoalik and Samuel Anukudluk would almost certainly have starved to death.

The journey to Resolute Bay was less eventful. By the following morning, 5 September 1953, the *d'Iberville* had already passed Coburg Island and she was steaming towards Lancaster Sound when Ross Gibson went up on deck to admire the cone of rock marked Princess Charlotte Monument on his map. Up ahead, the sun caught the glacier-capped mountains of east Devon Island and crimped their edges with rosy morning light. The clean air coming off the mountains made Ross feel loose and exhilarated. A pod of beluga appeared alongside the ship and there were still a few gulls overhead, even at this latitude. He waited until the *d'Iberville* turned across Cape Warrender and left the hilly terrain of Devon Island behind before going back down below to check the list of supplies the *d'Iberville* had dropped off on her pass through Resolute Bay a few weeks earlier. He noticed, among other things, that a new police launch had been ordered and was waiting for them at the campsite. As soon as they had set up camp, Gibson intended to take a party of hunters out walrus hunting. Henry Larsen had pointed out on a map a small inlet on the southern coast of Cornwallis Island to the west of Resolute Bay, where, he said, there were walrus to be found in their dozens, dozing on the beach. He had seen them there during the supply visit. Personally, Ross Gibson hated walrus meat—it was strong and fishy-tasting—and he knew that even the Inuit preferred to feed it to their dogs whenever they had the choice, but it would help their morale to begin to build their winter cache.

Gibson meant to run a tight ship on shore. He knew that Henry Larsen would have an eye on the new detachment and he also knew that Corporal Sargent and Constable Fryer at Craig Harbour had all the advantages; they had been around Ellesmere Island for a number of months and had an established detachment with a special constable. And there were two of them. All the same, Gibson intended to make Resolute the more successful camp. He planned to be fair and helpful to his "natives," but he would never cease to remind them of the single most important fact of their existence at Resolute Bay, which was that they were in the High Arctic to live off the land, and live off the land they must.

At seven o'clock on the evening of Sunday, 6 September, the *d'Iberville* dropped anchor three miles off Resolute Bay. It was a very bright, calm end to a long late summer day. A few large floes were making their way southwards in the current, accompanied by a group of ravens which spiralled up and down on the air currents around them. At the sea's edge, an arc of shale clutched the bay and rose slowly to meet the tuff. At one end of this arc lay a building marked on maps as the meteorological and radio station. Farther along the shoreline stood the ionosphere building, and in the distance, about four miles inland, there was a faint disturbance in the air marking the site of the RCAF base. The landscape was quite unlike the spectacular, feral cliffs of Ellesmere. It seemed gentler and more quiescent.

Cornwallis is a tiny, wind-torn island at the southwestern corner of the Queen Elizabeth Islands which stretch from Baffin almost to the North Pole. No one, including Henry Larsen, had ever had much good to say about the place, which was little more than a heap of flattened gravel from which the blasting Arctic wind had scooped a single, southern bay. Its weather was unpredictable, even by the chaotic climatic standards of the High Arctic. Winter blizzards brought frequent whiteouts and in the summer, storms threw fists of hail across the land and stirred up deep and instant fogs which could last for days. The coastline was a series of poor harbours and treacherous beachings. The coastal waters were often ice-bound and choppy and the shore was often obscured by bruise-coloured cloud. Its exposure to the polar winds meant that little grew on Cornwallis. You might find a clump of rock tripe or lousewort clinging to some sheltered southern slope but nothing of any size was able to find a purchase or protect itself from the parched bluster from the north and, as a consequence of this, caribou and musk ox were rare visitors. There were ptarmigan and Arctic hare and in spring and winter polar bears sometimes arrived from the south, but that was about it.

Six years before, in 1947, an icebreaker had slipped into the waters of Resolute Bay. The U.S.-registered *Edisto* had been escorting the cargo ship *Wyandot* towards Winter Harbour on Melville Island to establish a joint U.S.–Canadian weather station there when heavy ice had driven both ships back to Cornwallis. The navigation season was nearly over and the captains of both ships doubted they would make it to Winter Harbour before ice-up so they landed their cargo in Resolute and gave instructions to the crew to begin building the weather station there. Two years after that, the RCAF base arrived.

Before the unexpected appearance of the *Edisto* and the *Wyandot* in Cornwallis, no one had taken much notice of the place. The Thule had left it about four hundred years previously and the first white explorers who had come across the island in the nineteenth century could not see any reason to stay. When William Edward Parry passed by in 1819, looking for the Northwest Passage, he noted the long shale beaches and low, rolling plains in his log book but sailed on without even checking to see whether or not the beaches belonged to an island or were a part of some larger mainland peninsula. Hedging his bets, he named the place Cornwallis Land after his patron, Admiral the Honourable Sir William Cornwallis, and continued on his way in search of the passage.

The Arctic seemed to spawn bad ideas in white men, of which

the relocation of Inukjuamiut was only the latest. The idea of a northern seaway from the Atlantic to the Pacific had begun in 1497, when a Venetian adventurer known as John Cabot managed to convince Henry VII that by sailing westwards at high latitudes he would discover a short route to the spice and silk markets of the Orient. Cabot's reasoning has been obscured by the years. He may well have been familiar with the stories of the Greek trader Pytheas, who claimed he had travelled to a distant northern land he called Ultima Thule, the last place. Pytheas' ship was prevented from sailing farther, he later wrote, by some extraordinary natural phenomenon which had caused the earth, sea and air to pinch together, and he had had to turn back, but the experience had convinced him that Ultima Thule was the end of the known world and a passage into a new one. How far Cabot took his cue from Pytheas it is impossible to say but it is probably fair to presume that he wanted there to be a Northwest Passage so much that he made the idea up.

The first map of Ultima Thule was not drawn until seventy years later by the Flemish explorer Gerdus Mercator. The Flemish map showed a vast territory swarming with white bears and unicorns. He drew the North Pole as a tremendous mountain surrounded by open sea. Four northward-flowing and seasonally frozen channels divided the circumpolar continent and came together in a gigantic whirlpool round the polar mountain before draining into the interior of the earth. Close by but separated from the mountain by a broad strait was another mountain made of iron and it was this, Mercator speculated, which attracted compasses. Mercator's version of Ultima Thule was not so much the end of the world or a passage into a new one as one giant drain.

If the Flemish map had been available to Cabot he might not have bothered to look for the Passage. In any case, he did not find it, but the fact that he had tried piqued the interest of others, not least of whom was Henry Hudson, and over the years the search took on the quality of a mythic quest. Taking advantage of the large naval fleet Britain had acquired during the Napoleonic Wars and did not quite know what to do with once the wars were over, the Royal Society in London sent John Ross to the Arctic in 1818 and 1829. In 1819 and 1821 Captain William Edward Parry set off in the same direction and, in 1824, Parry and his acquaintance George Lyon led competing expeditions. A year after that, John Franklin went out on the first of his three attempts over twenty years, which ended only when he died, in mysterious circumstances, in the Arctic in 1845.

On 3 May 1850, a 410-ton vessel, the *Resolute,* flagship of the British Seaborne Squadron under the command of Captain Horatio Austin, left England to search for Franklin and his men. The *Resolute* was accompanied by the *Assistance, Pioneer* and *Intrepid.* The expedition encountered drifting floes near Cornwallis Island and decided to overwinter on an ice field between Cornwallis and Griffiths islands. The ships floated out on 8 August 1851 and sailed the length of Lancaster Sound looking for signs that Franklin and his crew had passed by, but they found nothing and were forced to sail back to England a week or so later. The following year, *Resolute* and her crew returned under Henry Kellett to Lancaster Sound and overwintered at Dealey Island, but she became stuck in ice and had to be abandoned. After the ice broke up, the ship, true to her name, drifted on the currents for a lonely nine hundred miles, until she at last reached the east coast of Baffin Island, where she was picked up by a whaler captained by James Buddington. The captain sailed her to New London, Connecticut, and sold her to the U.S. government for US$40,000. As a gesture of good will, the Americans refitted the *Resolute* and returned her to England in 1855. Queen Victoria later presented the White House with a desk carved from the *Resolute*'s timbers, which still sits in the Oval Office and serves as the President's desk today, and when the *Edisto* and *Wyandot* arrived on the southern coast of Cornwallis all those years later, they named the area of shale beach and low rock Resolute Bay after that doughty little ghost ship who had protested her exile and found her way back home.

Three Inukjuak families disembarked from the *d'Iberville* at

Resolute Bay in summer 1953, including Simeonie Amagoalik, his wife Sarah and their son Paul, who had been born on the *C. D. Howe*. Simeonie and Jaybeddie Amagoalik had been separated from their brother Thomasie who had already been dropped at Craig Harbour. Accompanying them were Jaybeddie Amagoalik from Pond Inlet and his family. A party from the icebreaker's crew went ashore and sang "O Canada" with their shins buried in the shale while others unloaded the families' raggedy tents and pots and pans. Then the migrants began to unwrap their tents and look for stones with which to secure them, while an angry northwest wind blew up round them. Henry Larsen gave a few instructions to the crew of the *d'Iberville,* shook a few hands, saluted the new detachment's flag, clambered back into the *d'Iberville*'s skiff and was gone.

On his first visit to Resolute Bay, Larsen had arranged for Ross Gibson to stay at the meteorological station until such time as he could set himself up at the air force base. The manager of the met station had laid out a camp bed for the policeman among a drift of old oil cans and there the constable stored his uniform, his gun and his personal effects. A while later he returned to the bleak spot where the Inuit were busy erecting their tents. The wind whipped his skin, which was already raw and flaky. The first job as camp boss—for that is how he now saw himself—was to check the supplies which had been left on the beach under a tarpaulin during the *d'Iberville*'s first visit. Before doing that, though, he wanted to take a look at the new police whaleboat which sat along the beach on timber stays, so he trudged off, his arm shielding his face from the worst of the snow, his legs sinking deep in the sharp, loose shale. It was not until his second turn round the boat that he noticed the space where the propeller should have been. He made his way back across the shale to the native camp. Already, the stones had begun pricking the Inuit through their *kamiks* and they complained that in a day or two there would be nothing left of the soles and the women would have to sew in a new set. It would be hard to keep the natives in traditional clothing, as Henry Larsen had insisted. They would have to bag a good few seal.

The next day, the problem of the boat remained. Gibson would have to beg a craft of some sort from the air base. It would not look good but he did not see he had a choice. Few of the Inuit seemed to have *kayaks* and, in any case, the ice looked too risky for kayaking. If they were to catch any walrus or seal they would need a boat. Fortunately, the air base had just the thing, it was free, and they seemed willing to lend it, and, later that day, Ross Gibson set off in it with a party of hunters. They motored along the coast for a while, taking note of the shape of the coastline and the inlets for future hunting expeditions, then they headed into the bay Larsen had marked on the map, expecting to find the walrus the superintendent had promised were there. But the bay was empty. A summer storm had hit the coast about a week before and the walrus had headed south for their winter grounds.

By then, the *C. D. Howe* was already well on her way to Quebec. On board was Doug Wilkinson, a film-maker hired by the Canadian Broadcast Company to film the historic landings of Inuit in the High Arctic. Years later, Wilkinson remembered the scene in Resolute like this:

> There was stuff piled everywhere . . . the whole thing was a smozzle from beginning to end . . . Everyone thought the Eskimo could live in their land anywhere. No one gave much thought to what really went into what it took to get the kind of knowledge to exist in an Arctic land as a hunter. As far as Alex Stevenson . . . was concerned . . . certainly as far as Jim Cantley and the rest of the people in Arctic Services were concerned, all you had to do was get hold of the RCMP and the Department of Transport to arrange for these people to be on the boat at a certain time, walk them off the other end and everything would be fine . . . There was no forethought put into it at all. You know, they just thought, well, all we have to do is get in touch with

these people and they're going to go . . . [There was] no planning at all. There was absolutely nothing. I don't know how
they ever expected those people to live.

Some time later that afternoon, the hunting party arrived back
at Resolute Bay. A freezing wind blew across the camp. "I'll tell you,"
Ross Gibson said, years later. "If I could have walked back to Ottawa
the next day, I think I would have gone."

CHAPTER TEN

PADDY AQIATUSUK surveyed the scene. Already the long voyage seemed curiously abstract; it lived in his mind as something he dreamed. The real sense of how far they had come hit him only now, as he took in the landscape of Ellesmere Island, which was like nothing he had ever seen. The view before him was, even by Arctic standards, ethereal and other-worldly. He and the other migrants were completely hemmed in. To the west of the spot where they had landed hung shields of granite laced with grey-green ice. To the east lay the clapboard houses of the Craig Harbour police detachment and beyond them, what looked like a glacier. The waters of Jones Sound shivered and, though it was still summer, clumps of pebble-dashed ice slewed in and out of the foam. A thin and bitter wind whipped in from the east on which Paddy Aqiatusuk could smell nothing. He looked to the north and saw a curtain of crumbly cliffs and, behind them, a regiment of ice-glazed peaks below scudding blue clouds before his attention was drawn to the tiny blades of shale digging through his boots, shale which contained no bone or hair or fragment of fur, no root or leaf or finger of lichen, no remnant of some summer past, nor hint of any to come.

Ellesmere is the world's ninth largest island, an area about the same size as Great Britain. It is also the most mountainous of the Arctic islands, home to the highest and longest alpine ranges in the eastern North American continent. Three-quarters of Ellesmere

Island is an impenetrable mass of frozen crags, deep fiords and terrible, green-ice valleys topped in the northern interior by forbidding, age-old ice caps up to a half-mile deep. Combined, Ellesmere's glaciers cover 40 per cent of its surface area. In the north the ice caps stretch all the way to the mountains beside the sea, gouging great fiords as they push into the Arctic Ocean. In the south the caps are patchier, and confined to inland peaks. The southeast corner of the island is, comparatively speaking, the least unfriendly. There are a few lakes there, and the fiords are less forbidding. Run-off allows some vegetation to grow in the sheltered, south-facing spots. The Hazen Plateau gives out to a series of rounded peaks around Discovery Harbour before rising again to form the steep cliffs and scree slopes along the coasts of Archer, Conybeare and Chandler fiords, tributary channels of Lady Franklin Bay. The southwest is more rugged. Around Greely Fiord and its tributaries, Borup, Otto and Hare fiords, the cliffs rise as high as three thousand feet.

If it were not for the North Water of Smith Sound which runs between Ellesmere and northwestern Greenland, then there would probably be no life at all on southern Ellesmere. The North Water has its beginnings southwest of Iceland, where the cold East Greenland Current meets the warm Atlantic Gulf Stream and becomes the Irminger Current, which flows in a southerly direction to the southern tip of Greenland, rounds the horn then flows upwards as the West Greenland Current and becomes, at Smith Sound, the North Water, colliding with the colder waters of the Arctic Ocean and carving out areas of permanently open water, or polynyas, sometimes called Arctic oases, off the northeast coast of Ellesmere Island from Eureka to the Hazen Plateau. From Smith Sound the current swings southwest to cup Ellesmere's southern coast, where there is another, shore-fast polynya at Makinson Inlet, before it culminates in a three to five mile stretch of turbulent water, the Hell Gate polynya, off Ellesmere's southwest coast. Even though they are surrounded almost all year round by ice, the polynyas themselves never quite freeze over and in their slowly swishing waters phytoplankton and zooplankton flourish. At Hell Gate, the plankton attracts Arctic char which bring in harp, bearded and ringed seal as well as migratory walrus, narwhal and beluga whales. Polar bears are regular visitors. The clear water raises the temperature and the levels of precipitation at Hell Gate and allows a few plant species to survive in stunted form. Arctic poppies living on Ellesmere take twenty years to reach adult size and what few Arctic char survive there are a quarter of a century old before they are mature enough to breed. The vegetation on the land side of the polynyas sustains a thin population of Arctic mammals: a few hares, a sprinkling of small, white Peary caribou and a few thousand musk ox. Greenlandic Inuit call the area Umingmaknuna or Musk Ox Land, which makes it sound more fruitful than it is. The musk ox populations are confined to those areas where scrubby heathland vegetation grows. No one knows how many caribou or hares there are, partly because their populations are very widely scattered, divided, as are the musk ox, into northern and southern groupings separated by the central ice caps. The formidable frozen zone of Ellesmere's interior has permitted only very limited study and there had been none at all by 1953. What was known from the expeditions of explorers and whalers in the region was that the turbulent currents were made worse by winds. They are heaviest in winter but blow all year round; the prevailing easterlies cross the huge Greenlandic ice caps and pick up frigid air. They produce such dreadful windchill that on Ellesmere Island the temperature in the wind can feel thirty degrees lower than the ambient reading.

In 1882 the U.S. Lady Franklin Bay expedition to northern Ellesmere recorded gusts of more than ninety miles per hour. Thirty years later, the Danish Inuit explorer Knud Rasmussen was in the area when:

> I received so violent a blow in the back that I was unable to get up for a moment, but when at last I succeeded in rising to my knees, I saw that all the many sledges which a moment ago had

driven in a long string one behind the other, were swept together into one huge pile . . . As it was quite impossible to stand upright, not to mention driving, we let ourselves be blown up on land with sledges and dogs, until we found some little shelter in a clough by a broad tongue of ice where the sledges could be anchored and the dogs tethered. Hardly was this done when the *Föhn*, with the roar of a hurricane, swept down upon us from the mountains and the inland-ice and made us suspect that the world itself was going under.

The high winds break open the ice and send the liberated sea into whirling whitecaps. One feature of the ice around Ellesmere is its mobility. The pack ice rarely stabilises before February. Before then it is in constant motion, floes smashing together, rafting one upon the other, grinding and jamming together.

Ellesmere Island had been claimed for Canada, near to where Paddy Aqiatusuk and the other Inuit were brought to shore, by the captain of the *Arctic*, J. E. Bernier, only fifty years previously. Early human populations used Ellesmere as a bridge into Greenland, coming up from the south and west, crossing on to Ellesmere from across the Cardigan Strait in the west and up past Coburg Island in the east. They travelled principally on the ice foot, a belt of ice formed between the high and low water marks of the tides. The ice on the foot is stable and relatively smooth. Later, when polar explorers came to Ellesmere Island, they named this characteristic feature "The Highway to the Pole." A thousand years ago or more, Thule settled there for a while, but moved south when the Little Ice Age of the fifteenth century blew in. A tiny group of survivors persisted in the extreme northwest of Greenland and it was these the Baffin Islanders came across in the mid-nineteenth century. Some years later, the American explorer, Robert E. Peary, stumbled on them, named them the Polar Eskimo and hired a few as guides on his expeditions to the North Pole.

Paddy Aqiatusuk knew none of this. *His* first thought was to presume there had been some mistake. The *qalunaat* had brought them to the wrong place. He decided to confront the detachment policemen. Until then, the priority had to be to establish the tents. The wind was icy.

The men hauled the group's possessions from where the *d'Iberville*'s cargo barge had dumped them, tethering their dogs, and rolling out their canvas while the women and children hastily unravelled the guy ropes.

An RCMP Peterhead appeared from the gloom and headed towards them. An Inuk man leaped out into shallows and made fast the boat, followed by two policemen, one huge and massy, the other thin and reedy, and the trio made their way to the shore. The large policeman scanned the group setting up camp on the beach.

"Which one of you is Fatty?" the big fellow asked in Inuktitut.

Paddy Aqiatusuk bristled. He sensed Ross Gibson had been talking about him to this new fellow. Now neither could be trusted.

"Are you the boss?" The policeman introduced himself as Corporal Glenn Sargent and the white man beside him as Constable Clay Fryer. The Inuit special constable's name was Areak. Sargent was a well-built, powerfully handsome man, the kind women pick out in a crowd. He had cut his teeth on the *St. Roch*. After that he had been posted to the police detachment at Herschel Island on the northern edge of the Yukon and had followed this with a stint at Spence Bay before finding himself commanding the RCMP's most northerly detachment at Craig Harbour.

Aqiatusuk looked about him. "I think you have brought us to the wrong place," he said.

Glenn Sargent sensed better than anyone how tough life on Ellesmere was likely to be for the newcomers. He found it hard enough himself, and his living conditions were very different from those of the newcomers. The *qalunaat* policemen were barracked in solid, insulated detachment buildings warmed by coal-burning stoves. They had constant and plentiful supplies of food and ammunition and access to radio, boats and other equipment. "G" Division police enjoyed several weeks' paid leave every year along with hardship and isolation pay. They could keep in touch with colleagues and family over the radio. Each posting was for two years only, after which they had the option to transfer out to another detachment and at the end of it all, a Mountie knew he would pick up a pretty good pension.

Sargent knew that if Paddy Aqiatusuk and his family were to survive, they would have to be successful at hunting the marine mammals living in Ellesmere's waters. This would be no simple matter. Wildlife studies have now shown that groups of walrus regularly overwinter in the polynya at the western entrance to Jones Sound and there are narwhal in the area of the North Water. In the autumn belugas swim from Lancaster Sound into Jones Sound along the coast of Ellesmere before crossing over to Greenland, but this was not known in 1953. The staple food of the new migrants, Sargent thought, would have to be the ringed seal which gathered around fast ice along the outer coast and in the sounds, bays and inlets. Sargent knew there would be no time to lose. Winter came on fast and early and the new arrivals had no store of meat to see them through. He would have to take them out hunting in the Peterhead the moment they had settled. After that, he would follow orders to move them forty miles away, to a spot on the Lindstrom Peninsula staked out by Henry Larsen, near enough for them to be able to make it back to the detachment in an emergency or to trade fox pelts but not so near that they would be able to drop in on the detachment any time they wanted something. There on Lindstrom they would have to stay and meet their fate, whatever that might be.

Twilight hung off the cloud and the day seeped gradually into the night. The temperature fell to freezing, the winds began to fluster the tents and the cold slid under the ropes and came creeping across the mattresses lying on the shale. Everyone began to feel very hungry. Sargent had promised the campers traditional stone stoves or *qulliqs* but the discharged cargo still lay under tarpaulins on the beach beside the detachment. Anukudluk, from Pond Inlet, had a primus stove but no one had any matches with which to light it. For tonight they would just have to eat whatever Sargent had given them. They unpacked flour, sugar, lard and settled on hardtack biscuits and a couple of tins of sardines and ate their meagre first meal on Ellesmere Island in turns, passing Anukudluk's torch between the tents. Exhausted, Aqiatusuk and his family lay together in the fog of their exhalations and told each other stories and as the night deepened they gradually drifted into unconsciousness.

Paddy Aqiatusuk woke the next day to the hum of the Peterhead. The mattress he had been lying on had sucked up water during the night, his back and kidneys throbbed and his gallstones were troubling him. The men pulled on their *kamiks,* went outside and stumbled over shale towards the boat. Greyish clouds slumped across the sound and spilled on to the beach, obscuring the view of the detachment. Sargent wanted some of the men to help unload the supplies the *d'Iberville* had dropped off on her first pass. The crates would need to be checked off against the bill of lading and loaded into the detachment store before the weather got to them. James Cantley had ordered the year's supplies for the High Arctic in Ottawa in May, but until Sargent unpacked them and checked them off it would not be clear exactly what and how much had been sent. After that, they would all go out hunting.

Having been assured that the Department would supply whatever they would need in the north, the Inuit had left most of their gear at camp in Inukjuak, for the benefit of their relatives, and Sargent was shocked to discover some serious shortages. Some had brought their *kayaks,* presumably because no one had told them that the ice conditions up in the High Arctic were too dangerous for kayaking, but no one had brought an *umiak* or a whaleboat, which would have been more useful. Many of the hunters did have their rifles with them, but for the most part these were ancient, low-calibre .22s and their bullets would be almost useless against walrus and polar bear. Sargent hoped that Cantley had been generous with his order of supplies.

His hopes were dashed the moment the men cracked open the crates. There appeared to be no duck for mending the tents, nor any first aid supplies, rifles, oil lamps, fish hooks, soapstone or snow-knives. The three hundred caribou skins promised on the bill of lading had been reduced to a few dozen buffalo pelts. Some of the supplies were completely inappropriate. There were dozens of men's overalls in sizes far too large for any Inuk, boys' fingerless wool mittens that were an invitation to frostbite and batteries for pieces of equipment the Inuit did not possess. Sargent radioed through to the *C. D. Howe* and the *d'Iberville* to establish that the missing cargo had not been loaded on to the wrong ship in error, but both vessels reported an empty hold. In Resolute Bay, Ross Gibson was noting down similar anomalies. Either the correct cargo had not been loaded while the *C. D. Howe* and the *d'Iberville* were in port at Quebec or it had been mistakenly offloaded somewhere else en route, or, worse than either of these, Cantley had not ordered it.

There was nothing to be done for now. The new arrivals needed to get out and hunt. It was already well into September and the new camp had no meat and none stored for the winter cache. For the next six weeks, until the light gave out and the dark period came upon them, the men would have to go out hunting every day to stand a chance of gathering sufficient food for the winter. While they remained near the detachment Sargent would take them out in the Peterhead. Once they moved out to the Lindstrom Peninsula, they would be on their own. A party set off the next day before light with Sargent and Areak. Fryer stayed behind sorting the supplies. The women and children watched the Peterhead disappear over the horizon, then gathered their bags and began to walk towards the cliffs in search of grass, willow twigs and a source of fresh water. For several hours they scrambled over the moraine, clambered along the rocks, until they finally reached the cliffhead around midday. From there a series of tremendous, barren peaks stood together like teeth and between them were valleys filled with greenish-grey glaciers, heavy with debris. A few crows observed the group's progress, their presence indicating that somewhere, in a sheltered inlet or on a south-facing plateau, the women would find lemmings or Arctic hare or at least a few small birds, but none was visible. They pressed on along the cliff, eyes set on the boulders and gullies until they came upon a rock basin and there, at its lowest point, where water and blown soil had accumulated, were tufts of wild heather and the spore of Arctic hare. The air felt as dry as old leather and it had a peculiar empty chill. They looked out for any sign which might lead them to a water source but there were none of the patchwork stains and rock moulds which usually indicated the presence of a summer run-off. The only source of fresh water appeared to be from the green-grey glaciers or from the stone-ridden bergy bits which had collected in turquoise piles along the shore. Ungava was full of lakes and rivers, but here there were none. They returned to the camp full of foreboding.

The men arrived later, in a more upbeat mood. Sargent had taken them out beyond Jakeman Glacier to the east of the detachment and there they had shot three fat walrus and seen plenty more. The coast was very ice-bound, but there appeared to be seal about too. While the men flensed and butchered the animals, took their heads and lay them facing the sea, pulled out the stomach contents and gave the gristle to the dogs, the women cleaned the entrails to bury under rocks for winter. Tonight, they would set up their *qulliqs* and by the deep-orange light that walrus blubber gives they would boil up blood soup and make a stew. The next day, when the walrus spirits had left their heads, and they were safe to touch, Paddy Aqiatusuk would pull out the tusks and begin to carve in walrus ivory.

That night it was so cold in the tent that Aqiatusuk dreamed frozen dreams. By the morning, though, the temperature had clambered above freezing and the group was feeling more cheerful than they had been since leaving Inukjuak. Sargent decided that the best use of the camp's time would be to pass the next few days unloading and checking the stores. After that he would take the hunters out for caribou before moving them to the permanent campsite on the Lindstrom Peninsula.

The lack of caribou skins in Cantley's supplies was particularly worrying. Buffalo hides did provide some insulation, though not as much as caribou, but they were heavy. Once the snow arrived, they would have to be removed lest they collapse the tents. Besides that, the black skins cut out the light inside the tents and the women would be forced to do their work sitting on the shale outside. This would prove particularly difficult for Anna Nungaq, stepdaughter of Paddy Aqiatusuk, who had been crippled by polio at the age of two, was largely immobile, and found it hard to keep herself warm. She would have to spend her days in the darkness inside the tents and, when winter arrived, the other women would have to join her. The cold would be too savage to remain outdoors. They would need lanterns, but there were none among the cargo. The caribou skins were also urgently required for clothing because buffalo hide was too inflexible to wear. Their supplies of winter clothing were perilously short. The previous summer the Inuit boats had all been hired out to scientists up in Inukjuak and the Inuit had not been able to find a boat to take them down to Richmond Gulf, near Kuujjuarapik, to hunt the caribou there. For a winter such as the one they were facing on Ellesmere, each hunter would require a new set of caribou clothes, each of which used up six caribou skins, the children would have to be kitted out in caribou undergarments and every family would need new caribou sleeping bags. In all, the camp would require at least 150 skins.

Sargent contacted James Cantley in Ottawa, but the reply was not encouraging. Cantley had been let down by his supplier somewhere in western Canada. He said he would endeavour to find some more skins and have them airlifted to Craig Harbour before the winter was out but he could not guarantee how many or when they would arrive. As for the rest, he did not really see there was a problem. The Inuit had been moved to Grise Fiord to enable them to lead traditional lives. So far as Cantley was concerned, lanterns, soap, washtubs and most of the other things Sargent said were missing were really just luxuries and he had judged that the Inuit could do without them.

The issue of the skins remained urgent. The Canadian government had declared the whole of Ellesmere Island a nature preserve and the new preserve rules set seasons and quotas for big game animals and made it altogether illegal to hunt musk ox. In practice, these rules had never been enforced because there had been no permanent population on Ellesmere but the RCMP could not be seen openly to flout the law. As the caribou season had already closed on Ellesmere, Henry Larsen had given Glenn Sargent strict instructions to allow each Inuit family to take only one buck caribou.

Sargent had himself hunted caribou in a spot beside Fram Fiord, a little to the west of Craig Harbour on the way to Grise Fiord, and this was where he decided to take them now. The fiord was only a short trip in the Peterhead and Sargent knew the route very well. He usually motored as far as the eastern headland of the fiord, then cut the Peterhead's engines and made his way to shore in the whaleboat, so the caribou would not be frightened off by noise. There was a south-facing slope, about an hour's scramble up cliffs, where the lichen grew and where a small herd of Peary's caribou, smaller, whiter and hardier than their more southerly cousins, could often be found grazing. There was an old Thule settlement en route. Sargent had found skulls and human bones there, as well as the ribs of blue and bowhead whales. Their antique presence tickled Sargent; on an island as bleak and lonely as Ellesmere, even a heap of old bones could provide companionship and a feeling of solidarity.

Sargent allowed the hunters to take ten bucks. When they got back to camp, the women were already sharpening their *ulus*, knives, in anticipation of the meal ahead. The walrus and the caribou cheered the camp enormously. It was a dry land, and a mountainous one, and despite the vast space you could not see far, but it seemed then that, at the very least, no one would starve. They did not altogether understand Sargent's quotas and they did not imagine that he would stick to them in any case. The hunters laid the bodies of the caribou out on the beach with their heads facing the mountain so their spirits would find their way back to the Fram, and set about the complicated business of butchering and flensing. Out of curiosity, Aqiatusuk went among the creatures. He noticed that the pelts were free from the bites of warble flies and there were no bots in the animals' ears or noses, also that there were no flies around the carcasses, and he decided it must be too cold for insects. Their hooves were already growing and the pads of the feet shrinking in preparation for winter. In Inukjuak, that never happened before October. Clearly, the season arrived early on Ellesmere. Still, the beasts were strong and fit with stomachs full of sedge and lichen, and it cheered Aqiatusuk to see that. He reached down and took a slice of liver with his knife as he was entitled to do and ate it just as it was, fresh and clean-tasting, with an iron tang. By the time the sun set on the following day, the creatures' sinews would already be boiled and bundled up to be used as sewing thread and the sedge and lichen would be in a pot somewhere, simmering away in blood to make soup. Sooner or later, they would use the skins for clothing and sleeping and the antlers for carving. They would roast the heads and make combs from the hooves and not a single part of the catch, not one fragment of flesh or bone or ligament or blood, would be wasted.

A week later, on a clear, sunny day in mid-September, the Inuit moved to the permanent campsite on Lindstrom Peninsula. The spot had been chosen by Henry Larsen on the basis that Otto Sverdrup's expedition had managed to overwinter there only a few years before. (The peninsula had been named after the expedition's Norwegian cook, who had kept his colleagues alive and healthy over the coldest winter they had ever known.) Sverdrup's expedition had been much better equipped and supplied than the Inuit, but Henry

Larsen had an overweening confidence in Inuit resilience and stamina and he was pretty sure the natives would be able to cope. At Lindstrom Peninsula the waters are turbulent and leads open up all winter and this, Larsen figured, would make it easier to hunt seal, though it would also make it very dangerous. In any case, the Inuit were given no choice in the matter. They went in shifts in the detachment Peterhead, dragging a little skiff containing their belongings behind them. The skiff had been abandoned by the detachment decades before but Sargent thought that, with a bit of restoration, it might make a seaworthy vessel for the new camp.

The beach at Lindstrom Peninsula was, if anything, even narrower than the one at Craig Harbour. It was certainly much steeper and Sargent had trouble finding a landing spot that would not damage the Peterhead's hull and had to make several approaches before the waves would allow the boat to get in near the shore. They did get in eventually, and dragged their possessions and finally the skiff itself up on to the slope. There Sargent left them, with the remains of the walrus and the caribou, some stone lamps and a box of rations each. The Peterhead disappeared around the headland and soon enough the new settlers could no longer feel the throb of its engine through the shale. Once again, they began to erect their tents. They set up stone lamps and began to cook caribou meat on them. When the light failed they sat under their caribou skins and rubbed each other warm. There was no time, then, to think much about the place they had come to, or how they would live in it.

The following day they woke to the sound of wind scudding over the cliffs and the sighing of the sea. They could see no signs of human life, no animals and no vegetation around them, just the green shale and the green cliffs and sharp, cold sun clinging to the horizon. They were utterly alone. Mary Aqiatusuk turned to her husband then and said, "Sailarjuarmiinginaaqitaa?" Are we still in the same world?

CHAPTER ELEVEN

IN ALMOST ALL RESPECTS, Lindstrom Peninsula was a bad choice for a camp. The beach was so small and narrow that the Inuit had to string their tents along it in single file, a formation that made communication between the tents difficult and gave the wind free rein to bluster around them. The beach itself was made of large pebbles and it was very steep, backing on to sheer cliffs. The tide appeared to be enormous. If a huge wind pushed in the waves, the settlers could easily find themselves sucked out to sea and those fierce currents which kept the water open in places even in winter would also make the ice pack unstable and dangerous. But it had not been chosen for its homely qualities. The real reason the six families had been moved from Craig Harbour to Lindstrom Peninsula was not that it was likely to offer a good living, but that it was far enough away from the police detachment to deter the Inuit from visiting.

The immediate tasks were to hunt and collect fuel and water. The camp had enough food for three or four weeks, but once the dark period set in, their hunting would be severely restricted. But there still was not enough snow on the land to sledge and the sea was neither open nor yet fast with ice. They would have to walk or go out by boat. Samwillie and Elijah took off along the cliffs but they returned without making a kill. They reported that the land above the cliffs looked parched and mean and there were few tracks or other signs of animal occupation. They had seen two musk ox, they said, grazing on some mossy rocks to the west of the peninsula and raised their rifles but then remembered Sargent's warning that if they shot an ox they would be fined C$500 or sent to jail. If game was abundant, as Ross Gibson had promised them it would be, it must be concentrated in scattered sheltered pockets where there were grasses or lichen, but where these pockets were the hunters could not tell. They had seen *inukshuks* on some of the distant mountains and the man-shaped cairns had told them that Inuit had passed by at some time and marked sled routes into the interior. Of those Inuit there was no trace, the men said, and the hunters could only assume they had gone away or died. It seemed that they would have to depend on marine mammals for their cache.

They figured they could use the old police skiff to return to the spot where they had seen seal and, perhaps, if they could find a way of bringing the massive carcass home, they might even bag a walrus. Once they had collected enough meat for a winter cache, they would begin setting their trap lines and establishing sledging paths with route-side caches. By then, they would know the coastline rather better. But it was a formidable job. Survival on the land was so dependent on their being familiar with it, and here they knew nothing.

On a clear morning soon after they arrived, a party of hunters set off into Jones Sound. Despite the clement weather, the swell was exceptionally rough and awash with floating ice. Making very slow progress they headed towards the area where they had found seals when they had first arrived, but the animals had moved on and no amount of searching revealed their new location. After a few hours and soaked in freezing water, the group returned to camp empty-handed.

While they were out, the women set themselves to the task of finding water and fuel. It seemed that any chunks of freshwater ice from bergs broke up before they reached the shore or got crushed by the pebbles at the shoreline. In any case, there were no bergy bits on the beach they could profitably melt down for sweet water and nowhere within sight to collect heather for fuel, so the women decided to clamber up the cliffs and go looking in the mountains in the hope of finding a stream and a sheltered spot where grasses or willow might grow. Leaving their children in the care of Anna, the crippled woman, they slung flour sacks over their shoulders and began the long climb upwards. At the top of the cliffs they paused a while to catch breath. Up here the air trembled and quivered with almost spectral energy. It was as if they had inadvertently stepped into a dead world restless with old and sleepless souls. Between the peaks were the greyish glaciers they had first spotted at Craig Harbour, which would at least provide some sweet-water ice, so they moved further inland, stumbling across the shale and scree until they arrived at an overhang. There, on the other side, they saw a deep hollow whose sides were ragged with dry moss. At the base of the hollow, sheltered from the whipping wind, there were humps of stunted willow the size of a newborn baby's thumb. They lowered themselves inside and began to pick. For several hours they gathered the moss and willow nubs until, eventually, their sacks began to bulge, then they scrambled back up the ridge, pulling the sacks behind them on sealskin ropes. It was a hard climb, the rock was ice-worn and slippery and along the way the scree bit into the soles of their *kamiks*. They knew they would not be able to carry ice in addition to the willow in the sacks, so they retraced their steps and reached the top of the cliff above the camp, intending to drop off their burdens and start out afresh. It was only then, looking down on the camp, that it really hit them how vulnerable they now were. In Inukjuak they were used to being able to spot a distant camp or a hunting path or sled track from any high vantage point, and the coast was specked with the remains of old *kayaks* and *umiaks* which the weak Arctic sun had been unable to rot. Out on the Ungava tundra, there were the leavings of generations of hunting trips: skulls and leg bones picked clean by the wind and bleached by the sun.

There were piles of rocks under which lay the remains of the hunters and their families and every hill and inlet told a story. Here on Ellesmere, the land had no voice and spoke of nothing.

They rolled the bags of moss and willow down the cliff and followed after. On reaching the camp, some of the younger women went off once more to find water, taking their sealskin carriers with them. They returned late with a few pieces of old glacier ice, so ancient and wind-compacted that the women had been forced to prise them out with ice picks. The ice took a long time to melt over their blubber *qulliqs* and the resulting water tasted as old as time, but the air was so arid that, in spite of the taste, they drank until their stomachs bulged.

And so the days passed and after the second or third week of patchy hunting and endless trips into the mountains for ice and heather, Paddy Aqiatusuk, as camp leader, came to the conclusion that the Lindstrom Peninsula was unsurvivable. He had serious misgivings about the camp's ability to last out the winter unless they were moved. The shale beach was too narrow and steep and the sheer cliffs behind made it impossible to watch for caribou or polar bears. There was no proper water source and insufficient heather or plant material for fuel. Sooner or later the moon would pull the waves up the beach and when that happened there would be no escaping the tide. And while there were signs of seal and beluga and even narwhal in the sea, the waters were so turbulent that hunting from the boat had proven too dangerous. True, the sea would ice up quickly but the pack would always be prone to movement and pressure cracks. The only large land mammals the hunters had found evidence of were musk ox and these they were forbidden to shoot. They had not seen any lemmings and only a few spoor of Arctic hare which meant there was unlikely to be a large fox population. Even ptarmigan, the little Arctic grouse, which sprang from the tundra around Inukjuak in great sprays, were a rare sight here.

He made up his mind to sail by the old police skiff to the Craig Harbour detachment. It was already late in the navigation season

and the journey would be dangerous, but it would be more dangerous to stay and do nothing. He would take some others along and
they would explain to Sargent that the Lindstrom Peninsula was a
poor spot for a camp and ask him to find another, or, better still,
take them out on the Peterhead along the coast so they could select
their own. Paddy would say that they had expected to be better supported with supplies and equipment, they had been promised these
and if they were not forthcoming, he was prepared to suggest they
take some food supplies, plus ammunition and traps, to be set
against future earnings on fox pelts and carvings. And so he set out
the following day in cloudy weather with his stepsons and brother in
the rickety old police skiff. The sea was rough and their passage
from the shore was slowed by slushy water and shards of ice. Entering a clear channel, they turned east, the little boat pitched violently
and its ancient motor began to struggle against the pull of water,
coughing and pluming black smoke. The men arranged themselves
round the sides to balance their weight and for hour after hour they
sat like that, in the freezing salty spray, until the clouds, which had
begun the day as soft as goose down, began to heap together and
darken. They had passed Grise Fiord and were already in the deep
waters of the sound when the weather really turned and a freezing
wind began to gust across the little boat's bows. The waves crested
white and the boat started to dive but they dared not slow the engine
for fear that the storm would overcome them before they reached
Craig Harbour. They hung on, grimly avoiding eye contact with
each other lest their fear become infectious. When water began
crashing into the boat they seized the bailing buckets and frantically
scooped it back out over the bows. Gradually the skiff advanced and
the rocky spit beside Craig Harbour came into view. The Inuit tried
to turn the boat against the current towards the shore but were
pushed back. The little motor cranked and spluttered and they
advanced for a while northeastwards towards the harbour. The wind
blustered and for an instant the fog cleared and they saw on all sides
an armada of icebergs afloat on the currents. Once again they

approached the harbour and once again they were pushed back. The men tried to hold their position, hoping that someone from the detachment would eventually see them. If no one spotted them pretty soon, they were doomed. The boat was taking in water and they had more or less lost control of her in the swell. For what seemed like an infinity they danced crazily on the waves while the wind whipped ice crystals into their faces.

Suddenly they heard the trill of another engine and the sound grew until it became a generous rumble and from out of the gloom the detachment Peterhead appeared, not twenty yards distant. The special constable slung out a rope and the skiff was towed to shore. The men were given hot sweet tea, a pinch of tobacco and a strong warning from Corporal Sargent not to try to come into Craig Harbour by boat again. Taking his cue, Aqiatusuk spoke up then, listing the faults of the campsite and explaining why it was that the Inukjuamiut felt they could not stay there. Sargent listened, then shrugged. He told them to come back to the detachment when the ice had settled and they had some pelts and carvings to sell and he would discuss the possibility of moving the camp then. In the meantime, he would advance them credit on some ammunition, a few dozen steel-sprung fox traps and, for Aqiatusuk, a few pieces of soapstone he had found among the supplies. Aqiatusuk, who was by Inuit standards assertive and self-confident in the company of *qalunaat*, knew that this was the moment he should insist and that if he did not Sargent would continue to dictate what the newcomers could and could not do, but even he found Corporal Sargent forbidding. Umilik towered over them and in certain lights his beard made him look wild and ursine. He was never far from a gun and he had a way about him Aqiatusuk found menacing. Besides, they now found themselves completely dependent on him. He had become, in effect, their guardian and their jailer.

The men returned to camp. The following few weeks passed uneventfully. Hunting and setting traps took the men's hours and the women spent their time collecting water and fuel and sewing new clothes for the winter. They began to travel farther and farther from the camp, leaving a couple of people behind to tend to the children and guard against bears, trying to familiarise themselves with the land. The lack of snow on the land confined the men to the sea ice. By October a thick ice foot had built up along the coast, forming a highway of old ice smoothed by new. This made travel a good deal easier and the men were able to sledge out as far as Hell Gate to the west and to Grise Fiord in the east, setting their trap lines and travelling on the shore-fast ice far out to sea in order to shoot and harpoon seal at the floe edge.

During those early hunting trips, Aqiatusuk quite often remained behind. He felt too old to explore such a new and challenging terrain, his gallstones bothered him and he knew he could be more useful to his family carving walrus ivory and the little bits of soapstone Sargent had advanced him. The dark period would be on them very soon now, and he was anxious to carve as much as he could before the light failed. His eyes were weakened by the smoke of cooking fires, the blaze of the Arctic sun on the snow and by all the carving he had had to do by lantern light. Still he carved. It seemed that his life and the lives of his family might depend on it. Just before the light gave out completely, Aqiatusuk decided to return with three dog teams to the RCMP detachment at Craig to trade pelts and try to persuade Sargent to move them to somewhere more hospitable. He laid out his *komatik* and retied the sealskin knots between the battens, then greased them with seal fat as a guard against freezing. He melted ice in his mouth and spat it slowly on to the rails, rubbing as he went so the water froze in smooth layers. He laid his sealskins on top of the battens, tied them in and loaded his bundle of spare clothes, his caribou sleeping bag and his bag full of carvings. On top of those he put the fox pelts he had managed to trap. In a few weeks from now, the animals' guard hairs would already have been pulled out by the ice and the fur would be patched and tatty, but right now, in the freezing autumn of the High Arctic, the pelts were mossy and luxuriant and, although they were few, he anticipated getting a good price for them. He took a step back to gauge the distribution of the weight, then covered the pelts with a final layer of skins and secured them down with sealskin ropes. He set the dogs into their customary harnesses, cracked his whip, urged them on with a *hai hai* and was off at the front of the younger men.

The Inukjuamiut's *komatiks* were strikingly different from Akpaliapik's and Anukudluk's, and, as they discovered, less suited to the conditions in the High Arctic. They were more tightly battened, which made them less flexible in pressure ice, and they were longer and thinner, which made them more liable to tipping. Their dog traces were shorter and each fanned out separately from the sled where Akpaliapik's and Anukudluk's dogs were harnessed off a single, thick, central sealskin rope. And the dogs themselves were different. The Pond Inlet animals had Greenlandic blood. They were shorter, hardier and more placid, their coats were thicker and they had a tough covering on their pads which limited the damage done to their feet by candle ice or sharp scree. At some point, the Inukjuamiut knew, they would have to make a new set of *komatiks* and start breeding their animals in with Greenlandic stock.

It was a slow journey. Though the ground had long since frozen there was almost no snow and the surface of the land was still too rough for sleds. The sea had been deeply frozen for three weeks but the ice was rough there, too, and the southern Arctic *komatiks* kept overturning and had to be laboriously repacked and retied before the party could go on. The dogs would not settle well. The dry air very quickly had them panting with thirst and the glassy ice along the shore broke their pads. Their leads soon became tangled and one or two of the weaker animals found themselves constantly dragged along whimpering on their backs or bellies by the momentum of the others. Farther out from shore, the ice in the sound seemed to be in a state of perpetual motion and they advanced with caution, watching for the black holes and drum ice which would sink the *komatiks*. Here and there, water burst through the surface ice and wet the dogs' paws and the men had to stop to wipe the ice crystals from between the creatures' pads to prevent them being cut to shreds. After a while, the animals began to lose heart, and Aqiatusuk, Samwillie, Elijah and the other men were forced to run ahead of the *komatiks* encouraging them. They passed Grise Fiord and pressed on towards Lee Point, where the dogs flagged and the men had to take to them with their whips. They were eager to complete the outgoing trip in a day, rest overnight and begin the journey back again the following morning. Aqiatusuk was worried about his wife, Mary, whose health had begun to deteriorate and he did not want to leave her for longer than he had to. Besides that, few of the men had new caribou clothes, and they knew they would be vulnerable to frostbite in a blizzard. So they pressed on, and by a very great effort they reached Craig Harbour late, by moonlight, and began to set up camp. They fed their dogs with frozen meat and went into the detachment.

They were greeted by Areak, the special constable, who set water on to boil and for a while the Inuit men sat in the detachment building drinking sugary tea and smoking and recovering from the trip. To the Inuit the detachment seemed impossibly luxurious. An arrangement of low stilts kept out the permafrost and the building was warmed with coal-burning stoves. It was separated into rooms and from the centre of each hung a coal-oil lamp. There were other comforts, too, such as beds and hot and cold water. Even the air smelled of comfort, a predominance of coffee and tinned stew. Areak found them a few sardines and heated something from a can. They sat and ate while Sargent inspected the pelts and carvings, decided how much store credit to give, then issued each man another fifty traps on credit. He was hoping that once the snow came the camp would be able to extend their trap lines into the interior and out across the west coast of the island. Foxes were more likely to be found out on the sea ice, living off the carcasses left by polar bears. As for moving the camp, for the moment, Sargent said, that was impractical.

The journey back to Lindstrom began slowly. The days were mostly twilight now and the men were forced to navigate their way round pressure ridges by feeling the contours of the snow. Every so often they had to stop to untangle the dogs from their traces and the problem of the *komatiks'* overturning slowed them down. They had been going a few hours when they came on a huge lead of open water, where the smooth, shore-fast ice had been blown from the ice foot at the shore. Samwillie went ahead, following the line of the lead in the half-light, but he could find no end to the open water. It was too wide to cross so there was nothing for it but to return to the safety of Craig Harbour for the night before setting off the next day by a different route. As the men turned back another storm began brewing, flinging hailstones down on the sea ice which hurt the dogs and the men had to use their whips to make them move ahead. The ice was soon followed by snow falling in flakes as big as the pieces of shale on the beach and within minutes their tracks were obliterated. There was no choice now but to head for land and camp wherever they could, so they turned their *komatiks* and whipped the dogs towards the shore, coming in near Fielder Point. There they remained for more than three days, while the wind and the hail flustered and savaged their tents.

And it was there, on the second day, that Akpaliapik and Anukudluk found them. When they had not returned as expected, the women of the Inukjuamiut camp had persuaded the two Ingluligmiut to go out looking for their men and now they were all caught in the storm. They sat in the dark together. The Inukjuamiut cheered themselves by telling stories and cleaning their guns while the Pond Inlet men, who could not readily follow the conversations, slept, dreaming, perhaps, of better days. The next day the dog food ran out and by the following morning the poor animals were slinking miserably around the tents. During the early hours of the fourth day the Inuit woke to frantic yelping and, grabbing their guns, they rushed outside just in time to see a pack of dogs disappearing along a rocky ridge. They gave chase, sliding and tumbling across the snowy scree, until they came upon two startled musk ox standing in their defensive position, with their heads lowered and horns presented. The dogs, agitated by starvation, began lunging at the oxen with their teeth bared, and the oxen responded by adopting fighting positions, scuffing at the snow and swinging their horns to and fro, one of which caught a dog and sunk into the flesh on its shoulder. Pulling back, the ox lifted the dog in the air and began trying to shake the unfortunate creature free. One of the lead dogs was by now snapping at the hooves of the second ox, which picked it up in its horns and flung it, as though weightless, across the snow where it landed, its guts blooming red and black on the snow. The musk oxen snorted, then lumbered away into the darkness. Once they were at a safe distance, the men approached the scene and, finishing off the first dog with the back of a rifle, they picked up the animals' bodies and headed back down the slope. Later, they butchered the flesh and distributed it evenly among the sled teams. Henry Larsen's decision to site the Inuit camp at Lindstrom Peninsula had now cost them four days and two dogs. Sooner or later, it was clear, someone or other would die.

On 15 October 1953, the sun set over Ellesmere Island for the last time that year. For the next four months the Inuit would be living in perpetual darkness. On good days, when the clouds were drawn back, the sea ice reflected the moon's glow and so long as the Inuit were out on the ice, they could see their footprints. On bad days, and most days were bad days, they could not tell what was beneath or above or around them, nor in which direction they were travelling or even when their journey, however short, might end. The Inuit of Inukjuak had no word for the void that opened up around them. At first, they tried to carry on with the routine they had worked so hard to establish while there was still light. The men left to go hunting in the dark and returned in the dark. They ate and pissed and shat and made love and sewed and cooked and swapped stories and fed their dogs and cleaned their equipment in the dark or by the dim yellow light of a *qulliq*. To cheer themselves they made bone flutes and lutes with sinew for strings and they sang and played music and told stories. But the dark exhausted them and pretty soon it was almost impossible to maintain a routine. Their body clocks broke down and the brain could not tell whether it was day or night or something in between. The absence of light made hunting an almost daily terror. Though they could no longer see it, the constant creaking and cracking of the ice reminded them that they were surrounded. The ice around the Lindstrom Peninsula often broke open without warning and floes were blown away on the high winds. Rime frost and beached ice collected at the shore and right at the sea's edge the smooth spread of the ancient ice foot gave way to rough ice rubble and pressure ridges. The hunters had not had time to learn the position of all the contradictory currents and eddies in the sound before the dark came down, and they did not know where the ice was at its most unstable. Around the cracks there were patches of rotting ice and, beyond these, smooth fields of the open sea ice interrupted by immense, embedded icebergs.

The land was no refuge. It was rocky and covered in loose boulders and scree and there was barely enough snow to sledge across it without the *komatik* runners' catching on some upstanding piece of rock or ice. In the darkness it was almost impossible to tell where the cliff edge lay and there were no established hunting paths or customary routes.

Even out on the sea ice, they often had to rely on their dogs to scent the way home and they would find themselves trapped on moving ice floes or lost in the fiords, waiting for a moonlit day or night. Sometimes they were away for days at a time, leaving the women and children alone at camp to fend for themselves, not knowing where their men were, if they were still alive, or how long they would be gone.

With the dark came the cold. In Inukjuak the snow always fell heavily at the end of September and by the beginning of October the Inukjuamiut were living in snowhouses, but here in the High Arctic the snow arrived in sporadic and unpredictable bursts, and when it did come the wind refused to allow it to settle so they were forced to remain in their flimsy canvas tents. The temperature hovered around −30°C and when November arrived, it plunged even lower. With winds roaring from the Arctic Ocean the windchill could drop the air temperature on the sea ice to −55°C. Whenever they went outside, their heads pounded, their eyelashes froze together and little ice balls collected around the tear ducts in their eyes. The hairs inside their noses stuck together and pulled apart each time they breathed and the breath came as a shallow pant. The lungs burned, the eardrums ached and the brain struggled to locate the body's extremities.

November merged into December and the Inuit were still in tents. The inside temperature rarely rose above −15°C and the women were forever breaking the icicles from the inside of the tent canvas. Everyone was constantly cold but there was not enough fuel to light fires and the only warmth they could generate came from the blubber *qulliqs* and their own breath. At night, the children slept bundled together with the adults and, during the day, their skin turned raw from all the rubbing their mothers had to do to keep them warm. The men caught a few wolves and the women sewed little suits from the pelts of these, and from the skins of dogs that died and the scraps of spoiled fox pelts, but the hunters had to be given first priority for caribou skin clothes. If they died, the whole camp would die with them, and so the children had to make do with whatever was left over.

By December, the camp was struggling to stay alive. There was not enough meat and for weeks at a time they had to live on bannock bread and tea, but the bannock did not fill their stomachs and the tea did not keep them warm. Their bellies demanded *niqi*, fresh meat, *nirimarik* or real food, flesh and blubber, but by December there was no *niqi* to be had. To satisfy their cravings they began to eat the carcasses of starved wolves or foxes they found lying in the ice. They ate ptarmigan feathers and bladders and heather, they boiled up hareskin boot liners and made broths from old pairs of sealskin *kamiks.* They chewed seagull bones and dog harnesses. They ate fur and lemming tails. They consumed their sick dogs and the bodies of their aborted pups. But nothing was ever enough. Before long some kind of stomach sickness began to spread among them. Their bellies knotted into fists, and their muscles trembled. The children leaked diarrhoea then vomit which the women in the camp fed to the dogs rather than have it go to waste. Sargent came to see them, leaving rations of flour, tea and a little sugar, but it all raced through their stomachs and out of their bowels more or less undigested. The illness dimmed their spirits further. Everyone grew so demoralised that not even songs and music could cheer them up. They began to fret and pine for the people they had left behind, and to talk about them constantly, remembering old times, events, celebrations. They came up with a new word to describe the dark period, Qausuittualuk, the Great Dark Time, and they named their new home Qausuittuq, the Place that Never Thaws. In the dark, their loneliness and isolation took on a peculiarly schizophrenic quality so that they were no longer able to distinguish what was real and what not. Qausuittualuk was more than mere physical blackout, it was a blind drawn across their souls.

Glenn Sargent reported the situation in his monthly dispatch to headquarters under the heading "Stomach Influenza," but he played down the cause and severity of the sickness. He was under pressure to make the experiment work and he was mindful of the competition at Resolute Bay. In truth, he didn't really know the worst of it. The camp was forty miles distant and the Inuit rarely made the trip into the detachment. When they did, they were often too afraid of Sargent's authority, his temper and his gun to speak out.

Often, in the later days of the winter, Aqiatusuk would take off up the cliff and sit in the darkness with his face to the south. Whenever he thought about the situation he was in, he felt gusts of angry resentment against the *qalunaat* and their promises. They were wrong. There was no better life to be had in Qausuittuq. He missed his stepson, Josephie. He missed Inukjuak and his old hunting grounds. It was time, he decided, that he and his family went home.

Halfway across the world in London, at about the same time, an exhibition of Inuit sculpture was opening to tremendous acclaim. The exhibition included works from several Inuit artists, but chief among the pieces on display were Aqiatusuk's wonderfully understated depictions of hunters. The *Art and News Review* commented that the pieces were "astonishingly subtle, these are works of art in the fullest meaning of the word." The *Manchester Guardian* went further. "Remarkable," said their critic. "Powerful enough to make the most fervent admirer of Henry Moore pause a moment." The exhibition proved so successful that galleries in Edinburgh and Paris asked for it on loan and Aqiatusuk's name became well known in certain art circles. Aqiatusuk knew nothing of this exhibition. No one had thought to tell him it was on. He was stuck at the top of the world, barely surviving.

CHAPTER TWELVE

Six months into the relocation experiment, two very different stories were emerging. According to the Department the whole thing was proving a great success. Larsen, Stevenson and Departmental administrator Ben Sivertz had visited Resolute Bay and Craig Harbour and made inspections of the camps. At the detachments, Corporal Glenn Sargent and Constable Ross Gibson had been encouraged to submit positive quarterly reports and to play down any problems. The Canadian Broadcast Company's film of the drop-off had been well received in the south and within weeks of the relocation, The *Toronto Sun*, the *Montreal Gazette* and the Hudson Bay Company's paper, *The Beaver*, had all published glowing accounts of the new, improved lives the Inuit were living on Cornwallis and Ellesmere islands. The good news had spread to the U.S., and a *National Geographic* journalist, Andrew Brown, had flown up to Resolute Bay to interview Ross Gibson.

None of these newspaper reporters or Departmental officials had asked the Inuit what they thought about the move in any detail. If they had, their stories would not have been admiring tales of pluck and grit but something more shocking, a detailing of the privations of more or less abandoned families trying to survive in the harshest terrain human beings had ever inhabited. These stories would have mentioned the disorientating, demoralising darkness which made hunting and trapping not only tremendously difficult but extremely dangerous and the huge distances hunters were having to travel on mobile pack ice in order to be able to hunt and trap enough to survive. Had they been asked, the Inuit might well have told the reporters and Departmental officials that while the hunters were away, the women and children were often forced to survive on bannock and thin broth made from seal heads, and that everyone regularly went hungry and thirsty. The group on the Lindstrom Peninsula might have pointed out that the women of the camp were having to walk miles out on the floating pack to chip freshwater ice from bergs mired in the floe and at the Resolute Bay camp they might have mentioned that no large game ever came on to the island and that they had been reduced to sneaking up to the air-base rubbish dumps under cover of darkness and stealing the remains of the pilots' packed lunches in order to stave off starvation. The Inuit would have certainly reported that both camps were too small and too remote to be viable and that the attempt to mix the Inukjuamiut and the Ingluligmiut had been, all in all, a bad idea. Parents might have brought up the fact that their children were now being denied schooling or access to medical care and single men, like Samwillie, would perhaps have complained that it was going to be impossible to find a wife up there, among women who were either already married or close blood relations. They all would have said they were homesick and they wanted to go back home.

Over the months it became Glenn Sargent's unenviable task to navigate a path between this untold truth, only part of which he really knew or understood, and the Department version being fed to the press. Perhaps for this reason, he turned down the requests of Paddy Aqiatusuk and some of the other Inuit at Lindstrom Peninsula to make radio contact with their relatives in Inukjuak. Sargent said it would be too difficult to organise, but it may well be that he just did not want the awkward facts to emerge.

At Craig Harbour Christmas came and went. Corporal Sargent

put on a festive meal of corned beef and sent everyone away with tinned sardines, some sugar and a few hardtack biscuits. Shortly afterwards, snow arrived and within days the biting winds had compacted it down so that it could be cut into snowbricks. This was a turning point in the new migrants' fortunes. With a sense of relief, the Inukjuamiut began building their snowhouses along the beach in a neat line topped off at one end by the sod houses of the two Pond Inlet families. The Aqiatusuk family snowhouse was, like most of the others, about twelve feet in diameter and about six feet high. Its entrance was elevated above the level of the living space, which was accessed by a tunnel so that warm air would not escape from it. The tunnel led from the outside first to a kind of porch, where Paddy, Samwillie and Elijah stored their dog harnesses, snowknives, harpoons and floats and frozen clothes. Another tunnel opened out to the living area, which had an ice floor and snowbrick walls lined with caribou and buffalo skins. At one end of the living area, the ice floor was built up into a sleeping platform and covered in more skins. In the centre of the house sat the *qulliq* over which Mary Aqiatusuk had built a simple wire frame on which to hang the cooking pot. By the side of that sat a large stone which acted as a store for frozen meat and blubber, when there was any. The space was cramped and often thick with the fumes from the *qulliq* but at least it was possible to stay warm inside, for the temperature in the snowhouses often rose as high as −5°C. As the winter progressed and the sea ice stabilised, the camp hoped they would be able to build more snowhouses out on the sea ice, away from the permafrost, where it would be a few degrees warmer and they would be nearer the edge of the shore-fast ice where most seals were to be found.

The men now felt able to leave the settlement for longer periods in the knowledge that their families would probably not freeze to death. They passed the late winter carving out new hunting routes, as far as Hell Gate in the west and south across the great ice sea to Devon Island. For week after week, they hunted seals at their breathing holes and in nets hung under tight leads in the ice and, though they were never able to catch enough meat to fill the bellies of their families, the camp did at least draw back from starvation. And so they passed the remainder of that winter, hanging on to life by a few threads of sealskin, some snowblocks and a stone blubber lamp.

At winter's end, when the immediate crises of survival were over, Paddy Aqiatusuk began to realise that something powerful had happened to him. For the first time in his life, he had been overcome by the thing that every Inuk dreads, often even more than death. The feeling had begun as a slow thump in the chest then strengthened until it became a sickness. Paddy Aqiatusuk was *hujuujaq*, homesick. Not any ordinary homesickness, but the deep, griping longing for kith and kin to which Inuit, perhaps of all people, are most prone. Paddy's *hujuujaq* was not merely a sense of missing. As it worked its way inside him, he felt himself invaded by a savage absence, a sense not simply of not being but of never having been. Away from his homeland he no longer really knew who he was. There was no escape from it. Working on his sculpture only furthered his distress, since so much of what he carved related to his life back in Inukjuak. He realised that to retrieve some sense of himself and restore some equilibrium to an existence which tottered dangerously towards the abyss he would have to go home.

He relayed his disquiet to Corporal Sargent, but the policeman did not seem to take any account of it, instead repeating the same excuse he had given over the matter of radio access, that sending Aqiatusuk and his family back to Inukjuak would be too logistically difficult. Aqiatusuk reminded him that the travellers had been made a specific promise that the Department would help them return if they did not like life in the High Arctic but Sargent merely shrugged.

On 14 February 1954 the sun poked a first, experimental ray beyond the confines of its winter hiding place and the Inuit at Lindstrom Peninsula ran from their snowhouses and sod houses to greet it. Over the days that followed, the sun did nothing more than wanly circle the horizon but the camp welcomed its return as that of a long-absent friend. Piece by piece the world quietly reappeared and they were reminded just how beautiful it was. The winter had renewed the land. Icicles sparkled off the *komatiks* and icebergs shone blue-green in the distance and the sea was as white as a fox.

The return of the light seemed to impress upon Aqiatusuk more fully than ever that in spite of its beauty, Ellesmere Island was not his land. Once more, he took himself off up the cliff at the back of the beach and, gazing southward, set his sights on Inukjuak. He was feeling old and tired, his gallbladder ached and the signs of his age only made him more determined to return home. No Inuk would countenance dying in a foreign land, full of unknown spirits and unfamiliar stories. When the time came Aqiatusuk wanted to leave the world among friends and the spirits of his ancestors. And he wanted desperately to see Josephie.

He passed his days carving and looking out across Jones Sound but the ache would not leave him and, when he could finally stand his *hujuujaq* no longer, he returned to the detachment to ask Glenn Sargent one more time to help him go back home. If it proved impossible to send him home permanently, he asked if a visit could be arranged so that he could see his family and his stepson again.

But Sargent had his instructions and they were to keep the Inuit where they were. He told Aqiatusuk that there were only two ways out of Ellesmere. One was by sled to Resolute Bay and from there by plane to the south, then north again to Inukjuak, which would be tremendously expensive and difficult to organise. The other was by sea on the *C. D. Howe,* but that too had its problems. After she left Craig Harbour the *C. D. Howe's* route took her *all the way* to Montreal. If she were to pick up Paddy and his family, they would all have to remain in Montreal for twelve months before boarding the *C. D. Howe* on the following year's patrol. The navigation season was too short for the *C. D. Howe* to sail back into Hudson Bay after calling in at Craig Harbour and such a huge diversion would, in any case, prove prohibitively expensive. There was no money to support the whole family to live in Montreal for a year and, Sargent surmised, they would be very unhappy there. What Sargent *did* suggest was that if Paddy was missing his relatives as much as he said he was, then he could write to them and ask them to join him on Ellesmere Island. The government, he said, would sponsor their journey north on the *C. D. Howe*, just as it had Paddy Aqiatusuk's. It was the best he could do.

Over the weeks that followed, Aqiatusuk considered his options and after searching his heart he decided reluctantly that since he could not speak to Josephie Flaherty on the radio, and he could not return to Inukjuak, he would do as Sargent had suggested and ask his stepson to come up to Ellesmere Island. The sculptor knew it was a lot to ask of the young man, more than Josephie would realise, but the way he thought about it, the whole camp would be sent back to Inukjuak sooner or later and, until then, having the Flahertys on Ellesmere would bring great comfort to the family as well as adding another hunter to their number. If Josephie were with him, Aqiatusuk felt he could manage his *hujuujaq*. The mail usually left the Craig Harbour detachment with the spring patrol at the end of March by dog teams and took two weeks to reach Resolute Bay from where it travelled by air to the south. If Aqiatusuk wrote a letter at once it would probably find its way on to the *C. D. Howe* that year and Josephie would get it in July.

Spring arrived on Ellesmere Island. Temperatures rose and remained stable at around −25°C. The sun dazzled and bounced off the ice and the whole of the sound solidified into a hard, white plate, as smooth as marble, as the sea ice settled. Everyone who had them took to wearing their snowgoggles. Those who had none were forced to bind their eyes with strips of sacking to ward off the dazzle. Even then, hunters routinely came in off the ice snow blind. Ice crystals spangled the air. Forests of little ice fronds sprang up from the land, icicles hung from the roofs of the sod huts and the wind transformed them into little glockenspiels. Ellesmere Island became almost unbearably beautiful.

Seals began to gather in the open water at Hell Gate and, before long, the hunters were able to abandon their hunting at *agluit*, the seals' winter breathing holes, and turn instead to stalking the creatures when they came up on to the ice to bask. From time to time whale and narwhal appeared on their spring migrations north and, when they did, everyone ate well. The hunters picked up aborted premature seal pups on the ice and by May they were hunting female seals and their live, full-term young in their dens under the snow. For the first time there was enough meat at camp for everyone at least to have a little. The improvement in the conditions brought the husky bitches into heat and pretty soon they were producing pups.

But Aqiatusuk took no comfort in this small upturn in his family's fortunes. His decision to ask Josephie Flaherty to come up to join the camp weighed heavily on him. It had not done anything to ease his homesickness either. He needed his stepson but he felt bad about asking him to come. He passed much of his time now sitting on the cliff above the camp, staring out across the sound, carving and waiting. All late spring and early summer he waited until one cloudy day at the end of July, his head began to droop and he began to feel his legs prick. Thinking he had overexerted himself on a hunting trip the previous day, the old sculptor clambered down the cliff and went to rest in his family's tent. By the onset of evening he felt quite ill. His chest ached and his limbs were sluggish and unresponsive. Through the night, his condition deteriorated until the moment arrived from which there would be no turning back. He had seen this moment a thousand times in the dwindling lives of fox and hare and seal and he was not afraid of it. He had lost the will to live and his heart opened to his fate. On 31 July 1954, Paddy Aqiatusuk lay down for the last time and took in his final breath.

A few months later, when news of his death finally reached the south, *Time* magazine published an obituary. It read:

Akeeaktashuk, 56, one of the leaders of the small group of Eskimo primitive sculpturists whose work came to the attention of the outside world in recent years because of its fluent,

uncluttered simplicity; of drowning July 31, when he slipped
from an ice floe while hunting walrus off Ellesmere Island.

But Paddy Aqiatusuk did not die from a fall on an ice floe. He
died of a broken heart.

Paddy's stepsons buried their father at the foot of a south facing
cliff under red rocks. The loss of their leader hit everyone at the
Inuit camp on Ellesmere very hard. Aqiatusuk had pulled them
together and they were now afraid that there would be nothing to
stop them falling apart. There was no more talk about returning to
Inukjuak. In ten weeks the dark period would fall over Ellesmere
once more and they would have to build a winter cache of meat
before it did.

If Paddy's death ended all thoughts of return for a while, it also
strengthened the hunters' resolve to survive. The American adventurer, Lewis Cotlow, witnessing Akpaliapik and another Inuk track a
polar bear on Ellesmere several years after this, wrote:

> It seemed to me that the bear epitomised everything the Es-
> kimo had to struggle against in the open wilderness: hardship
> and uncertainty, an often pitiless nature which was for each
> member of the community a personal and implacable threat. It
> was that threat which made these people the most tightly-knit,
> yet most individualised human beings I had ever seen. It made
> them ready at any moment to give up possessions or comfort to
> help a stranger. Not because of some abstract idea; for them it
> was the only way of life that made sense. So each man threw
> into the communal lot his strength, wisdom and skill as if
> nature had decreed, cooperate or die!

Over that hard, second winter, and over the spring and the summer which followed it, the Inukjuamiut and the Ingluligmiut of
Ellesmere Island pooled their strength, their resources and their
knowledge into the raw business of survival. During the long and

often savage months, those thirty-three reluctant pioneers took stock of their new land. It was not their way to try to master the place, a goal they knew to be quite fruitless, but to understand it. Gradually, through many weeks and months of watching and listening, they learned how to live on Ellesmere Island.

Before the sun set for the final time that year, the camp moved to a larger stretch of beach beside Grise Fiord and there, using spare packing cases and bits of lumber dumped by the *C. D. Howe* on her annual supply, they constructed a huddle of little huts. Each was about 12 feet by 15 feet long and 8 feet high, with an outer structure of packing crates covered with sod and a roof constructed from canvas stretched over a wooden frame. There was no furniture in the huts, but those who could afford to bought a primus stove with the credits from their fox trapping and these supplied heat for cooking and light in the darkness.

They rebuilt their *komatiks* shorter and wider, better to withstand the pressure ridges, loosened the battens to make them more flexible over rough ice and fashioned upright handlebars from bone and bits of old wood, which made them much easier to control. They plaited together new sealskin harnesses for the dogs, with a single central rope, from which long individual traces fanned to give the animals better purchase on the rough ice. The owners of shotguns made fresh cartridges from spent ones by inserting new firing pins and points, and filling them up with gunpowder.

When the Inukjuamiut's bitches came in heat, they bred them to Akpaliapik's and Anukudluk's Greenlandic dogs and trained the pups to sniff out the breathing holes of seals and follow polar bear tracks. By the end of the year, most families had two sleds, one with steel runners for the compacted spring snow and another with whalebone ones for the winter. In the absence of water, they iced the runners with fresh caribou blood and filled the cracks in the whalebone runners with pieces of frozen walrus liver, rasped smooth.

Land mammals continued to be hard to find but marine mammals proved more plentiful. The big issue on Ellesmere Island, they came to see, was not so much the quantity of marine game as its accessibility. Like their land-based counterparts, the marine mammals around Ellesmere were living at the most northerly ranges of their species. They were mostly migratory and congregated in highly scattered pockets. As the hunters extended their ground, sketching hunting trails west along the sound from Grise Fiord, down into Devon Island as far west as the Grinnell Peninsula, then northeast to the Bjorne Peninsula and Baumann Fiord on southwest Ellesmere, they took note of the inlets and bays where they had seen narwhal, seal or beluga. They made trails inland from Grise Fiord across the south central tip of Ellesmere to meet the sea route at Baumann Fiord and ran their trap lines there. They travelled as far east as Coburg Island, then north all the way to the Bache Peninsula, a journey which had defeated the icebreaker *d'Iberville* only a couple of years before. Eventually, their hunting routes would traverse an area no less than 255,800 square miles and would include 750 miles of established winter routes and 3,200 miles of less regularly used paths. By the end of the 1950s, the average hunter in Grise Fiord was covering an area of 6,864 square miles every year, the largest hunting range of any Inuit people.

The hunters also began to adapt the way they hunted and trapped. In good fox years, they extended their trap lines, but learned to avoid those areas, such as Baumann Fiord, that were patrolled by wolves which would eat the trapped foxes. They learned how to stalk and hunt polar bear and then how to flense and butcher them, avoiding the livers which they knew would make them sick. When hunting for beluga, experience taught them to swap their harpoons for lassoes. The beluga living round Ellesmere had more fatty insulation than those in Hudson Bay and the harpoon heads would only find fragile purchase and work themselves out of the flesh, allowing the creatures to escape wounded. Lassoes gave the hunters a firmer grip but they also made sure that those whales which did slip away remained unhurt and would live to breed and perhaps to be hunted again. Instead of leaving their families behind, the hunters gathered the confidence to take them along, so the women could help in the hunt and make repairs to the hunters' clothing or sew a new pair of *kamiks* while they were en route.

By the close of 1954 the hunters had established a hunting cycle on Ellesmere which remains unchanged today. From mid-April to mid-July, they hunted ringed seals by stalking them on the ice from behind hunting screens, *utoq,* made of Arctic hare to blend in with the snow. During late April they began *nunajak* hunting, locating seal mothers and their pups in their dens with dogs, and by June they were hunting seals through open leads in the ice in Jones Sound in their old police detachment skiff. Whenever their journeys took them to Coburg and Smith islands, Makinson and Sverdrup inlets, Baumann, Grise and Starnes fiords or Cape Combermere, they would stop to collect the eggs of the glaucous gulls and Arctic terns which nested in thick clumps on the cliffs. During the brief Ellesmere summers they would concentrate their efforts on sealing at ice cracks and when the water opened up in mid-July they would hunt ringed seals on the open water, banging on the gunnels of the skiff to arouse the animals' curiosity. Noting that walrus moved from Baffin Bay into Jones Sound in June or July, they would take walrus-hunting parties out on to the open water, finding the females and their young at Jakeman Glacier and males at Hell Gate. In late July, they hunted narwhal migrating up into Jones Sound from Baffin Bay. The beluga arrived later and more reliably, they discovered, from areas of open water in Baffin Bay and Cardigan Strait and came into Grise Fiord to breed. In the early autumn they pursued walrus heading back down south on their migrations and when the ice came, and they were able to take their dog teams out, they hunted caribou around Bjorne Peninsula and Makinson Inlet, lightly at first, and more vigorously after Henry Larsen relaxed the hunting quotas. As soon as the ice reached a thickness of three or four inches, the hunters returned to catching seals through their *agluit* or breathing holes.

The women learned how to flense and scrape polar bear skins and picked up from some visiting Greenlanders the technique required to sew the thick pelts and make trousers with them. They also learned how to set their *qulliqs* with heather wicks and which kind of blubber to use for warmth and which for light or cooking. In their searches for freshwater they developed such a keen sense that they could often smell it out. They became more active in the hunt. Even the children mucked in, tending the fox trap lines and hauling buckets of freshwater ice.

Though life was still tremendously hard, the Inuit survived. But they never forgot Ross Gibson's promise that they were going to a better life, nor lost the dream that one day they would find themselves on their way back to Inukjuak.

CHAPTER THIRTEEN

AT THE TIME of Paddy Aqiatusuk's death, in 1954, *Nanook of the North* had been playing in one cinema or another continuously for thirty-two years. The man who had made the picture, Robert Flaherty, had never contacted any of the principals since leaving the Arctic, nor had he ever returned, though from time to time he had been sent news from Inukjuak and had a good idea of what was going on there. He knew, for example, that Alakariallak, the hunter who had played Nanook, had died of starvation. He had mentioned Alakariallak's death in interviews and always said he felt "bad about it." At some point, he had also discovered that Maggie Nujarluktuk had given birth to his son, Josephie, though on this topic he had remained resolutely silent. He never wrote to the boy, or, so far as we know, sent him any money or other token of affection.

Language experts describe Inuktitut, the Inuit language, as highly contextual and so structurally complex and minutely inter-leaved that nouns and verbs are formed as they are spoken, according to the current state of the thing or action they are describing. This feature of the language has made it very difficult to produce an Inuktitut dictionary. I mention it here because, in this regard at least, Inuktitut has parallels with Robert Flaherty's own life. As a film-maker and as a man, Flaherty lived for his next self-created instant. Once that instant had passed, another seamlessly took its place, and then another after that. He was not a man for ruminating on his past. He once told an interviewer that he found horizons poignant. What he meant by this, presumably, was that horizons fenced him in while at the same time hinting at the possibilities that lay beyond. He lived his life in a state of perpetual motion, his sights set on whatever was there on the other side of the next experience.

In Robert Flaherty's eyes, *Nanook* was the culmination of his love affair with the north, just as Josephie Flaherty was the culmination of his love affair with Maggie Nujarluktuk.

Inuktitut brings the things it speaks about into being, and in the same way the Inuit brought Robert Flaherty the film-maker into being. The people of the Barrenlands had taught him how to see. In a manner of speaking, he had returned the favour in *Nanook*. For a worldwide audience of *Nanook* fans Robert Flaherty would always be the man who first threw light on the Barrenlanders. It was his vision that became the accepted view of the Inuit and their lives.

Nanook of the North contrived to tail the film-maker. More and more it became an unwanted offspring, one that its creator was unable to shrug off. After *Nanook*, Robert would go on to make other moving pictures, take stills photographs, write books, but whatever he created would always invite comparison to that first, monumental effort. His fans, his backers and his audience never ceased to hope for another *Nanook*.

Not long after the première of *Nanook of the North,* Flaherty took a call from Jesse L. Lasky, the production head of Paramount. The mogul was an adventure fanatic. For years he had spent his vacations tramping the wildernesses of the Canadian northwest and Alaska, he had been camping with Zane Grey, the western writer, out in New Mexico, and the whole frontier myth fascinated him. In Flaherty, Lasky reckoned he had found a man on the same frequency as himself, someone whose adventures he might vicariously share. He told Flaherty to make him another *Nanook*. Flaherty could go where he wanted, do what he liked and Lasky would foot the bill. The call came at just the right time. Flaherty already had a plan for a follow-up to *Nanook*. Sometime before, he had been introduced to

Frederick O'Brien whose travelogue of his year in the remote Marquesas Islands, *White Shadows in the South Seas,* had been a big hit. During their conversation, Flaherty mentioned he was looking for a new project and O'Brien had suggested he might get on well in another part of Polynesia with which O'Brien was familiar, Samoa. There, O'Brien told Flaherty, he would find a kind of paradise of plenty. The breeze was always balmy, fish flopped into the nets and fruit fell off the trees, and the untroubled ease of Samoan life was reflected in its permissive, happy-go-lucky people. O'Brien observed that he had never been anywhere where human life was more natural and human beings were more free. The Arctic had been one kind of Eden. Samoa would be another.

By now Flaherty had a wife and three daughters and Polynesia was then still extremely remote and inaccessible. But the more he thought about it, the more determined he became to do it. And now he had a backer in Paramount. The Flaherty family, Robert, Frances, the three girls, and Robert's younger brother, David, boarded a steamer heading west out of San Francisco. A long voyage later, they landed at Safune, a small settlement on the island of Savaii in Samoa.

O'Brien had given them a letter of introduction to a German trader called Felix David. He lived just outside Safune in a two-storey building with a first-floor veranda overlooking a landscape of palms and sky-blue sea. Felix David was an old-school eccentric. He had roamed round the Pacific for years, hooking up with the local women, trading in whatever was tradeable and treating the islanders on whichever remote paradise he found himself to improvised amateur operatic performances. He and Robert Flaherty formed an instant bond and with Felix David's help the Flaherty family found a house to rent nearby. There, in the grounds, they built an open-air theatre where they showed movies they had brought over from New York. Within weeks, the Savaiians had forgotten all about Felix David's operatic performances.

Though conditions were a good deal more pleasant on Savaii

than they had been in the Arctic, Flaherty found it proved much harder to settle on a theme for the Samoan film. Life was so easy and the Samoans so peaceable that there was no real drama. Robert, Frances and David had to spend a good many weeks drifting about with the locals before they landed on a topic that might make an intriguing film. Before any Samoan boy could pass into manhood, he had to undergo a series of agonising tattoo rituals. Beautiful and elaborate patterns would be imprinted all over his body using plant dyes and hot shark bones. Flaherty had first become interested in tattooing in the Arctic. Although the practice was much frowned upon by missionaries there, many older Inuit women still bore tattoos in the form of seal or walrus whiskers on their faces. But the Samoan tattoos were much more elaborate, often taking years to complete and the results transformed Samoan men into living story books. From the tattoos, other Samoans could tell which family the young man belonged to and where he fitted into the family hierarchy. The skill and intricacy of the tattoos determined his status among his peers, his future prospects and his marriageability. The Flaherty brothers began filming. They spent two years making their Samoan movie and the result was *Moana of the South Seas* which remained, until his death, Robert Flaherty's favourite film.

The studio heads at Paramount were underwhelmed with *Moana*. They had been expecting another *Nanook*. "Where's the blizzards?" asked one Paramount executive. They found other reasons to nitpick, too. Having cheerfully waved off scenes of speared walruses and disembowelled seals in the Arctic picture, they now wondered if the tattooing sequences were not just a little distasteful. The Paramount booker scheduled *Moana* for a limited release in Lincoln, Nebraska; Pueblo, Colorado; Austin, Texas; Jacksonville, Florida; Asheville, North Carolina; and Poughkeepsie, New York, expecting it quietly to die, but it received enthusiastic audiences. The critics liked it, too. Surprised, and rather caught out, Paramount took another look at the film with a view to a national release. But the marketing department met with considerable resistance from Flaherty himself. He reasoned that *Nanook* had flourished on word of mouth and he wanted the same for *Moana*. Director and studio were gridlocked. Paramount did not want to leave the movie's success to chance; Flaherty did not want it aggressively marketed. In the impasse, *Moana* was shelved. It came out a while later in a few more towns around the U.S.A., but did not, in studio speak, "do business." Its moment had passed.

Hollywood had not quite given up on Robert Flaherty though. Sometime after *Moana*, Irving Thalberg, head at MGM, got in touch. Thalberg had optioned O'Brien's book, *White Shadows in the South Seas*, and it was about to go into production in Tahiti with W. S. Van Dyke as director. Thalberg wanted Flaherty to lend his expertise in the area and co-direct. Seeing no objection to this, Flaherty set out eagerly for Tahiti, but it was clear from the start that the relationship between Flaherty and Van Dyke was doomed. Flaherty was a miniaturist who dealt in epic ideas and, for all his liberal stretching of the truth, his instincts lay always in the direction of documentation. Van Dyke wanted a garden-variety Hollywood blockbuster in an exotic setting. Before long, Flaherty took himself off the picture and returned home to New Canaan, Connecticut.

He was to go back to Tahiti a couple of years later through a connection with the German director, Frederick Murnau, who was then working in Hollywood. Murnau had financial backing for a Flaherty-style observational film set in the South Seas and he wanted Flaherty to make it. For Robert, this meant leaving his family behind, because the girls were by now all at school, but he was not a man to be boxed in by his domestic circumstances, and he and his brother, David, took passage on a ship out of California, arriving in Tahiti on 7 July 1929.

The two men immediately set about finding a story and quickly settled on a seventeen-year-old beauty by the name of Reri to front the picture. Reri was a smiling, round-faced young woman with a thick mass of tarry hair, who might well have reminded Robert of Maggie Nujarluktuk. *Tabu* hung on a simple love story between a girl, played by Reri, forced to leave her island after a taboo is put on her, and a young pearl diver. Completed in eighteen months, the picture caused a sensation among critics. *Film News* called it "one of the most visually lovely films ever made." Reri was picked up, brought over to New York and put in the Ziegfeld Follies. From there she went on to Europe and danced hula to titillated urban audiences, before marrying a Polish actor. The couple lived the high life for a couple of years, then separated. Reri's work dried up and she eventually returned to Tahiti a broken woman. "I feel bad about it," Flaherty said later. "I guess in a way I'm partly responsible."

For all *Tabu*'s critical success, though, the picture failed to please its backers. Flaherty was completely undisciplined about money. Every film he made went over budget and he got into endless jams with financiers, but the overruns on *Tabu* really finished him so far as Hollywood was concerned. His next job came to him through the British office of the French film studio, Gaumont, which wanted Flaherty to take himself to the tiny island of Aran, off the west coast of Ireland, and make a film about traditional life among the fishermen there.

Around the same time a *Nanook* backlash began, kicked off by a woman called Iris Barry, who had once been secretary to the Arctic explorer, Vilhjalmur Stefansson. Barry was now working as the film critic of the *Daily Mail* in London. Writing on the tenth anniversary of *Nanook*'s première, Barry questioned the film's authenticity, calling it "an enchanting romance, which convinced us it was fact though it wasn't at all," and claimed that her erstwhile boss, Stefansson, had always considered it a set-up. The *Daily Telegraph* followed up with an article headlined "Is *Nanook* a Fake?" For a while the picture lost its respectability and it looked as though its creator might lose something of his reputation. Flaherty was baffled by the accusations. In *Nanook* he had wanted to capture the struggle for survival, because, for him, it was at the heart of Inuit life. How he achieved this was of less concern. "Sometimes you have to lie," he said. "One often has to distort a thing to catch its true spirit." It had never been his role, as he saw it, to depict actuality, only to relay its essence. He took it as a given that he had augmented reality. His responsibility as he saw it, began and ended at the lens. One of the first film-makers to wade in on Flaherty's side during the backlash was the radical leftist Sergei Eisenstein. Eisenstein had famously elaborated on historical events while filming both *Battleship Potemkin*, his rendition of the mutiny at Odessa during 1905, and *October*, a highly embellished account of the uprising of 1917, and he wrote that "we Russians learned more from *Nanook of the North* than from any other foreign film. We wore it out studying it. That was, in a way, our beginning." In the end, *Nanook* was too popular to be shouted down and to most of its global audience the arguments against it seemed rather academic.

Aran proved less easy to win round. Robert and David bought a patch of land on the main island in the Aran group, Inishmore, built two huts there and settled down for the duration, but for all Robert's celebrated bonhomie and charisma, the pair were never welcomed. Aran was an impoverished, backward little place whose population of Spanish-Irish still lived in a medieval world of feudalism and superstition. In the west of Ireland at the time, Flaherty was identified as a Protestant name and the Aran Islanders suspected the two Flaherty brothers of being descendants of the Soupers, that band of Protestants who had offered bowls of broth to starving Catholics during the potato famine on condition that they convert to Protestantism. Robert and David attempted to reassure the islanders but they remained wary all the same. They enjoyed the attention and the money the Flahertys were willing to give them though, and, in spite of a good deal of infighting between the leading man, a blacksmith with the enviable name of Tiger King, his on-screen wife, Maggie Dirrane, their on-screen son, Michael Dirrane, and other lesser members of the cast, the filming passed off as well as the fierce sea storms and rocky weather allowed. The result was a striking picture cast in what was now an established mould, the story of an everyday family living in extraordinary circumstances, surrounded, this time, not by ice, but by a stormy and intractable sea.

Man of Aran won the first prize at the 1934 International Venice Film Festival and, for a while, Robert Flaherty settled down with his own family in England. Even there, though, *Nanook* still haunted him. His audience wanted more from him on Arctic topics. He tried to satisfy this desire by writing two Arctic adventure books, *The Captain's Chair* and *White Master,* but they were, inevitably, held up against *Nanook* and pronounced midgets standing in the shadow of a giant. What Flaherty needed was a film project which would allow him to outgrow the Arctic hunter and his smiling family. He alighted on a story about a boy and a bull in Spain and presented it to Paramount, but Hollywood had other ideas.

Not long before, Alexander Korda had established a new production company with, among others, Douglas Fairbanks, and they were actively on the hunt for property. One of the fledgling company's first activities had been to buy up Rudyard Kipling's estate. Korda was taken by Flaherty's motif of a boy and his animal but he wanted to weave it in with his Kipling material, so he suggested Robert and David Flaherty go out to Mysore, where he needed some documentary footage to slot into director Zoltan Korda's fiction film. As always happened when Flaherty was asked to cooperate with anyone other than his wife and brother, he and Korda soon fell out. Flaherty wanted the film to centre on the relationship between the boy, Toomai, and his elephant. Korda wanted something on a much larger scale involving big game hunters. The venture continued to be an uneasy one and Flaherty soon returned to his family in England. On the eve of the Second World War, the family set sail for America, where Robert passed the war writing, lecturing and shooting a documentary called *The Land* for the Department of Agriculture.

By the time the war ended, Flaherty's incandescent energy was flagging. Now in his sixties, and still not much better off financially than he had been after *Nanook* came out, he took a small suite of rooms at the Chelsea Hotel on Manhattan's 23rd Street and began dividing his time between there and the 250-acre family farm in Brattleboro, Vermont. Frances had decided to quit travelling, pinning up a sampler over the fireplace at the farm which read "Wander No More," but wandering had become Robert Flaherty's life and from the relative privacy of his rooms at the Chelsea he planned his next move.

In *The Land*, Flaherty had tried to capture the romantic sweep of the American landscape, but the film was dour and went largely unnoticed. Flaherty still had a hankering to make a tribute to his homeland that would get more play. He needed to inject some drama, a sense of peril into his production. More than that, he needed money. The latter he found in the Standard Oil Company and the former in the Louisiana bayous.

At the time, the traditional Cajun way of life with its slow, dank backdrop of creeks and Spanish moss was coming under threat from oil companies, eager to get at the black gold that lay under the bayou. The story appealed to Flaherty's heart. Like most romantics, he generally preferred what had been lost or was about to be lost to what was about to come. In the America of the 1950s, with all its optimistic bluster and faith in new technology, this may have seemed a particularly anachronistic view to some, but it was by no means an unpopular one.

Flaherty took himself down to Louisiana and rented a house in Abbeville. Before long, he had found his lead, a bright-faced lad named Joseph Boudreaux who was to play Alexander Latour, a Cajun boy growing up somewhere between the bayou and the oil fields. The film, *Louisiana Story*, premièred in 1948. Shortly afterwards, a telegram arrived for Flaherty from California. "Just saw your magnificent film. Do it again and you will be immortal and excommunicated from Hollywood, which is a good fate. Congratulations. Signed Oona and Charlie Chaplin, Ester and Dudley Nichols, Dido and Jean Renoir." J. Donald Adams, the book critic of the *New York Times* Sunday edition, gave over his entire page to the picture. Flaherty was, he said, "the only creative genius yet to appear in the field of animated photography" and *Louisiana Story* won a commendation at the Venice festival that year.

In spite of his critical successes, Flaherty had really sidelined himself. A loner in a cooperative medium, he had fallen out with almost every studio, director and producer he had ever worked with. His stubbornness and dogmatism and his disdain for budgets sat ill in a world increasingly dominated by the money men. The eminent documentarist John Grierson once observed that Robert "wouldn't learn, or rather he wouldn't work at learning. Sometimes I thought he was too grand to learn or too indolent. But that was not really the secret. He just hated to conform to the disillusionments of the practical world."

In 1950, as the price of fox pelts in Inukjuak was taking a nose-dive, Flaherty's spirit was beginning to fade. For most of his life he had managed to get by in a world of his own creation, an intense and heightened wonderland centred on the great and mysterious romance of human existence. The presence of this world had made the ordinary, quotidian grind of the day to day seem drab to him. Holed up at his suite at the Chelsea Hotel, he lurched between financial crises and the next big project. In the evenings he would take his seat at the Coffee House Club or at Costello's Bar on Third Avenue, where he would sit with his cronies, the poet Oliver St. John Gogarty and the architect Harrie Lindeberg, endlessly rehearsing tales of his old adventures. By all critical measures, he was a success, but Hollywood had long since turned away from him and his reputation in the wider world was still as the director of *Nanook*. No matter what else he had made, and been applauded for, it was *Nanook* which, more than any other, was to fix Flaherty in the minds of film buffs and Americans as a great film-maker and also as a great American. He was trapped.

When John Grierson said, "He had the power of making you forget the trivial things in life and look only at the elemental things that build up the dignity of man. He has in him the expansiveness and generosity of the true American," he was thinking specifically about *Nanook*. When Orson Welles called him "one of the two or three greatest people who ever worked in the medium" he had Flaherty's first picture in mind, as did John Huston when he claimed that Flaherty had influenced not only him, but John Ford, William Wyler and Billy Wilder. After all these years, *Nanook*, that paean to the self-dramatising romance of masculinity, still clung to Flaherty like a sick puppy. Everyone who had ever spoken about Flaherty always came back to *Nanook*.

At the beginning of the fifties, the film-maker began to talk about going to Malaya or Borneo to make a movie about the tea plantations there, but *Louisiana Story* was to be his last work. His lifestyle had taken its toll on his health. In 1950, Flaherty was sixty-six but he looked older. Though he was still quick to smile and his blue eyes still shone, the skin on his face had been coarsened not just by age but also by alcohol and tobacco. His hair had gone ice-white, and a good deal of it had fallen out altogether. He was portly now and had trouble in his joints and he wheezed on his way up to his rooms in the Chelsea. Everyone round him knew that he would never make old bones. Only a couple of years before the *New Yorker* had given him an extended three-part profile which had, at the time, read rather like an obituary. A while later, the BBC had recorded a radio retrospective with him. He was himself well aware of the tick of the clock. At the urging of a publisher friend, he had begun an autobiography, but had quickly become self-conscious and given it up. Perhaps he sensed the interest in his private life that such a book would stir up, and wanted to avoid too much scrutiny. None of the profiles of him had yet revealed that he had fathered a half-breed son, much less that he had never supported the boy or his mother. Robert Flaherty was a big name in movie-going circles, an American hero. Nobody, not least Robert himself, would have welcomed a tarnish on the lustre.

Flaherty's final illness began gently enough, some fluish symptoms, a nasty cough. Typically, he did not report feeling unwell for several days and it was only when Frances called from Brattleboro and picked up a change in his voice that he confessed to feeling sick. She rushed down to New York, but Flaherty was never going to be one to hang around for long and on 23 July 1951, almost exactly three years before Paddy Aqiatusuk lay down inside his tent on Ellesmere Island, Robert Flaherty made his last and most mysterious journey.

By then Hollywood had almost forgotten him. He had been an innovator and his films had brought him prestige if not riches, but in the end he was someone who had too much of a sense of his own integrity as an artist to be able to work in a team or to budget and, so far as Hollywood was concerned, that made him too awkward a proposition. The *Hollywood Reporter* listed the death and printed an obituary, and it amounted only to three lines on page five, less than the space accorded to Paddy Aqiatusuk by *Time*.

Some while later, John Grierson wrote a tribute to his old friend. The theme running through Flaherty's films, he claimed, was boyhood. In each of his pictures there was a boy who hoped one day to grow into the kind of solid, everyday hero America had made its own. Maybe, Grierson speculated, the theme had drawn Robert because he was the eldest son of an eminent American or perhaps there was another explanation. Maybe, Grierson wrote, the boy who appeared in all of Robert Flaherty's films was "the son he never had."

CHAPTER FOURTEEN

THREE YEARS and three days after Robert Flaherty's death, on 26 July 1954, the *C. D. Howe* returned to Inukjuak on the annual Eastern Arctic Patrol with Paddy Aqiatusuk's letter to Josephie Flaherty.

The letter was taken to the police department. Word soon spread of its existence and, before long, Josephie Flaherty was on his way to pick it up. He had already guessed it was from his *attataksaq,* his stepfather, Paddy Aqiatusuk, because there was no one else who would write to him. The envelope was marked in Inuktitut syllabics, the system of swirls and hollow circles invented by a missionary for the Cree Indians over one hundred years previously. Before then, the Inuit had never written anything down, preferring to pass on their history and their news in stories and songs, for families had never been separated, as they were now, by hundreds of miles. It had been a year since Aqiatusuk left for the High Arctic and in all that time no one had heard any news of or from him. This fragile-looking letter was a reminder of his absence, but it was also, or so Josephie thought, welcome proof that Paddy Aqiatusuk was still alive. Josephie opened the envelope. He did not read well, but the point of the message was clear. Aqiatusuk missed his *irniksaq,* his beloved stepson, and he wanted to know if Josephie and his family would come up to the High Arctic to be with him.

Josephie Flaherty put the letter in his bag and began to make his way home along the banks of the Innuksuak River, where the muskeg gave out to shingle and made the going easier. It was midsummer, the river ran fast and wide but in only a few weeks from now it would begin to crust over with ice and, by November, it would be possible to drive a dog team along it far into the interior. It was a long trudge back to Davidee, Peter and Lazarusie's camp where Josephie, Rynee and their children, Martha and Mary, had been living for almost a year now, and he had to pick his way along the marshy bank on foot. If only he had been able to buy a boat or even a *kayak* the journey would have taken a quarter of the time. He might have tied up somewhere and dropped a jig and bagged a char or even a few trout for supper. He brushed at the clouds of summer mosquitoes wheeling about, but it was impossible to move without swallowing a few.

He edged past the landing dock that fed boats in and out of the waters of Hudson Bay. In the summer, a collection of ramshackle *kayaks* and *umiaks* were always tied up there and the air smelled of the fishing nets which were usually strung between the boats to dry. Men came down to the shoreline at this point to fish for bait or mend their nets and, in the navigation season, small groups of women often left from the same spot in their *umiaks* for the Hope Islands where they would go jigging for tommy cod or hunting eider ducks. Most of the river traffic was from Inukjuak, but from time to time an old boat would come growling in from Qikirtaq or the Sleeper Islands laden with hunters eager to trade skins and walrus ivory at the Hudson Bay store. It was Josephie's usual routine to pass the time with the fishermen or whoever else was there as he went by. Today he merely nodded a greeting. His mind was full of the letter.

In the year since Aqiatusuk's departure, much had changed. The Bay store was still the large, unkempt clapboard building with a red roof it had always been, and the Bay factor's wife, Lily Ploughman, had just given birth to the couple's first child.

Beside the Bay stood the cold clapboard Anglican church and beside that the unimposing minister's house, now empty, the job of minister having lain vacant for some months after the incumbent, the Reverend Donald Whitehead, had caused a scandal (at least among the whites) by running away from his fiancée, a young Inuk woman by the name of Sarah, and, so far as anyone could tell, disappearing off the face of the planet. Bishop Marsh, otherwise known as "Donald of the Arctic," who was head of the Anglican Church in the region, had threatened to separate Whitehead from his vocation if he did not return to keep his promise to Sarah but Whitehead remained missing and no one had yet been appointed to replace him. The little church still opened its doors a couple of times a week and services in Inuktitut were led by the lay catechist, an Inuk known as Old Willya, but the wool had been pulled from the eyes of the locals and the days when the place had managed to exude a sense of sanctimonious holiness were over. The Inuit were happy to go along for the music and for the Bible, too, but they kept their amulets tucked away under their sleeping skins.

The rules by which the settlement lived were now set by the police detachment. The clapboard building and its outlying sheds and stores served not only as the settlement's police station, but also as its post office and its departments of game and welfare. In 1954, the detachment Mounties were Corporal J. E. Decker and Constable Doug Moody, who had replaced Ross Gibson the year before. No one liked Moody much, but he was considered an improvement on his predecessor, whom the locals now openly referred to as Big Red. They did not miss him.

In spite of Moody's vigorous efforts to keep them out, there were more Inuit living in the settlement in 1954 than there had been in 1953, but these were still, by and large, employees and servants of the *qalunaat*. Noah worked as a choreboy at the school, Elijah from Labrador assisted Margery Hinds, Minnie helped out at the police station. There were others too. Until the year before, Josephie, Rynee and their family had occupied the choreboy's hut beside the Radiosonde station, but Josephie had been fired for refusing to fill the station manager's wife's coal bucket, and the Flaherty family were now living out at Lazarusie's camp. Trade or the weekly family allowance brought Josephie into the settlement from time to time.

The coal bucket incident remained something of a puzzle. Not long after Paddy Aqiatusuk's departure, Josephie had been working in the kitchen at the manager, Carter's, house. Mrs. Carter had been given the responsibility for preparing meals for a half dozen construction workers who had come up from the south to work on the station over the summer and she resented both the sudden intrusion on her time and the fact that she could not palm the job off on an Inuit woman because an Inuit woman would be unfamiliar with the kind of food the construction workers expected. It was a Sunday, supposedly the day of rest, and Mrs. Carter was in a funk about that, too. She had asked Josephie to keep the range topped up with coal from the coal store in the shed beside the station, but the coal bucket was tiny and all the shuttling to and fro was taking his time away from other tasks with Mrs. Carter barking at him that he wasn't working hard enough all the while. Josephie had seen plenty of managers and their wives come and go during his twelve years at the station, but there was something about the Carters, about Mrs. Carter in particular, which rubbed him raw. On that Sunday some long dormant rage stirred in him and when Mrs. Carter started shouting at him for allowing the bucket to run out of coal, the anger found its outlet and, almost before he was aware of it, he heard himself telling Mrs. Carter where to put her bucket. And, well, that was that. As Mrs. Carter later told Margery Hinds, the welfare teacher, Josephie's outburst was just one in a long line of prior insubordinations. From that point on, he was out of a job and out of a home and, so far as working in Inukjuak was concerned, out of a future, too. No *qalunaat* would take it on himself to employ another white man's reject.

Josephie missed his job or, rather, he missed the money, and he missed Inukjuak. He knew the old place as well as he knew the taste of Arctic cranberries or the patterns made by clouds. But he was no longer welcome in his former home. As soon as his business there was done, he was hustled out by the detachment police. He traipsed out along the river to where the granite gathered itself into a gentle hill and he often picked berries as a boy. At the summit of this hill he saw the neat clapboard home of Margery Hinds.

One of Margery Hinds' jobs had been to inspect the clothes, food stores and equipment of those Inuit heading north in 1953. That summer, just before the *Howe* arrived, she had borrowed the police detachment boat and gone on a long trip up and down the coast with Special Constable Kayak and the report she sent to the Department had made for rather stark reading. She recognised the Inukjuamiut were struggling and approved of moving them, but thought it was irresponsible to send the families north with so few caribou-skin clothes and such limited equipment.

If Margery Hinds had been writing a year later, in 1954, her report would have looked rather different. The winter of 1953 had been a very productive one for trapping around Inukjuak. Some of the better trappers had been able to order sewing machines and new dog chains, even to buy shares in whaleboats and outboard motors, with the proceeds of their winter catches, and by March 1954, so many Inuit had racked up credit at the store that Rueben Ploughman had almost run out of supplies. Certainly, no one was talking about starvation any more. For most of the Inuit living around Inukjuak, life was looking up. If the idea of moving Inukjuak to new hunting and trapping grounds had been mooted in 1954, rather than a year earlier, it would have seemed crazy.

That year had not passed so happily for the Flahertys though. For the past eleven months, Josephie had been trying to provide for himself, his wife Rynee and his little daughters Martha and Mary by living on the land, but in twelve years of choring he had lost a good deal of the hunting knowledge he had learned as a young man from Aqiatusuk and others and, in all those long months, he had barely been able to feed his family. Even as his neighbours were trapping more foxes and earning better credits in the store, he had seen his own income dwindle almost to nothing. His hunter's aggression, never pronounced, had been dulled by years living in the settlement. He was by nature too self-effacing, too sensitive ever to be able to pursue game as Alakariallak or even Aqiatusuk had. He would never have made a great hunter, but in the past he had had the support of Aqiatusuk and his job. Now he had neither. His only real recourse during the past year had been the government. Like all Canadians, the Flahertys were entitled to a family allowance. It was a very modest sum, particularly in the north where the price of everything from butter to ammunition was four or five times higher than it was in the south, but it was enough to buy a bag of flour and a few tins of powdered milk for the children and this, coupled with whatever Josephie and Rynee could catch, was what had been keeping them alive. For months together he and Rynee and the two children had lived on little more than flour-and-water bannock bread, supplemented by soup boiled from the meat of the foxes Josephie caught. Neighbours had sometimes brought round gifts of beluga skin or walrus fat and every so often Josephie had bagged a seal, but there had never been enough to keep everyone full for long and food remained a constant source of worry and insecurity, particularly as Rynee was pregnant once more. For Josephie, the year had been one long slide into frustration. If "to love" was the same as "to care for," as Inuktitut had it, then he wasn't doing a good job of loving his family.

It was summer now, and the berries would be ripening and the migratory birds would be passing on their way back down south, but soon it would be winter again, and there would be a new baby to feed. No amount of bannock bread and powdered milk would keep out the cold then. They would need meat and animal fat and the prospect of being unable to supply enough of either pressed against Josephie like a cold wind. Unless something changed and soon, the Flahertys might well find themselves standing on the precipice, overlooking a long, slow starvation. It would begin the way it always did, as a thinning of the nails and hair and a certain yellowing of the eyes, and for a while they would be able to stave it off but gradually, bit by bit, it would wear them down, so subtly, so softly, they would hardly know they had got to the end until they were already there.

The irony of all this was not lost on Robert Flaherty's son. If Ross Gibson had not strong-armed Aqiatusuk into going north in search of a better life, Aqiatusuk, his family and Josephie would almost certainly have found one right here at home in Inukjuak. Had they all stayed put the family might well have been looking forward to a bumper winter of hunting, trapping and carving. As it was Josephie could not see how his own situation was going to improve without his stepfather and stepbrothers. Besides, he loved Aqiatusuk and felt duty-bound to him. He did not want to leave Inukjuak. It was his family's *nunatuarigapku*, their homeland. His children had been born there, another child was on the way and the whole family had always expected to live out their days in Ungava. But the more he thought about it, the stronger his sense became that he had no option.

Paddy Aqiatusuk's letter was not the only thing waiting for Josephie on the *C. D. Howe* that year. David Flaherty was Robert's younger brother and collaborator. He was also Josephie Flaherty's white uncle. Exactly why he was on board the *Howe* remains unclear. When Rynee was asked about it many years later, she said simply that the man had come to take a photograph.

What really happened during this unlikely meeting between the two men will probably never be known. David Flaherty certainly took a picture of his half-breed nephew. What else went on can only be a matter of speculation. Irrespective of what was actually said, it can't have been easy, this coming together of two men joined by blood but sharing no ties of history, culture, values or habits. It is perfectly possible that David took Josephie's picture, shook his hand and went back on board the *C. D. Howe* and that was the end of it. Indeed, this seems most likely. Josephie had been brought up to be both wary and a little fearful of white men. His English was patchy and in the presence of *qalunaat* he found it hard to talk, still harder to assert himself. Many decades later, one of the white men who knew Josephie around this period described him as seeming "almost retarded" and this impression, if Josephie was aware of it, could hardly have encouraged Robert Flaherty's son to have been forthcoming. More likely than not, the meeting was an awkward encounter, full of thoughts and sentiments on both sides for which there is no language.

What does seem clear is that this was the moment Josephie first learned of his father's death. We can only guess what he thought and felt about this. Robert Flaherty must have seemed very abstract to Josephie, a concept, almost, rather than something he could call his own, his blood. He had never met the man, nor had he had any contact with him over the years. In 1954 Josephie wasn't even officially a Flaherty. That surname came later, after the Canadian government required Inuit to adopt surnames, in the 1960s. He was simply Josephie, E9701, the number handed to him by the Department as an identifier.

What is also clear is that not long after the arrival of the letter and the meeting with David Flaherty, Josephie decided to take his family north to join Paddy Aqiatusuk on Ellesmere Island. He did *not* know when he made this momentous decision that the man he was planning to join, the man who was his father in everything but blood, lay dead and buried under rocks. Nor did Josephie, E9701, have any idea that the trip would be his last and that he would never again set foot on the grey hills, the gravel eskers and dun-coloured tundra of his beloved homeland, his *nunatuarigapku.*

CHAPTER FIFTEEN

THE YEAR PASSED and, at the end of the following July, Josephie, Rynee, Martha and Mary Flaherty found themselves sitting in the *C. D. Howe*'s cargo barge among their few possessions. The couple's first son, Peter, born the previous winter, rested in Rynee's *amiut*. Behind them lay the Ungava tundra, lush with purple saxifrage and willow and clouded with whining mosquitoes. Early sun had made the air balmy, the waters of the bay were soft, swollen and grey, and clouds were beginning to gather. The sky buzzed with the cries of ducks and gulls and loons. Out on the open water, in the direction the Flahertys were headed, there was a light mist the colour of bone. In a few hours, that world would be gone for ever. On Ellesmere Island, their lives would be shaped by rock and ice, and they would look back on this last, busy summer with its cawing birds and blankets of mosquitoes with a terrible longing.

They knew now that Paddy Aqiatusuk was dead. Corporal Decker had approached Josephie with the news while he had been loading the barge at the quayside in Inukjuak. Josephie had stopped loading for a moment or two and then carried on with his task. It felt too late to change his plans. Something had been set in motion, which Josephie had no means to prevent. Perhaps he was afraid of a confrontation with the police if he changed his mind. Perhaps, he reasoned, with Aqiatusuk gone, Mary and the rest of the family would need his help more urgently than ever.

The Flahertys were one of four families moving north from Inukjuak that year. Levi Nungak, Johnnie Echalook, Mawa Iqaluk and their families were heading to Resolute Bay to be with relatives who had moved there in 1953 under the supervision of Ross Gibson. The *C. D. Howe* planned to pick up Joseph Idlout, his wife Kidlah and their extended family in Pond Inlet and take them up to Resolute Bay and there was the usual sorry cargo of consumptives and others being transferred to southern hospitals; but Josephie, Rynee and their children were the only family destined for Grise Fiord.

The ship soon passed the Belcher Islands, the largest of which had been renamed Flaherty Island after Robert Flaherty's expedition there. Now that Josephie Flaherty and his family were leaving the Ungava Peninsula, this rocky little island, with its blue cliffs and gravel beaches, would be the last physical reminder of Robert Flaherty's time there. By the end of the second day they were in Churchill, Manitoba. Camped on the empty side of the river, the Flahertys unrolled their sleeping skins and lit a willow fire to make some tea. During their twelve-year tenure at the Radiosonde hut they had had no need for camping equipment and most of what little they owned was old and worn or borrowed. Their tent was made from oddments of canvas patched here and there with duck and pieces of sealskin. It had served as their home during the summer months and was now in desperate need of replacing. They had no lantern or torch or primus stove. Clothes were a problem too. The girls possessed few warm caribou-skin clothes and they were short of *kamiks*. The baby, Peter, had no winter clothes at all. For twelve years Josephie had only ever hunted to supplement the family's diet of trade goods, and he had very little hunting gear. His .22 rifle regularly jammed and he was short of knives, traps and nets. The family did not own a *kayak* or an *umiak,* neither did they have a *komatik* or a dog team. But none of this concerned them because the police had assured them that once they reached Grise Fiord they would be provided with whatever they needed to survive on the land up there.

While medical examinations were being conducted on ship, the

Flahertys waited in camp. The family had been issued rations on board the *C. D. Howe* and a local had arrived sometime later with fresh whale meat. They had been at camp a couple of days when a policeman and a doctor arrived, asking to see Mary. During the inspection at Inukjuak, a nurse had noticed yellow spots in the little girl's eyes, one of the signs of the first onset of tuberculosis, and the doctor now wanted to take a closer look. An interpreter was summoned to explain the situation to the Flahertys. The news was bad. The yellow spots had got worse and the doctor felt he had no choice but to sign papers to have the two-year-old taken from her family and flown south for immediate treatment. Another, older girl, Dora Iqaluk, and her little sister, Mary, who were also staying in the same camp, had the same symptoms. Dora would be assigned to accompany the two younger girls. How long any of them would have to remain in the south it was impossible to say. Everything depended on how far the tuberculosis had progressed and how each child responded to treatment. Since TB was highly infectious, all three girls would have to be taken at once to the hospital at Churchill and isolated. The translator advised the Flahertys that they should say their goodbyes.

Josephie and Rynee Flaherty reeled at the news. They were in no doubt about what it actually meant. They had heard the stories and were prepared to believe them. Their daughter would be taken to some huge building full of sickness, then she would be stripped of her caribou-skin clothes, bathed and disinfected. From there she would be placed in an isolation ward and forbidden to speak Inuktitut. She might also be tied to the bed to prevent her from wandering off and spreading infection and to make it easier for the doctors to administer the great many very painful injections the treatment prescribed. For the duration of her stay in the south, the likelihood was that no one would tell her parents where she was or whether she was dead or alive. If they were lucky, she would be sent back to them months or years from now, dressed in a skimpy cotton outfit, bewildered and cold and unable to speak her parents' language. Otherwise, these few moments might be their last together as a family.

There was nothing Rynee and Josephie could do to stop their daughter's being taken away. If they resisted, the police would take her anyway and so they said their goodbyes and a frightened and tearful Mary Flaherty was removed from the camp with Dora and Mary Iqaluk and taken to the tiny hospital in Churchill. From there the girls were transferred on to a noisy cargo plane and sent south. Many years later, Dora recalled the journey. In all the rush, Mary's bottle had been left behind and she became so hungry during the flight she tried to eat a doll made from rabbit fur. The three girls were taken to a sanatorium which looked like a prison. The girls found it terrifying. Soon after their arrival, Mary was separated from the two sisters and put in a ward staffed by nurses who did not speak Inuktitut. One time Dora managed to sneak away from her own ward, she found Mary tied to the bed, crying. For the next three years Mary Flaherty neither saw nor had any news from or about her parents. She became *aattimajuq,* one who is separated from her family, cut adrift. According to Inuit custom she would not be talked about openly. Until she came back to them she would be a living ghost, at once a presence and an absence too painful to be acknowledged.

The *C. D. Howe* left Churchill and sailed on round Salisbury and Nottingham islands and out across the Hudson Strait. The strait was well known for producing rough weather, particularly during the August storm season and sure enough near Resolution Island, a fierce wind whipped up the swell and pretty soon they found themselves surrounded by huge slabs of churning pack ice. A half-dozen crew rushed down to the Inuit quarters to distribute lifejackets and, not long after, the ship began to lurch and roll alarmingly, clipping ice floes on either side. The blasting wind swept her up on to the crest of each wave of white water, then dashed her back down to the foot of the swell. Hail began drumming against the ship's hull, while up on deck the wind ripped the tie-downs from the tarpaulins, which began billowing and humming in the wind like rogue sails. The sound set off the sled dogs, who howled and scrabbled wild-eyed at the doors of their crates. Suddenly the ship seemed to come alive. Guns, fish hooks, stone lamps and sewing gear scurried across the floor. Fire extinguishers rattled in their clasps, doors swung and crashed shut. Water flowed out of some broken tank or tap and tore along the linoleum. In the Inuit quarters men, women and children threw up where they sat, unable to stand let alone make it to the washrooms. Everyone was terrified. They knew that if they were swept to sea, within two or three minutes in a high swell in Arctic waters they would all be dead. Rynee Flaherty clung to her bunk with Martha in her arms and little Peter tucked in her *amiut,* while Josephie tried to gather their possessions. There was no prospect of sleep. This was Torngak, the evil spirit who played havoc with those who broke taboos and he would not stop until he was done with them. They had to sit and pray and hope they would get through it.

After what seemed like days but was probably hours, the storm fell away, leaving them flattened and edgy. No one spoke. People fell, exhausted, on to their bunks. The *C. D. Howe* proceeded north in still waters towards Baffin Bay. A few hours later they found themselves above the 65th parallel. An empty cold filled the air. They were moving through an ethereal blue iceberg forest. Red Northern Lights shot across the sky. Once again they crossed the Arctic Circle. For the next day or so nothing seemed to move on the horizon. At the 70th parallel, where the West Greenland Current gave out, broken floes and bergy bits appeared in open water. Five degrees farther north the High Arctic began. From here the great polar desert rolled away a thousand miles north to the tip of Ellesmere Island.

At the beginning of September, forty days after the Flahertys left Inukjuak, the *C. D. Howe* finally swung into Resolute Bay and dropped anchor in the midst of a deep and sinister fog. Leo Manning, the Department interpreter, appeared in the Inuit quarters to tell the Nungaks, the Echalooks and the Iqaluks to pack their things and make ready for the cargo barge that would take them on shore. The Flahertys were to remain on ship until they reached the Craig Harbour detachment.

The Flahertys watched the others leave, then went to their bunks. The storm had unsettled them so much that they had barely slept or eaten. Peter had begun refusing his mother's breast. The Flahertys hadn't been able to bring themselves to imagine how Mary might be by this time. They felt drained and uneasy. For a few hours they took some rest. A while later, when the fog still showed no signs of clearing, Manning came back down to the quarters to tell them that the ship could not sail in current conditions and that they would be put ashore until it was safe for the *C. D. Howe* to continue on.

No one got much sleep that night but for the first time in forty days the Flahertys scarcely noticed how tired they were. There was two years' worth of news and gossip to catch up on. The Resolute Bay camp had been having a hard time of it, they said. The weather on Cornwallis was unlike anything they had ever encountered in Inukjuak. They could barely breathe the winter air, it was so cold, and in summer, dense fogs descended for days. A ceaseless wind ripped across the island and the hunting was hard. Polar bears came up from the south and crossed over on their way to Bathurst Island, but they were fearsome and the dogs were not trained to contain them. The hunters hated having to go after them, but in the winter, in particular, they had no choice. They had to grit their courage. They would much rather hunt caribou, and the meat was infinitely better, but they had to cross all the way over to Southampton Island to get any. The first winter they had gone very hungry and had been reduced to raiding the rubbish dumps at the air base and the weather station, which Ross Gibson had expressly forbidden them to do and seemed now determined to prevent.

The policeman had begun daily inspections of the tents, pulling up the sleeping skins and poking into the pots and pans, looking for stuff that might have been taken from the dump. They wondered if the extreme cold had not affected him in some way. He seemed even more agitated up here, constantly drilling them on the need to maintain the traditional Inuit way of life, as if he knew anything about it. In any case, most of the men were hoping to find work of some description at the air force base. At least the men got fed there, though their wives and children still had to be provided for. Right now, there was only the odd day or two of casual work and it paid badly, but they were pinning their hopes on being offered some formal waged employment at the base in the future.

They had not had much contact with the camp at Grise Fiord, they said. A few dog teams had come in during the spring, bringing the police for their annual leave. They had heard that Aqiatusuk had died. It was a different world up there. From what they had picked up there was game on Ellesmere Island but it was almost impossible to reach and the camp was completely cut off. There were no weather stations, no air bases and no prospects for employment whatsoever. The Grise Fiord camp was not really big enough to be viable but there was no other way for them to survive except to keep on hunting and trapping. The loss of just one hunter or carver like Aqiatusuk could put the whole camp in danger.

The following morning the fog had thinned considerably, though it was still misty and there were sharp spiny ice crystals in the air. Josephie Flaherty woke to the sound of boots on the shale and throwing back the tent flaps he saw the old Inukjuak detachment *pulisi*, Constable Ross Gibson, striding towards the camp. In two years Big Red had aged to an almost shocking degree. The policeman was still huge and powerful-looking but not much else remained of the man Josephie remembered. His face was livid with red blotches and darkened, leathery-looking spots and when he took off his hat to scratch his head Josephie could see that his hair had receded and thinned. He moved at a strange angle, like willow twigs in fierce wind. He did not seem happy.

Gibson had come to check on the newcomers and to make sure

the Flahertys were prepared to leave whenever the fog cleared, which it did, as if on command, shortly after. It was hard saying goodbye and strange boarding the ship alone. The previous night's discussions had been rather gloomy and the Flahertys were nervously anticipating arriving at their destination unsure of what they would find. The *C. D. Howe* moved out of the bay, cleared Barrow Strait and began to churn steadily through the waters of Lancaster Sound. By the end of the following day, she had turned northwest and was steaming along the east coast of Devon Island, where, two years before, Ross Gibson had noted the shadows on the cliffs and glaciers. The sun came out, refracting from the ice crystals in the air and scattering millions of tiny rainbows. The ship ploughed on, sliding finally through Lady Ann Strait and into Jones Sound. It was then that the Flahertys caught their first glimpse of Ellesmere Island. For two years now, the place had lived in their imaginations as an icier version of the gentle, willow-covered hills and sand strands of Inukjuak, but with more and larger game. The Ellesmere Island of their imagination boiled with seal and beluga, the rocks were white with the guano of plump snow-geese and the cliffs were dotted with their eggs. In this imaginary Ellesmere, caribou wandered along snowy paths to their grazing grounds and walrus lay sleeping soundly at the edge of the shore-fast ice. Blooming willow, pink saxifrage, purple heather and yellow Arctic poppies were watered from a hundred little streams and the muskeg was firm and not too hummocky, with cloudberries ripening on every south-facing slope. It was not fanciful, this imaginary Ellesmere, nor was it an amalgam of their hopes. It was rather what they had been led to expect.

The Ellesmere Island stretched out ahead confounded every expectation. Recalling the scene later, Rynee said she thought they would be crushed by rock and ice.

A cluster of tiny people appeared on the beach beside the police detachment and began waving. From where the Flahertys were standing on the deck of the *C. D. Howe* it was impossible to make out individual faces but the shapes and contours of these people, the way their bodies stirred the air as they moved about among the rocks, were so familiar to the Flahertys that it was hard, in spite of their surroundings, not to imagine they were back in Inukjuak and that Aqiatusuk's departure and death and their own long, exhausting journey were just elements in a dream from which they had at last awoken. The sense of being among fellows hit them like a sudden wind and in that single, tremendous moment of recognition, all the uncertainty and confusion of the past two years melted away and they were left with the only thing that mattered or had ever mattered: to be among family.

The ship dropped anchor and the crew came out on deck to prepare the cargo barge. Sometime later, Josephie, Rynee, Martha and Peter Flaherty were dropped on the beach. There were tears then, and wide, open grins from the men. The children ran between the newcomers' legs, laughing with excitement. Aside from a party of Greenlanders, these were the first Inuit the settlers had seen in two long years and they were bundled along to Mary Aqiatusuk's tent and offered hot sweet tea. A barrage of eager questions followed. The Inukjuamiut wanted to know everything about the camp at Resolute Bay. How was the hunting going? Where were the people camped? Was Big Red bothering them? Had they caught caribou or bear? Were there any foxes? Did they have trouble finding sweet water? Had anyone come down with illness? Was Cornwallis as empty as Ellesmere? And as cold? After a long series of investigations, they began more tentatively to enquire after Inukjuak and their relatives there, but their questions were now hesitant and oddly detached. It was as if their homeland had taken on the character of an ancestral place, revered but remote. Josephie could not know then that in a few years from now he too would find himself set loose and drifting whenever the old country was mentioned, reluctant to call up the image of a place to which he longed so fiercely to return.

While the Flahertys were enjoying their welcome, Corporal

Glenn Sargent was taking note of how little equipment or food the newcomers possessed. No boat, no *komatik,* no dogs, no lamps, the list went on. This worried him. He ordered the special constable to fetch some destitution rations and noted the donation of flour, oats, sugar, tobacco, lard and tea in his report book. When the time came to file his usual quarterly dispatch on "Conditions in general among the Natives," he would let HQ know, as diplomatically as he could, that he thought it had been irresponsible to allow this new family to travel to Ellesmere with so few clothes and such spartan supplies. His instructions were to interfere as little as possible but he knew the newcomers had not a hope of surviving the winter without a great deal of assistance and good will from their family already at the camp.

A new constable had come up on the *C. D. Howe* at the same time as the Flahertys as a replacement for Clay Fryer. He was Bob Pilot, a tall, genial man with a rocky exterior. Pilot was very young, only twenty-one or twenty-two. He had begun his police career in Calgary but his only Arctic stint prior to the posting at Craig Harbour had been in Iqaluit for summer duties the previous year. Still, he was very obviously keen to do whatever it took to earn his "G" man stripes. Sargent thought it would be good for him to get a feel for life on the land. Once he had had a chance to unpack his things and settle in a little at the detachment, Sargent resolved to dispatch his new junior to live in Akpaliapik's sod house at the camp, where he could learn how to handle a dog team on the ice before the winter came. Once the dark period arrived, he could return to the comforts of the detachment, but while he was out with Akpaliapik, Pilot would be able to keep an eye on things in general and on the Flahertys in particular. It seemed like a good solution to their concerns.

By evening the new Inuit arrivals had settled in their tent. The baby began to cry. Rynee cooked up some porridge, dipped an Arctic hare's foot into the mixture and held it to the lips of her son, who took it in his mouth and sucked a little. She had no milk of her own for him now. The journey north had dried her up. Twilight fell and the cliffs closed in around them, blocking their view of what lay behind. It seemed to Josephie and Rynee then that all the events of the past few months, the arrival of Aqiatusuk's letter, his death, the *qalunaat* uncle, the journey north and the loss of Mary had already blurred into a past that felt all the more remote in time for having happened so far away. An atmosphere of abstraction, a thin, life-denying feeling crept into their tent that night. In the half-light, only Martha still seemed full of spirit. They fell on to their few sleeping skins, exhausted, and woke the next day to a floury sky. Out in the sound, the *C. D. Howe* had finished unloading her cargo, and was preparing to weigh anchor and head back down south to Montreal.

CHAPTER SIXTEEN

THE NEXT DAY the Inuit moved from the detachment to their camp. In the past year, they had shifted from the site chosen by Henry Larsen and were now established along a small beach twenty miles east of Lindstrom looking out to the southeast across Jones Sound at the folds of the Devon Island mountains, just visible nearly a hundred miles away. A fierce blue sky loomed overhead, punctured here and there by high, drifting cloud and the sun clung to the safety of the horizon line. A few crows soared by as the Flahertys began erecting their tent, the sea sighed and flopped against the beach but these small sounds were no match for the clank and groan of the loose ice pan. The Flahertys had never seen so much summer ice as there remained in the waters of Jones Sound and at the mouth of nearby Grise Fiord, nor had they ever heard ice growl and moan with more anguish than here, where it never melted.

The winter before, the camp's second in the High Arctic, Simon Akpaliapik and Samuel Anukudluk had shown the Inukjuak families how to build the sod huts, *qarnaq,* typical of the inhabitants of the Arctic's arid zones, where there was often too little wind-packed snow to build snowhouses until late in the winter. In Pond Inlet, Akpaliapik and Anukudluk had built their *qarnaqs* into the rock, but here they had had to rely on scrap lumber from the supply ship and improvise roofs from pieces of old canvas. Now, as it was summer, the huts lay unused, their roofs put to use as tents. The

Inukjuamiut and the Ingluligmiut were living separately, the Inuk-juamiut tents zigzagging along the shoreline at some distance from where the smaller group of Ingluligmiut was camped. The two groups had discovered they had less in common than Henry Larsen had supposed and they had gradually drifted apart. More experienced in high-latitude survival, the Ingluligmiut were the favourites of the police detachment, which showed them greater consideration and respect. The Inukjuamiut resented this. For their part, the Ingluligmiut were still waiting for the payment they had been led to believe would follow their efforts to help the Inukjuamiut settle in and could only imagine that the Inukjuamiut were in some way responsible for the fact that they had never been paid.

From the camp, Josephie set off directly to Paddy Aqiatusuk's grave, a rubble of stones piled up on a nearby slope where some loose rock formed a gentle, upward curve and Josephie had to scramble to reach the spot, which was marked by a red stone *inuk-shuk*. It looked unbearably lonely. There were a few patches of vegetation growing there but nothing else and everything living seemed to point southwards.

He returned from his first sortie subdued. He missed his stepfather greatly. To him, the land was *nangijuanngittuq*, empty, not in any literal way, but in the more profound sense of having no meaning. Paddy Aqiatusuk was, or, rather, would have been, the meaning whose presence would have filled the land. Now he was gone, buried not among his ancestors, but here, surrounded by emptiness. The *qalunaat* place names—Grise Fiord, Craig Harbour, Lindstrom—said nothing to Josephie about the land. In the absence of Aqiatusuk's tales of hunting routes and traplines, Ellesmere Island felt like a place that did not really exist.

There was only one way to make it exist and that was to experience it. Josephie knew the task ahead would be enormous. Learning the land here would be as much a lifetime's work as it had been in Ungava. He already sensed there were conditions here that he had never before had to confront. Elijah, Samwillie, Joadamie and the other men at camp later told him that he would have to get used to very dynamic ice and moving floes, to whirling winds and rip tides. He had already seen how the movement of light through the thin air baffled distance and produced strange mirages out at sea. He would have to learn how the currents moved and where there were safe beachings. When winter came, he would need to familiarise himself with the way the ice heaved up into pressure ridges and the places where the tides broke through. The hunting conditions on Ellesmere were very different from anything he had ever known. The game was so scattered that he would find himself having to be away from the settlement for days, sometimes weeks, at a time, leaving Rynee and the children to manage with whatever cache of meat remained. He would have to learn how to hunt narwhal, creatures with which he was completely unfamiliar. Occasionally, the men advised him, he would run into musk ox, which would think nothing of charging the sled if they felt cornered. If he shot one, he would risk being sent to prison. Before long, he would come face to face with a hungry polar bear. He would be afraid. Trapping would be no easier. The foxes often followed bears way out on to the sea ice to scavenge from their leavings and Josephie would have to follow them. Food was so scarce that crows and wolves would often get to the bodies of trapped foxes before he would be able to retrieve them. The men had discovered that the only way to work was to go out hunting in pairs during the summer months and split up during the winter to work their separate trap lines. For months at a time, the only animals they would get, aside from the foxes, would be seal.

Rynee and the children would have to adapt themselves to *their* new conditions too. In Inukjuak, Rynee and Martha had only to venture out so far as the river to find sweet water or freshwater ice, but on Ellesmere Island, the women of the camp warned them, it could take hours to gather enough ice for a couple of days. Heather and grass were hard to come by and there were no berries to be found, no insect grubs and very few ptarmigan or hare. It was rare to find gull eggs or sculpin. For protein, they would be dependent on whatever Josephie could bring back from his hunting trips and they would have to get used to Josephie's being away for days, sometimes weeks, not knowing where he was, or even if he was still alive.

Josephie would need harpoons with *avataqs*, or floats, for spearing seal, traps, seal nets and ammunition, harpoon heads, fishing line and hooks, holland twine for mending nets, a lamp, a flashlight, a hare-skin baffle, fox-fur *kamik* soles to soften the sound of his step across the shale, a seal breath detector for hunting the animals at their breathing holes, a spare snowknife, a new flensing knife, a *komatik* and dog team with the attendant harnesses and equipment, and access to a boat. Rynee would need a couple of dozen stretched sealskins with which to make *kamiks,* hare skins for baffles and underwear, caribou skins for parkas and other winter clothes and sinews for sewing, blubber for the *qulliq* and, eventually, a primus stove. They could only hope the detachment would supply them.

A few days after the Flahertys arrived, Bob Pilot and Special Constable Kayak, who had replaced Areak, turned up in the detachment Peterhead, bringing tea and sugar and hardtack biscuits and offering to take the men hunting. Just as they had done in the previous two years, they would cache walrus for winter dog food and any seal they caught they would use immediately. The men climbed on board the boat. If Josephie hoped to see his new equipment there, he was disappointed. There was nothing resembling traps or a lamp or a snowknife.

The few weeks between summer and winter streaked by in a fury of activity. There was much to do to patch up the tents, prepare the winter caches, repair the *qarnaqs,* spruce up the *komatiks,* feed the dogs, look after the pups, haul water, make walrus-meat cheese, and sew new sets of clothes to prepare the camp for the onset of the dark period. When freeze-up came, Josephie and Joadamie went out along the coast, setting traps and going after seal where the shore-fast ice gave out to the pack. While he was away, Rynee moved part time into Mary Aqiatusuk's tent and the two women shared the burden of searching for grass and heather for the *qulliq* and ice for water. When twilight fell, as it did earlier and earlier, they sat inside scraping skins and sewing sealskin clothes. Neither woman mentioned her troubles, though each sensed the wound in the heart of the other. Work activity took their minds off the sudden fall-off in temperatures and the spiralling winds which came with the start of the autumn and it shielded them a little from the painful memories of people lost to them.

One day in mid-October the sun did not rise and an inky gloam took the place of dawn. Moonlight reflected in the frozen sea and picked out the silhouette of the tied-up sled dogs. Above the sea the sky was dark grey and powdery, but on land every living and dead thing melted into the same impenetrable black swell. The absence of light seemed to slow down everything. All the ordinary markers of the passing of time disappeared. Nothing moved, nothing changed, but everything sounded oddly unfamiliar. Strange barks ricocheted off the rock, rattled across the shale and bounced along the shoreline before disappearing somewhere inside the folds of the pressure ice out at sea. Primus stoves hissed and *qulliqs* stuttered and the guy ropes of the Flahertys' tent clinked in the wind. The shale under foot cracked, the piss pots echoed. The sled dogs scraped and pawed and howled as the ice drummed and thumped. The tides wheezed and guttered, snowflakes hummed. Human breath made crisp little gasps as it turned to ice crystals.

After a few days, the Flahertys discovered that their internal clocks had broken, waking them at all hours and disturbing their sleep. In the dark, everything seemed at the same time simpler and more complex. Objects became silhouettes whose sharp outlines obscured detail. Their own fingers dissolved into tentacles floating in a sea of contradictory impressions. Adults felt shorter, children taller, eyelashes felt thicker, noses more fleshy. The others, who had gone through it all before, attempted to reassure them, but there were so many bewildering new sensations that it was impossible to feel comforted.

At the end of October, temperatures began to plunge. Bob Pilot left Simon Akpaliapik's *qarnaq* and returned to the detachment. Thomasie and Mary Amagoalik and their sons Allie, Salluviniq and Charlie moved into the choreboy's hut nearby. Samwillie and Elijah Aqiatusuk moved into their *qarnaq* with Mary, Minnie and Larry Audlaluk. Phillipoosie and Annie Novalinga and their family followed suit. Last into their own *qarnaq* were Joadamie and Ekoomak Aqiatusuk, and their daughter Lizzie. In the frenzy of activity during the summer and autumn, no one had got round to showing Josephie how to build his own hut but there was an old one left over from a previous year so the Flahertys moved into that. The place took some getting used to. Unlike a snowhouse, which had windows and a spacious aspect, the sod hut was windowless and claustrophobic. The constant burning of the *qulliq* filled the space with blubber fumes which seared the eyes and the back of the throat. The whole structure proved unstable. Rynee Flaherty returned one day from a trip out collecting heather to discover that the sod bricks had caved in. It was far too cold to live in the tent, so the Flahertys were obliged to move in with Joadamie. There were now two families, seven people, living in a single earth room twelve feet by ten feet, and with nowhere to escape one another even for a moment because it was too cold to stand outside. The adults had to take turns sleeping. There were no complaints, though. Josephie and Rynee both knew that without Joadamie and Ekoomak's generosity they would freeze. For Rynee, the move was particularly hard. Josephie's relatives were kind to her, but these were not her people and this was not her home and she was already lonely.

The cold made everyone much hungrier. Each hunter was having to go out hunting alone, now, or with his own family. The scarcity of the game did not justify hunting in pairs. Joadamie loaned Josephie some of his dogs, his *komatik* and harnesses. The detachment advanced him some traps and ammunition but he soon discovered that it was almost impossible to control the dogs. The animals had to be kept very hungry to make them move and, even when they were starved, they considered Joadamie their master and would not obey Josephie's instructions. Often he would have to trudge ahead and, crouching low, imitate the movements of a seal to get them going. They remained uneasy in their new fan harnesses, which were more suited to High Arctic conditions than the longer harnesses of Ungava, as a result of which the *komatik* was always overturning and Josephie would have to stop to repack it in the dark. The dry air made the dogs' lungs bleed and the dry ice ground against their paws, even, sometimes, after Josephie tied sealskin booties over them. On several occasions he took them out along the coast with the intention of setting his trap lines and from there sledging out to the edge of the shore-fast ice where the dogs could scent out seals' breathing holes, but each time the team lost control and bolted or refused to move and he had to return home empty-handed.

In the dark he felt completely bewildered. He could not see the end of his own outstretched hand. Walking out on the ice blind was terrifying. At any moment, he expected to fall through some thin patch or opening lead. For mile after mile he had to trust the dogs, beasts who, it seemed, were as disoriented and as demoralised as himself. It were as if he suddenly had no body, but existed only as a shadow, unable to get any purchase on the world around him, aware that at any time the world could swallow him up. When it was clear and the moon gave off a strong light, he felt his chances rising, an intimation, a possibility that he might get out of it all alive, but the cloud had only to come over and a baleful gloom would settle back in and despair would sneak into his heart. What had he brought himself and his family to? It was too dark to see his way to an answer.

As the days and weeks wore on, the cold deepened into a hard, inescapable crust which seemed to work its way into his vital organs. Sometimes Josephie would return from a trip struggling for breath which had frozen his lungs. The dark, the dogs and his own lack of experience after twelve years as a choreboy seemed constantly to doom his efforts. He had to fight the temptation to give in to brooding or despondency but this new life was a terrible shock to him. One of his hopes in travelling north had been to be able to make himself useful to his stepfather's family. Now, after only a few weeks on Ellesmere, he began to sense that there was very little he could do to make any difference. On the contrary, unless he could change his situation, he would be forced to accept the humiliating truth that the Flaherty family's survival would for some time depend on help from the Aqiatusuk family. The conditions stretched him beyond his limits. As they edged further into the dark period, he grew more anxious. Without help he would not be able to keep his family fed through the winter. He needed a hunting partner, but there was no one he could turn to. Rynee had to remain at home to feed the children, clean skins and patch their clothes and it was as much as the other men could do to keep their own families alive. The detachment appeared to have no interest in his plight. There was only one person left. His daughter Martha.

And so, at the age of six or so, the granddaughter of Robert Flaherty and Maggie Nujarluktuk began her hunting career, in temperatures cold enough to freeze the breath, to curdle the blood and murder the bones.

Father and daughter made an odd couple. Forced together by circumstances, they rose together in the black dawn, pulled on their outdoor caribou underclothes with the fur on the inside and rolled on another pair of hare-skin stockings, while Rynee lit the *qulliq* to melt water and chewed their *kamiks* to make them supple. Once they were dressed, they ate a piece of seal meat or a little slice of blubber and took a piece of bannock bread to pocket for the journey. When breakfast was over, Josephie went out to fetch the dogs and ice the runners of the *komatik* while Martha pulled on her caribou overclothes—still frozen so they would resist condensation and damp—and yanked up her *kamiks* and waited for her mother to check that there were no holes and no little pieces of skin exposed. Once that was done, Rynee would help her daughter put on her sealskin mitts and her dog-fur mitts and she would go out to meet her father on the ice.

If the cold was terrorising for Josephie, how much more so was it for his little daughter. Frost cramped the muscles in Martha's throat and froze her eyelashes, her brows and the hairs inside her ears. Out there on the High Arctic ice, her breath scoured her lungs like gravel and her brain rattled hard and frosty in its little box. This fierce, black world made no sense to her. As she bumped along on the sled across Jones Sound in pewter light, with Josephie up ahead encouraging on the reluctant dogs, almost invisible in the gloom, she would feel as though she had somehow died and entered a limbo world and tears of horror would fall down her cheeks, freeze and form forests of ice crystals on her face. When that happened, her father would grab her arms and say, "What do you want? Do you want us to starve?"

Then Martha would wipe her cheeks and focus on the way ahead because she was strong, stronger than Josephie would ever know, and because she had no choice.

All through that early winter they sledged, past Christmas and on into the New Year. They went east to Smith Sound and south to Devon Island, then north as far as Norwegian Bay and west to Hell Gate, till there was no patch of ice, no glacier or fiord or shale beach around southern Ellesmere that was not tattooed with their tracks. On and on father and daughter moved, endlessly in motion, bound by fear, hunger and the incalculable ties of family.

What Martha Flaherty would have given for it all to stop! At times all she wanted was not to have to face another day out on the frozen land. But, tiny child though she was, she knew already that to give in to this impulse would mean her death and those of her mother and brother, and so she would muster the resilience which was both her genetic legacy and her cultural heritage, gather herself and set her sights ahead.

From time to time, Bob Pilot would turn up at camp, bringing little offerings of flour, tobacco or lard. Sargent came too, though less frequently. They had not, as Josephie had supposed, washed their hands of the Flahertys. In fact they were anxious about the family. But their hands were tied by their orders, which were to keep the Inuit out on the land. Besides, they never saw the whole truth of the situation. The Inuit were too wary of the policemen to tell them everything. If they were asked, they would say only that conditions were hard but they were managing. Neither Sargent nor Pilot could understand what they were asking of a gentle man with only a few years' experience of hunting was impossible. All the same, the two policemen knew that the family were hungry and vulnerable, and that winter was not over yet. If the Flahertys were to last it out, Sargent and Pilot decided, then, orders or no, something more would have to be done.

CHAPTER SEVENTEEN

SNOW ARRIVED and the families deserted their sod huts for snow-houses. All through the early weeks of the winter they hunted and trapped, their days reduced, as they had been during every winter on Ellesmere Island, to a stark and brutal regimen of survival. At Christmas the detachment threw them a party. They swallowed tinned sardines and chocolate, watched a film and danced a few lacklustre reels. Corporal Sargent and Constable Pilot took pictures. No one smiled much. Afterwards, they returned to camp and resumed hunting and trapping and by January the sardines and the chocolate were already distant memories.

Josephie and Martha were now able more often than not to bring back a ringed seal, but there were four human mouths and several dogs to feed and blubber to be kept aside for the *qulliq* and still barely a day passed when the family's stomachs did not ache and their minds grow dizzy with hunger. All the talk was of food and how to get it. The dark days tumbled relentlessly one upon the other and discovered the Flahertys, huddled in the cold, picking at the bones of seal flippers. Technically, they were not starving, but their faces had taken on the soft, bloodless look of malnutrition and their eyes were matt and empty. Sleep provided them no relief. Under frozen sleeping skins they dreamed of duck and eggs and cloud-berries and of all the luscious bounty of a life now gone.

If Josephie regretted making the journey up to Ellesmere Island he never said so. On the few occasions Rynee brought the topic up, he merely observed that they had to make the most of their situation. All the same, he was preoccupied. As winter wore on he seemed to lose interest in the world beyond what might be extracted from it to feed his family. He took no pleasure in stories or songs, things he had always loved. The beauty of the land escaped him and his manner became sharp and unpredictable, particularly round Martha. Gradually, over the months, Josephie Flaherty, the hard-working, cheerful, somewhat introspective man who loved his homeland and his stepfather, began to dwindle and in his place a bitter, vindictive and moody creature took shape.

In February the sun arrived again, revealing devastation in the Inukjuamiut camp. Old bones, antlers and pieces of flensed seal and bearskin were scattered between the sod huts and snowhouses, there were broken piss pails and harpoon handles, bits of tattered sealskin harness and walrus skulls strewn about. Bits and pieces of butchered animal were stuck on ledges and rock outcrops out of range of the dogs. Over to the side where the Ingluligmiut had built their *qarnaqs*, the beach was cleaner and more ordered. The mess seemed to echo the peculiar desperation of the Inukjuamiut, who had been brought to a land in comparison to which Ungava, which had in turn seemed so relentless and raw to Robert Flaherty, appeared infinitely forgiving. In their camp's dishevelment could be discovered the great shake-up which the move north had wrought not only in their everyday lives but also in their hearts. As they went about restoring the camp to something like order, it was clear that the order was as fragile as the new roots they were trying to lay down. They had survived another winter, but they were in a mess.

The return of the sun spurred the detachment into action on behalf of the Flahertys. Not long after the first sunrise, Bob Pilot appeared to ask the Flaherty family to move. Corporal Sargent had decided that Josephie would take Thomasie Amagoalik's place as the detachment's storeman. The job involved stacking shelves, counting stock and keeping the store clean. In return for his labour, Josephie

Flaherty would receive a small wage and the right to live in the store-man's hut beside the detachment building. Thomasie Amagoalik would have to return to the camp and make his living once more on the land. Corporal Sargent was insistent. He did not want any star-vation cases on his hands, and the Flahertys' situation was more des-perate than the Amagoaliks'. For now, there was help at hand. The Flaherty family had won a reprieve. Later Josephie Flaherty would have to learn to grasp their new situation. He was Inuk, and to the planners in the Department this meant that sooner or later he would have to support his family by hunting and trapping.

And so the Flahertys moved into the hut beside the detachment building and found themselves in the strange position of having gone full circle, only it was a very odd kind of circle indeed which had taken them so far from home. For the first time in months, Jose-phie seemed a little more like his usual self. The family relaxed. Their new situation did not put them out of danger altogether and they were still hungry, but it at least meant they were unlikely to die of starvation any time soon. Bit by bit they began gathering their strength and after a month or so had passed and they felt settled in the hut, Josephie and Rynee turned their attentions to their missing daughter, Mary. Josephie still found it too painful to speak much about the little girl, though Rynee always knew when he was think-ing about her because he would pace up and down the hut with his eyes gazing at nothing, his paddle hands tied in knots behind his back. But he could never bring himself to ask Corporal Sargent or Constable Pilot for news. In all his years, he had spoken out only once, and he had lost his job as a result. He remained mute, at least in front of qalunaat, but Rynee said afterwards that there was not a day when they did not think about their daughter, miss her desper-ately and long for news of her return.

At the detachment, Constable Bob Pilot readied himself for the spring patrol. The patrol carried the settlement's mail and official documents to Resolute Bay and it was also the chance for the detachment constables from Craig Harbour and Alexandra Fiord (which had been re-established after Henry Larsen had failed to reach it in the *d'Iberville*) to take their annual southern leave. The patrol took about ten weeks, two weeks or so to get from Craig Harbour to Resolute, six weeks while the Mounties were in the south, then a further two weeks for the return trip to Craig Harbour. Royal Canadian Mounted Police rules stated that *qalunaat* police must always be accompanied by at least one Inuit guide when they were out on patrol. On short trips this would be Special Constable Kayak, but Sargent did not like him to be away from the detachment for long periods and so for the spring patrol he generally hired two guides, who were also dog-team drivers, from among the Inuit living at the camp on Ellesmere Island. This year he asked Josephie Flaherty. There was a small stipend attached to the work and Sargent knew Josephie needed the money. The other Inuk would be Simon Akpaliapik from Pond Inlet.

The four men, Bob Pilot, the Mountie from Alexandra Fiord, Josephie Flaherty and Simon Akpaliapik, started out on a fine day at the beginning of March. They headed west to Cape Storm and crossed Jones Sound, reaching West Fiord on Devon Island at the end of the third day. The going on Devon was tough, but they got across without incident and continued on south along the west coast, stopping every night in a temporary snowhouse to rest the dogs and catch a few hours' sleep before setting off again in the early morning. It was light almost twenty-four hours a day now, and in good weather they would make the most of the sun by skipping a night or two's rest and taking it in turns to cat nap on the *komatiks*. So they made good progress and in ten days they had reached Beechey Island off the southwest tip of Devon Island and were navigating their way across the sea ice when a fierce wind started up and the two Mounties became disorientated in blowing snow and lost their bearings. Visibility was poor and the wind was loud enough to drown out the men's whistles and, for quite a while, Josephie and Simon carried on, unaware that the two Mounties were no longer following. When they finally realised they could neither see nor hear the men, they stopped their *komatik* and called and whistled for them, but by now the wind was at such a pitch that it blanked out any human noise and the ashy air made it impossible to see farther than their own hands. The two Inuit had no idea when they had become separated, but they knew that in the current conditions the Mounties were in a great deal of danger. There was no horizon or coastline to be seen now and their tracks were covered by snow almost the instant they made them. The Mounties' compasses would be no good to them at this latitude and they would not be able to get a purchase on the sun. The *qalunaat* would quite likely get themselves tangled in the weather and perhaps forget the first rule of Arctic survival: to build a shelter in a lee and sit out the storm.

The two Inuit decided to begin a methodical search for the missing men. Dividing the area between them, they walked in diminishing circles, looking for tracks or any other sign that the men might have passed that way. The wind was gusting so strongly now that it was often hard to stay upright and they were being pelted with snow and pieces of ice. Wet snow heaped rapidly into piles, making the going very difficult. For hours they searched, calling and whistling, until the ominous heat of frostbite began to bother their fingers and toes. The coastline of Devon Island loomed out of the fog and they realised they had gone the wrong way and there was little hope for the *qalunaat*. They could barely breathe now for the force of the wind. It was hopeless. The world round them had been transformed into a vast spectral city of snowy towers. No human being could live for long outside in such conditions and the two men considered that it was time to look to their own survival.

They were about to give up the search and build a snowhouse for themselves when the dogs alerted them to two nearby mounds. They approached and, scraping at the soft snow, not knowing what they would find, the two Inuit came at last on the bodies of the two Mounties, alive but sliding in and out of consciousness. With hail and snow pounding their heads and the wind punching their faces, the two Inuit men untied two caribou skins from their *komatiks,* wrapped their charges in them and placed them beside the dogs for warmth, then they pulled out their snowknives and began to cut snowblocks for a snowhouse. The snow was wet and unstable but it was all they had and they worked with it as best they could, finally fashioning a small dome with a rudimentary entrance tunnel. The two Inuit dragged the policemen inside and brewed up some hot tea. The Mounties were shaken and a little frostbitten but the tea seemed to revive them very quickly and it did not look as though they had suffered any permanent injury.

For three days the storm continued to blow and the four men holed up inside the dome, surviving on tea and pemmican and sleeping sitting up because there was no space for them all to lie down. To occupy themselves the two Inuit sang songs and told stories, and although each had only a rudimentary grasp of the other's dialect, the stories and the songs helped muffle the tormented screams of the wind and the terrified whimpering of the dogs.

When the travellers failed to arrive at Resolute Bay on the appointed day, Ross Gibson of the Resolute detachment sent out a couple of Inuit men to look for tracks. When the scouts returned, saying the wind had blown so much snow across the sea ice that there would be no prospect of picking up any tracks, he radioed headquarters to ask for advice and was told to hold fast for a couple of days and see if the expedition turned up. Until the weather conditions improved it would be pointless sending out a rescue team by land and too dangerous to scramble a plane.

It was Ross Gibson's final year in the Resolute detachment. He had asked for a transfer and was due to be posted back to Inukjuak in 1957. The years since his first arrival in 1953 had been the most formative ones not only of his career, but, in all probability, of his life. Under the most difficult conditions and with virtually no backup or support from the RCMP in Ottawa, Gibson had helped construct in Resolute a community from what was initially a holding camp. And while it was true that his idea of what the "natives" needed or wanted was primitive and arrogant, no one could have accused him of being cynical or lazy. It was he who had come up with the idea of clearing out an old toilet block and using it as a community room and rudimentary school. It was he, too, who had written to the Coca-Cola company and persuaded them to send pencils and he who had suggested that Leah Idlout from Pond Inlet be allowed to teach Resolute's Inuit children. He had encouraged the migrants to make a camp of scrap-lumber huts and advised the Department not to waste money on sending prefabs when the Inuit were so resourceful with what discarded planks and packing crates were already at the air-force dump. Once the huts were up, he had even had each fitted with its own single light bulb and connected up the ionosphere station's electricity supply (Gibson felt one light bulb per household was plenty for the native home).

Never a man to take much account of the bigger picture, Ross Gibson was supremely proud of his achievements. In his view, he had had to pay a high price for them. His knees were acting up from having to scramble in and out of snowhouses to check on whether or not things had been taken from the air-force dumps and his skin, which had always been delicate, was now so roughened and sore from the dry, High Arctic winds that it regularly broke out into bloody rashes. He had lost the one great battle Henry Larsen had laid at his door: to protect the innocence of the Inuit and keep them away from the air base. Worse still, the many hours and days and years of intense scrutiny the endeavour had taken had left him worn and anxious. His superiors had admonished him for poor record-keeping and blocked his promotion but he remained resolutely unrepentant about his actions. He sensed, in the way that only someone who has been pushed to the edge of his limits can sense, that he had done his best. He did not regret his time in Resolute Bay, not yet anyway, and the Arctic was still the place he most wanted to be, but it was time to return to Inukjuak where conditions were eas-ier. Until then he intended to keep things ticking over for the next man. He was keen not to leave behind a legacy of incompetence or recklessness, but that would be what would happen if the spring patrol failed to show.

On the fourth day, the four travellers woke to a changed world. The storm had abated and everything was silent and swollen where the snow clung to it. It was time to move on. The men brewed some tea and got their bearings, then broke camp, harnessed the dogs and began to move slowly out across the wet snow. The animals struggled through the deeps and the men had to whip them on, but they soon sensed they were nearing their destination and began to pull with the great, life-affirming enthusiasm only Arctic dogs know. The men, exhausted, could do nothing but cling to the *komatiks* and hope.

At Resolute Bay the detachment had begun to consider the real possibility that the men were dead. Then someone at camp spotted something moving at a distance on the ice. The movement resolved into what looked like two tiny specks. A couple of scouts went out on a *komatik* and returned, saying the specks were definitely dog teams, but it was hard to know how many men were with them. Ross Gibson fetched his binoculars and trained them on the horizon, but it was the Inuit who first identified the party as the missing patrol. They loaded their guns, put bannock bread in their parkas and went out to meet it.

Later, in the safety of the Resolute Bay detachment, the two Mounties related the tale of the storm. Even now, Bob Pilot underplays the danger he was in, but he felt sufficiently grateful to Simon Akpaliapik and Josephie Flaherty at the time to give them a knife and a watch as thanks and it seems clear that the two Inuit saved the Mounties' lives. The policemen flew south shortly after and for the next six weeks, Simon and Josephie stayed at Resolute Bay, hunting for their own food and for the dogs and waiting for the return of the constables from the south.

The journey back to Grise Fiord was uneventful enough, though it was so cold that the men coughed blood. Sometime in late April they saw the cliffs of Ellesmere Island come into view and a tremendous sense of relief fell across the party that the journey was finally over. Rynee Flaherty later said her husband was so cold from the trip that his muscles convulsed for two or three days. Not long after their arrival Josephie Flaherty and Simon Akpaliapik went to collect their money from Corporal Sargent. They had agreed a fee of C$5 a day while out on patrol and though they were not to be paid for their six-week stay at Resolute Bay, their families were given rations while they were gone. Energised by the rescue, the two men asked if Sargent might consider giving them another C$10, in recognition of their endeavours. Simon Akpaliapik recalled later that Sargent stared at them for a while, then he turned and went back into his warm, heated quarters and very firmly closed the door. It was dishonourable, Sargent thought, to expect payment in such circumstances. The two Inuit never received any extra money for their efforts and from then on, when it came to dealing with *qalunaat*, Josephie Flaherty most often kept his mouth shut.

CHAPTER EIGHTEEN

BY 1958, what had begun five years before as a makeshift camp on a lonely outcrop on Ellesmere Island had grown into a more permanent-looking settlement of wooden-framed huts neatly positioned along the beach beside Grise Fiord. The settlement could almost have been any one of the many remote hamlets dotted about Arctic Canada, though no other hamlet in Canada had a backdrop as fearsome as this, no other was more isolated or more northerly, there was no other where survival came at such a high price. Grise Fiord was as far from anywhere as anywhere could be. No one came to the tiny settlement and no one left it. It was a staging post to nowhere, its inhabitants a group of obscure flags fluttering in a forlorn breeze.

It was midsummer, the sun had stirred the damp inside the huts, and most families had moved into canvas tents. The Flahertys were living next door to the Aqiatusuks and Josephie Flaherty was back making his living on the land. He had his own dog team now and a *komatik* made from scrap lumber. Otherwise, things were much the same. All the hardships of the earlier years remained: the harshness of the climate, the struggle to hunt and trap, the numbing dark and isolation and the persistent failure of supplies. What *had* changed was that Josephie had given up on the promise of a good life and had learned to adapt to what was before him, so that the situation no longer felt like a game he was bound to lose. He could tolerate his new life only by giving up any dreams he might have had for it. He longed, now, only to be reunited with Mary, and to go home. He and Rynee rarely spoke about Inukjuak and the families they had left behind, nor about Mary or Paddy Aqiatusuk whose absences were acknowledged only in so far as they were understood to be too painful to be named. He and Rynee were talking less and less now about everything. Mostly, Rynee left Josephie alone. His moods had become frightening. Day after day he waited for news from the detachment that they would be returning to Inukjuak, but so far no such news had come. He still had not asked after Mary, too fearful of the response he might get. Instead he brooded, drifting out across the seas of his imagination, where no one else could reach him.

Nineteen fifty-eight became a turning point for the inhabitants of Grise Fiord. On 27 July of that year, only a few days before ship time, Thomasie Amagoalik rose early from his tent to go out hunting. His two sons, Allie, aged twelve, and Salluviniq, aged nine, were keen to accompany their father but Thomasie did not want his sons holding him up and told the boys to stay in camp. Sometime later that morning, after their father had left, Allie and Salluviniq spotted their cousins, Elisapee Novalinga and Larry Audlaluk, carrying their sculpin lines and hooks. In any ordinary situation the boys might not have bothered with sculpin fish which were as wiry as bunch grass, but July was a thin month for hunting on Ellesmere and the Amagoaliks were hungry and the children reasoned that if their father returned from his hunt empty-handed, they might at least have some fish soup to eat and so they begged their mother to let them go along with Elisapee and Larry to try their luck.

The Amagoalik boys were not dressed for a day out so Elisapee and Larry agreed to wait while they put on their outdoor clothes. It was a long wait. The boys' mother, Mary Amagoalik, had made her children a new set of caribou trousers and parkas but, at the request of the detachment who liked their "natives" to look their best for the benefit of the visiting Department officials and police officers, she was saving these for ship time. Until the arrival of the *C. D. Howe,* the two boys would have to manage with their rags, arranging the torn layers in such a way that the holes did not leave parts of their bodies exposed because, even in July, the weather at Grise Fiord was unpredictable. Before they left, their mother reminded them to stay close to the others and come home the moment they felt cold.

The four children made their way across the plateau and along the folds of the cliffs into the fiord. As a precaution, they kept to the ice foot under the rocks, where the ice was ancient and never melted. The plan was to walk to the spot where a little stream emptied out on to the scree. It would lead them to a brackish inlet where sculpin sometimes gathered and where they could cut a hole through the ice and sink their lines. Elisapee and Larry had been to the place many times and knew it well. The weather on this day was fair and the way was unobstructed by meltwater or rockfall, and by mid-morning the children had reached the inlet. There they stayed for a few hours, playing games with bones they found and waiting for the fish to appear, but by the afternoon when they had caught very little and were all beginning to feel hungry and cold, Elisapee suggested they go home. The two Amagoalik boys were not content to return without bringing some fish, however, and made up their minds to go looking elsewhere, so Larry and Elisapee turned back to camp, leaving Allie and Salluviniq to work their way deeper into the fiord.

There was no particular reason to worry. The weather was clear, the children knew the path and polar bears kept away from the fiord during the summer. They often went out for a day at a time collecting heather or hunting for eggs or ptarmigan, so no one in camp thought anything much of it when the two Amagoalik boys failed to return home at the end of the afternoon. It was only as evening set in, with the sun still ablaze, that the children's mother began to get worried and went down to the beach with a telescope to scan the area round the fiord and see if she could see the boys or their tracks. Sometime later a handful of the men in the camp set out to look for the boys while someone else went to alert the police detachment.

The women stayed behind to look after the boys' mother. For what seemed an eternity, they sat and waited. Every so often they thought they heard the yap of a dog coming from inside the fiord, but the sounds became muddled with their thoughts. Time slid by. Suddenly, a lone figure appeared from the direction of the fiord and began trudging along the shale towards them and they hurried out to meet him, their feet bringing up little fountains of stones behind. The news was as bad as they had feared. The body of one of the boys had been found in the water and it looked as though he had fallen through a soft patch in the ice and drowned. He had been dead a while. His brother was still missing.

By the next morning there was still no sign of the missing boy and the men were forced to give up their search so they could hunt for food for their families. In keeping with Inuit custom, Mary Aqiatusuk burned the clothes which the boys' mother had been saving for the arrival of the *C. D. Howe*. The women cried at the waste of new clothes. It was easier than crying for the boys when the tears shed might never have ended. There it was: Allie and Salluviniq Amagoalik would never see another ship time.

The report of the Grise Fiord police detachment to Henry Larsen in Ottawa in September of that year noted, with regret, that the Amagoalik boys had died "while out playing." But, like Aqiatusuk's obituary in *Time* magazine, this was not true. The boys had died while out looking for fish to feed their family.

The deaths of the two boys brought to mind a story the camp had been told by a party of Greenlandic hunters and their families who had passed by Grise Fiord the year before. One of them was an old woman called Padloo. Padloo's father had been among the travellers who had made their way from Baffin Island to Etah in northern Greenland under the leadership of Qillaq. It was a story familiar to most Baffin Islanders but to the Inukjuamiut it was new. After several years' travelling, and just before the party reached Greenland, Qillaq's friend Oqe became disillusioned with the search and decided to return to Baffin, taking twenty-four of his supporters with him. It was summer, but there was enough ice to sledge and the group turned back at Makinson Inlet on the east coast of Ellesmere Island and began heading south, stopping at Goose and Fram fiords on the southern coast to set up hunting camps to gather a cache for the winter. But high winds followed by bad autumn weather made hunting hard and the people began to go hungry. When the dark period and the cold set in, their meat stores were empty and by the end of the year they had eaten their dogs and their surplus skins and were starving. One by one they began to die.

Of all the travellers, a man called Qimmingajak was the most determined to save himself. Under cover of the perpetual dark he went out collecting the corpses of those who had died. When he and his family had eaten all the dead, Qimmingajak looked about to see whom he could eat next. His first victim was his young brother-in-law, Qallutsiaq. The boy had already eaten all his clothes with the exception of the sealskin boots and trousers his grandmother had given him, and he was in a pitiful state. After Qallutsiaq, killing came easier to Qimmingajak, and before too long, he had murdered everyone in the camp except his wife, Angiliq, and their two sons.

For a while the family lived off the frozen corpses of Qimmingajak's victims, but hunger eventually returned. Stringing a cord through the roof of his *qarnaq* and fashioning the loose end into a noose, one day Qimmingajak instructed Angiliq to fix the noose round their elder son's neck. The boy and his mother both protested, but Qimmingajak threatened to kill Angiliq if she refused to do as he commanded and so, after a great deal of crying and shaking Angiliq pushed the rope over her son's head and Qimmingajak tightened it. Then he cut up the body of his son and gave the hands to his wife just as, in happier days, he had presented her with the flippers of a seal.

Now only Angiliq and Qimmingajak and their younger son were left alive. In the hope of saving her remaining child, Angiliq took off hunting. Till then she had never hunted anything much except sea birds, hares and lemmings and there seemed very few of any of these on Ellesmere Island, but she took off across the sea ice in Jones Sound, checking the *agluit* and begging Sedna, the sea spirit, to send her a fat harp seal. All night she walked and waited and towards dawn she put her testing feather in one last *aglu*. Within minutes, the feather moved with the breath of the creature beneath it, and Angiliq raised her harpoon and brought up a small struggling seal. Angiliq whooped for joy and, half running, half stumbling, dragged the animal behind her to camp. When she reached the *qarnaq* she crushed a little of the seal's fat to light a fire and in the low flame of the *qulliq* she suddenly saw Qimmingajak sitting in a corner watching her. It was then she knew it was too late. Her younger boy was dead and his father had already begun to eat his body.

Spring came and the sea melted into blue, Padloo said, but a *tuurngaaluk,* an evil spirit, had taken over Qimmingajak and he no longer even tried to hunt. Knowing who her husband's next victim would be, Angiliq went out to sea in Qimmingajak's *kayak* looking for walrus. She knew what she was doing was dangerous but she had nothing to lose, so she paddled round the sound, searching for signs of life. After many hours, she saw a ship in the distance, and, racing back to camp, she began to pile the clothing of the dead into a huge mound before setting it on fire to make a beacon. Spotting the smoke, the captain of the whaler sent his ship's skiff to investigate. He picked up the survivors and dropped the pair at Pond Inlet on Baffin Island from where they wandered into a nearby camp at Igarjuaq. The people there offered them *muktuk* and polar bear meat. Angiliq ate the meat but Qimmingajak refused and was later seen inspecting an area of graves. He did not live long in Igarjuaq. Some said Angiliq killed him, others said it was a relative of one of the bodies he had scavenged. No one knew what had become of the *tuurngaaluk* which had occupied Qimmingajak and given him his terrible taste for human blood, but it was possible, Padloo said, that the *tuurngaaluk* of Fram Fiord remained there, waiting for its next victim.

A rumour began that the spirits did not want the Inuit on Ellesmere Island. Something bad had happened to every group of Inuit who had ever camped there. The deaths of the Amagoalik boys were just two in a series which stretched back past Paddy Aqiatusuk and Special Constable Kakto and his wife, Ooarloo's two children, to Oqe's followers and the Thule themselves. The Inuit did not want to be in a place which so manifestly did not welcome them. They needed to get back home. But how?

Just over a month after the boys' death, a faint pucker appeared on the horizon, as if someone had pinched two clouds together. The lookout let off two rifle shots to warn the camp that the C. D. Howe was on her way towards them and the camp Inuit changed into their best clothes and came down on to the beach to wait, speaking excitedly, as they always did, about who and what the ship might bring, and for a moment they forgot their sadness.

The detachment store had run out of most of the things they needed. For a few heady weeks after the ship's departure those who had the credits would be able to get their hands on all the staples plus such wonderful luxuries as currants, tobacco, sugar and even cookies. After months of living on nothing but polar bear and seal meat, and little enough of that, families looked foward to enjoying some currant bannock and sweet tea. The ship was also bringing the previous year's special orders for those families who had had particular luck in trapping and had managed to tuck away enough credits for a sewing machine, a gramophone or a set of new needles. There were not many special orders at Grise Fiord but the few there were had been eagerly anticipated and when they finally arrived it felt like a sudden fall of rain in the midst of drought.

This year, as usual, there was also the hope that the C. D. Howe would be returning relatives from southern sanatoria, newly cured and brimful of tales about the crowds and mayhem south of the tree line. The families were not told whether or not their relatives were on board ship, so the first they would know about it would be when their missing son or mother appeared on deck. By 1958, the Flahertys were not the only family who had lost a relative to the south and for all those who had, the interval between the ship's announcement and the opening of the passenger quarters seemed interminable, as full of anxiety as anticipation. For three long years the Flahertys had clung to the hope that Mary would be on the next supply ship. But she never had been and they had had no word from her.

As the *C. D. Howe* sat in Jones Sound, the Flahertys tried to prepare themselves for every eventuality. They heard the sound of an engine starting up and saw the detachment Peterhead begin motoring towards the ship. Moments later a handful of crew members came up on the *C. D. Howe*'s deck and began untying ropes. The Peterhead disappeared round the far side of the ship and the two detachment Mounties reappeared on the deck of the *C. D. Howe* accompanied by some other *qalunaat*. The men appeared to be in conversation for a while before disappearing back down below. Sometime later, the Flahertys saw figures moving beside the ship's hull and caught the cough of the Peterhead's engine. A puff of blue exhaust fumes made its way into the sky as the boat began to swing round towards the shore. She dropped anchor shy of the beach and Constable Bob Pilot transferred to the skiff and took hold of a bundle passed over the side, then the boat began to edge towards the beach. At the shoreline, Pilot got out and lifted the bundle, which, it was now clear, was a girl of about five or six, on to the shale. No one dared approach. Pilot stood there for a moment, then, taking his charge's hand, he began to move towards them.

Josephie and Rynee Flaherty exchanged a worried glance. The girl was swinging her head about, trying to take in the mountains, the red cliffs and the row of little huts. She seemed distressed. Could it be?

"Mary?" said Josephie.

In all the flurry it was hard to recall exactly what happened next. At some point the girl tried to loose herself from Pilot's grasp and began to call out for Jackoosie Iqaluk.

Josephie and Rynee stood on the beach and said nothing. Was this their daughter after all? They were not the people she was crying out for. The little girl looked terrified. There was no glint of recognition in her eyes. Again, she called for Jackoosie, and began to scream and kick out.

Josephie and Rynee looked at one another. Rynee nodded. The wind brought a cold blast down from the mountains. They took Mary back to their tent. When the girl had run dry of tears, she fell into a fitful sleep broken by gasps and sobs. She refused to eat or drink or even to catch anyone else's eye. Eventually she stopped protesting and sank into a profound gloom, as if she hoped they would forget about her.

It would be difficult to believe what had happened to Mary during her time away, were it not the incontestable truth. She had been transferred from Churchill, Manitoba, with Dora and Mary Iqaluk to the tuberculosis sanatorium. The three girls were quickly separated, stripped, bathed, deloused and put into different wards. None of the nurses in the sanatorium spoke Inuktitut and the girls spoke no English, so they had no idea what was happening to them. At one point, Dora found Mary Flaherty strapped to a bed and sobbing. She was two years old. Luckily for Mary, her illness had been caught early. After some months at the sanatorium, she had made a swift recovery and had been transferred in due course to Montreal. In July 1956 she was placed on board the *C. D. Howe* for the trip north and was put ashore at Inukjuak. According to the records, the Flahertys were still living in the settlement and Mary was then three years old and not in a position to argue with anyone about it. By the time the mistake was spotted the *C. D. Howe* was already making her way across Hudson Bay and it was too late to call her back.

For a year, Mary lived with relatives. In 1957, when the *C. D. Howe* returned to Inukjuak on the annual supply, the little girl was put back on board the ship and sent north. For forty days she sailed without parents or guardians until the *C. D. Howe* finally put in at Resolute Bay. The *C. D. Howe*'s own records seemed to suggest that Josephie and Rynee Flaherty had been landed at Resolute Bay and they were now living at the Inuit camp there. A quick check would have established that this was not the case, but no one made it. Four-year-old Mary was left with the cargo on the beach. Mary was taken in by Dora's family, the Iqaluks. For a year, she lived with the Iqaluks in Resolute Bay. No one bothered to contact her real parents. Confused and full of contradictory impressions, she took the Iqaluk family to be her own. She was now five and had been in transit from Manitoba to Grise Fiord for more than half her life. When she finally arrived in Grise Fiord she had no idea who her parents were. No one apologised to Mary or to her parents for her treatment and there was no investigation of the incident.

As the fifties ground into the sixties, obscure and lonely though it was, the settlement at Grise Fiord began to transform itself into a remote but respectable little community. On her 1959 visit, the *C. D. Howe* dropped off a pallet of 12-foot-by-6-foot prefabricated houses, which the Inuit modified for the extreme conditions by reangling the slope of the roofs and altering the guttering, then reconstructed them along the beach facing the sea. A year or two later, a few more of the prefabs arrived and, pretty soon, Grise Fiord boasted eight houses arranged in two parallel streets and the scrap-timber huts that had formerly been their homes were converted into stores or torn down. In 1962, a day school opened and a welfare teacher endeavoured to instruct children who had had no schooling at all for nine years, using the only two books the Department sent him, *How to Run a Successful Bank* and *The Roads of Texas*. While he struggled with his lessons, the teacher's wife organised adult classes in sewing, cooking, art and music and was surprised when women turned up at some of them. In the spirit of community, the police detachment set up a branch of the Wolf Clubs where young Inuit boys learned how to skin seals and put up summer tents. Twice a month they screened a film at the detachment and when CBC Radio began broadcasting Anne Pedlo's weekly show in Inuktitut, they invited everyone along to the detachment to listen.

Grise Fiord developed politics. Agendas emerged and competed. Men and women took positions and argued them out among themselves. Disputes were resolved, reparations made and alliances forged. Leaders sprang up and followers followed them. Hunters accustomed themselves to the terrain and began to be more successful at their hunting. More fox were trapped. The settlement remained poor, people continued to die in accidents and of the cold and disease but, for most, everyday existence no longer teetered on the edge of survival. But Grise Fiord was never able to escape the fact that it was a made-up world, a *terra nullius* whose population had been tricked into living there. It remained somewhere with no history, no context, no soul and nobody really wanted to stay there.

Ever since the deaths of the Amagoalik boys, people had been asking the detachment when they could go back. Some wanted to return to Inukjuak to look after elderly relatives or to be reunited with their families or they needed wives or were homesick or feared that the fate of the Amagoalik boys would fall on their children, or they simply found the life on Ellesmere Island too lonely and difficult and remembered that they had been promised they could go back. Bob Pilot, who took over the post of head of detachment after Glenn Sargent left, had no doubt that such a promise *had* been made, but his hands were tied. The Royal Canadian Mounted Police and the Department refused to do anything.

There were only two ways out of Ellesmere Island, by ship or dog sled. The only ship that ever called into Ellesmere, the *C. D. Howe,* would not have time in the navigation season to call into Inukjuak on its way back to Montreal. If it took the Inuit all the way down south, they would have to support themselves until the following year, when the *C. D. Howe* set off for the north once more. To leave the settlement by dog team, each family would have to carry themselves and all their equipment to Resolute Bay. Josephie Flaherty knew first hand how perilous that journey was. With children, it might well be impossible. Supposing the families made it to Resolute Bay, they would have to wait for the RCAF plane which left Resolute air base four times a year for the air base in Kuujuak in northeast Ungava. The plane always carried a lot of air-force cargo, so there would not be room to take Inuit equipment. Once they were landed at Kuujuak, any Inuit family wanting to get to Inukjuak would have to travel by dog sled inland across Ungava, a trip which had nearly ended the lives of both A. P. Low and Robert Flaherty and *had* killed Alakariallak forty years before. The Inuit would have to pay their own passage. And if all that were not sufficient, the Department inserted a new condition. Every family who left Ellesmere Island would have to recruit another family to take their place. It was important to Canada that the settlement remain populated.

What the people of Grise Fiord were never told was that from Montreal, the Inukjuamiut could have travelled by train to the railhead at Moose Factory in James Bay and from there picked up one of the Department of Transport's Norsemen which made supply flights to Inukjuak every two months. The journey would have taken some energy to organise but it would have been relatively cheap and easy. This option was never offered to the Flahertys or to anyone else because despite their assurances of a return, both the Department and the RCMP had interests in keeping the Inuit right where they were. The most northerly settlement in the Americas had become, in effect, an icy prison, one whose bars were made of space and broken promises.

The Inuit living at Grise continued to ask to leave through the late 1950s and into the 1960s, but the detachment only repeated the argument that it had used on Paddy Aqiatusuk. If the people of Grise Fiord wanted to see their relatives, then the best—and only—way would be to invite them up to live in Grise Fiord. This was not what had been promised, and the inhabitants of Grise Fiord did not wish to submit their relatives to the kind of conditions they would find on Ellesmere Island. On the other hand, they felt the separation very keenly. They dreaded dying without ever seeing their homeland or speaking to the loved relatives they had left behind. Their children would grow up cut off, not knowing where they came from, and with no connection to their history or their families. The Ungava Peninsula was and always would be their home. It held their stories and the spirits of their ancestors. However harsh their lives, and however challenging their terrain, there remained this one great truth which the fiercest winter storm could never take from them. Ungava was who and what they were. Separated from it they were no better than the adventurers who had come from Europe only to discover that their compasses had failed and that they were now adrift.

Josephie and others had gathered themselves many times and, through the police, begged the Canadian government to take them home, but they were afraid of insisting. They looked on those gangling officials with their brisk uniforms, their expensive boats, their baffling laws and jails and they felt *ilira,* awe and unease. If the thousand years of contact between Inuit and *qalunaat* had taught them anything it was never to confront the whites directly.

But as Josephie's desperation grew, so did his courage. He returned to the police detachment several times during 1959 and 1960 and asked in a quiet voice if the Canadian government would help him to get back home. He had six children now, and no matter how often he went out with his sled and no matter how many traps he set or how many seals he harpooned, he could not hunt enough on Ellesmere Island to keep his growing family fed. He was watching his children grow up half starved, isolated and uneducated.

Listening to him, Bob Pilot detected a calm, almost dangerous need. Until recently, he had marked Josephie down as meek and malleable. Now the man seemed driven, even obsessed. He appeared to think that the police detachment owed him something on account of that time when he and Akpaliapik had dragged the two RCMP constables out of the snow. Over the years he had become fuelled almost to the point of madness by this determination to see Inukjuak. Although Pilot had a good deal of sympathy for the man, and for all the Inuit living in Grise Fiord who wanted to get back home, he knew that the RCMP would never recognise any such obligation. It was a matter of realpolitik. Josephie Flaherty lived in the most isolated settlement in Canada and the RCMP and the Department wanted him to stay there. He had no power against them. So far as anyone knew, he had no contact with his rather influential family in Vermont and his greatest ally, Paddy Aqiatusuk, was dead and buried. As a Canadian, he had a vote, but only in theory since there was no voting constituency in the eastern Arctic. The man was illiterate and helpless. The reality was that no one was going to do anything for him or for any of the growing band of people who wanted to return to Inukjuak.

By 1960 Josephie Flaherty was becoming unstable. The same thoughts were driving in circles round his head. He saw himself as a choreboy, sitting on the stoop of his little hut mending his nets, surrounded by all the old, familiar hills, watching his children growing up, in the company of his wife, his relatives and his people. The sense of having been cheated out of the life he had been born to began to overtake his days and trample on his nights. All he could think about from the time he first got up in the morning till the time he settled on his sleeping skin was how to get his life back.

Gradually, over the years that followed, this gentle, unassuming man began to turn toxic. For days he would rage like a wounded bear, unpredictable and terrifying, then at other times he would be reduced to a baleful silence punctuated by sighing. When he did open his mouth to speak it was to find fault in everything, until everyone around, even Rynee and his own children, began keeping out of his way, a strategy that appeared to inflame him all the more. Perhaps in revenge for his loneliness he began to hit out, first with his tongue then, later, with his fists. Within the space of a decade, Josephie Flaherty had turned from a gentle, passive man into someone violent, anxious and unrecognisable.

If she was to have any chance in the world, Martha Flaherty quickly saw that she would have to get out. She was twelve years old, beautiful, bright as a button and as tough and as fragile as an egg. She was also determined to change her destiny. The moment she reached high school age, she applied to a residential school in Churchill and was accepted. Taking up her place meant leaving her mother, her siblings and everything she now looked upon as home. But it also meant surviving. Martha packed her bag.

In Martha's absence, Rynee took the brunt of her husband's fearsome temper, his outlandish rages, his sullen depressions and bullying tantrums. For sweet, tiny, tough Rynee, separated from her family in Inukjuak, still penniless, living at the top of the world, and with six children to keep, there was no getting out. She was stuck with it. Her friends were sympathetic. No one in Grise Fiord had failed to notice the change in Josephie Flaherty but no one really understood it either. Those who believed in such things claimed that the old Greenlandic woman, Padloo, had raised a bad spirit by telling the story of Qimmingajak. Others said Josephie had been possessed by *nuliarsait,* the spirit wives who sew chaos inside people's heads. There was talk of *pibloktoq,* the Polar Madness, which was well known to afflict northern Greenlanders and dwellers at high latitudes. Certainly, Josephie exhibited many of the signs: mood swings, violent depressions and irrational thoughts. Some made a connection between *pibloktoq* and feelings of impotence, others put it down to the biorhythmic disturbances caused by the long dark period. Most people who knew Josephie had a more straightforward explanation. They said it was hardly surprising that a man whose father had abandoned him to such a fate as Josephie's would go crazy sooner or later. He was a dry stalk, they said, ripped from its root, unable to recall the time, long since past, when it had borne leaves and sprung back from the wind.

The son Robert Flaherty "never had" never got to see Inukjuak. In 1968, he had a mental breakdown, from which he never fully recovered and, in 1984, he died of lung cancer in Grise Fiord, caused, so his family said, by the burning his lungs had received during all those hunting expeditions on the sea ice. He was buried under a little cross in what is now a growing graveyard beside the airstrip, at the foot of Ellesmere's mountains.

CHAPTER NINETEEN

THE DEATH of Josephie Flaherty was, in part, a liberation for his daughter. For a long time, Martha Flaherty's overwhelming feeling was one of relief. In those last years of his life, he had caused too much unhappiness to be immediately missed. Much later when she understood more about his life then she would mourn him. But at the time a part of her was glad he was gone.

For all its benign intention, residential school had been a difficult experience. In many residential schools Inuit children were forbidden to speak their own language and had no means of contacting their parents or relatives. They were put beside Indian children, with whom, historically, they did not get along. The most common currency of discipline was beating. Fights, bullying and an atmosphere of threat and mutual hostility were the norm. Though most staff were doubtless well meaning, the schools attracted more than the usual helping of perverts and child predators. The children, whose own traditions were considered primitive, were taught southern history and southern customs. They fell prey to southern diseases. Many were returned to the north in flimsy clothes and shoes completely unsuited to the conditions, unable to speak the same language as their parents. Damaged by their experiences at the schools and often entirely ignorant of the Inuit way of life, the children found it hard to fit in, let alone to settle in the Arctic, but impossible to go back to the south. They became rootless and drifting, cut off by language and by habit both from their families and from the traditions into which they had been returned. Residential school, for many, was residential hell.

Martha's experience had been as miserable as most, but it had taught her a great deal about the *qalunaat*. She had come to realise that, despite centuries of expeditions, the Arctic remained a fearful and enticing mystery to most of those who lived below the tree line. Even the more curious and better informed often based their notions of the north and its people on her grandfather, Robert Flaherty's, vision of the place. It seemed ironic that the global popularity of *Nanook* had served to freeze the Arctic and the people who lived in it, including Robert's own son and granddaughter, in a version of a past that never was, in a land that could never be. For Martha and her people, the north was a region of complex, dynamic conversations between ice, land and living things in which human beings were incidentals, at the centre only of their own lives. There were no heroes among the Inuit. There were only human beings getting by.

In their own environment, southerners suddenly seemed less powerful to Martha than they once had. For all their forests of buildings and human rookeries, the young Martha discerned that these southern men and women were often leading lives of almost unbearable sadness and isolation, living away from their families and from everything they knew, more deeply exiled, even, than the inhabitants of Grise Fiord and Resolute Bay, who at least recognised their banishment. To an Inuit mind, southern city life was not any kind of life to aspire to. Grise Fiord might well be frozen, but people's hearts somehow seemed warmer up there.

By the late sixties, Martha Flaherty had been through enough to sense that what her family had suffered was not in the usual run of things. Her brother Peter, half starved as a baby, was still afflicted, spending much of his time staring out to sea. Her sister Mary had not forgotten being taken from her parents. Then there was Martha herself, a trembling child-hunter, bumping along on the sea ice doing her best to avoid the polar bears. How she felt for her mother, Rynee, whose smile did not come as fast now as it once did, bringing up so many children with so little and none of her family to help and with Josephie slowly going mad with anguish and frustration, it is difficult to say. Even now, she finds it hard to talk about it. For many years she could barely bring herself to think about Josephie.

For the Flahertys there was still no hope of going home though. From the late sixties on, a few families in Resolute Bay managed to get enough work at the air base to raise the cost of their airline tickets and, abandoning their homes and belongings, flew back to Inukjuak and settled there. Jackoosie Iqaluk and his family, who had looked after Mary Flaherty in Resolute Bay, returned in 1977. Jaybeddie Amagoalik left in 1979 and Paddy Aqiatusuk's stepson, Samwillie Elijasialuk, who had been given permission to move from Grise Fiord to Resolute Bay in the early sixties to look for a wife, arrived back in Inukjuak in the same year. Even by Canadian standards, the High Arctic to Inukjuak is quite a distance, the equivalent of moving, say, from New York City to Cuba, and Arctic travel is extremely expensive. The majority of the exiles, as they had begun to call themselves, still longed to return home but remained trapped in their isolated, icy prisons with no means to make the journey and with Department officials refusing to accept that they had any duty to help them.

For Martha Flaherty, returning to Grise Fiord felt too much like revisiting old wounds. She moved to Fort Smith in the Northwest Territories to study nursing, and wound up acting as a translator between Inuit patients and southern doctors, moving, as she had learned to do, between two worlds. Before long she joined the Northwest Territories Interpreters Corps and moved to Yellowknife. It was there, in the capital of the Northwest Territories, that Martha began to organise.

In 1973, a group of men and women representing Grise Fiord

and Resolute Bay wrote to Bob Pilot, who was then working in Yellowknife as an adviser to the Commissioner of the Northwest Territories, asking for help to get back to Inukujak. Pilot was one of the few *qalunaat* in the northern administration to have lived among the Inuit in the High Arctic and, unlike Ross Gibson, he had always seen himself as a social worker first and a lawman second. It was as a welfare-minded rookie policeman that he had witnessed at first hand what isolation, homesickness and hunger had done to the people of Grise Fiord. He was clear in his own mind that the Inuit had been promised a return to Inukjuak and sensed that, if it ever came to court, the federal government would have a case to answer. The arrival of the letter came as no surprise to him. His own view was that it would save time and trouble in the long run if the funds were found to help those people who wanted to return. Holding out would haunt the Department further down the line. With that in mind, he recommended that the government of the Northwest Territories organise a charter flight from Grise Fiord and Resolute Bay to Inukjuak so that the exiles could take a look at the homeland they had last seen twenty years before and decide whether or not they really did want to return. If they did, Pilot felt that the federal government should stump up the considerable expense attaching to such a move because it had been the federal government's idea to send the exiles north and the federal government which had promised, all those years ago, to help the Inuit get back home. In any case, it was the federal government which had most benefited from the settlements at Grise Fiord and Resolute Bay because they had helped to establish Canadian sovereignty in the region. Those families had planted the flag for Canada and Canada had a duty to return the favour.

Bob Pilot's plane never left the runway. Between them, the governments of the Northwest Territories and Quebec and the federal government in Ottawa could not agree on who should pay for the flight. They knew that whoever took the initial responsibility would be lumbered with the entire move and it would be difficult and expensive. In any case, none of the governmental agencies were particularly troubled by the Inuit claim. Grise Fiord and Resolute Bay seemed a long way off. The exiles were easy to ignore.

It would take another twenty years, and numerous reports and appeals to the Department, the House of Commons Standing Committee on Aboriginal Affairs, and the Canadian Rights Commission before the High Arctic exiles would get a just hearing.

All through those years, Martha Flaherty helped keep up the pressure, speaking at meetings, drafting letters, translating for those among the exiles who could not speak English, continuing to insist on the merit of the Inuit case, and refusing, despite the intransigence of the authorities, to be discouraged or turned away. Even when at times it would have been easier to capitulate, to label herself and her family hopeless victims and be done with it she refused to give up. Her experience among *qalunaat* had taught her that ignorance was no excuse for injustice, and she was now in no doubt that what had happened to her family had been unjust.

The federal government continued to insist otherwise. Its arguments rested on intent. A government report stated that "records indicate, quite simply, that there was no malice or wrongdoing by departmental officers in the relocation project . . . it is 37 years since the first people moved from Inukjuak to Resolute Bay and Grise Fiord. With the passage of time, the facts surrounding the project have become altered in the memories of the people concerned." In spite of the overwhelming evidence against it, the federal government's official line was that it had no reason to apologise to the Inuit because its intentions had been benign. Even as it accepted that the move had been ill-prepared and those who had been moved had suffered emotional and physical stress it claimed that the Inuit were exaggerating or that their memories were playing tricks. In 1990, it finally agreed to help those who wanted to return to Inukjuak, but refused under any circumstances to pay the exiles compensation.

It was particularly ironic to accuse the Inuit of forgetting. A hundred and forty years before, a British rescue party looking for

the Franklin expedition, which had got lost in the Arctic the previous year, had begun talking to a group of Inuit on Baffin Island
about Martin Frobisher's Arctic voyage of 1576. At that time the
Inuit had no written language and had never recorded anything
about the voyage on paper. Nonetheless, they seemed to know a
great deal about it. Intrigued, the rescue party took notes and when
they returned to England they checked the Inuit version of the story
against the documentation and found that the former was not only
a perfect rendition of the established facts, but also that it added
credible detail to various of the official accounts which lacked it.
Amazingly, the tale of the Frobisher expedition had been handed
down by mouth from generation to generation of Inuit for nearly
three hundred years without any loss of detail or accuracy. The Inuit
are rememberers. They hold history fast to them. For anyone to suggest they have forgotten details of events within living memory was
nothing short of fantastic.

What was being lost in this game of accusation and counter
accusation was what had always been lost or trampled on or just
plain neglected, which is to say, the opinions of ordinary Inuit. Over
twenty years, reports had been commissioned, documents sifted
through, legal opinions sought, but the Inuit had never been given a
chance to bear witness in a formal setting, in circumstances where
they would likely be heard. On 15 January 1993, the Royal Commission on Aboriginal Peoples in Ottawa attempted to set that right. It
was all very well relying on documentary evidence, but, the Commission said, the documentary evidence was almost all from one
side. The Commission undertook to hold a definitive series of hearings which would adjudicate on the matter for good. It would take
testimony from the Inuit and from the various Departmental officials who had been involved at the time, as well as from police,
experts and anyone else with a view to give. For the first time in its
dealings with Inuit people, the government of Canada would find
itself, in effect, on trial.

It was an extraordinary achievement. After all the approaches to

High Arctic constables, the appeals to Eastern Arctic Patrol officials, to interpreters, missionaries, teachers and welfare officers, which had for forty years fallen on deaf ears, the Inuit of Inukjuak, Resolute Bay and Grise Fiord were finally about to be heard. What they had to say would provoke one of the most explosive controversies in Canadian history.

CHAPTER TWENTY

THE TV CREWS stationed outside the Château Laurier in Ottawa on Monday, 5 April 1993, were anticipating a good day ahead. The weather was sunny and the forecasters were predicting a respectable high of 8°C. The Château was looking its usual fantastical self, a good backdrop for the cameras, its Indiana limestone towers shining in the morning sun. The hotel opened quietly in 1912, after the man who commissioned it, American-born Charles Melville Hays, died on the *Titanic* while bringing over English dining furniture, but there was nothing quiet about the building, built in grand French Renaissance style with Italian marble floors and English walnut-wood fittings. Over the years the place had gained a reputation as the third chamber of parliament, its labyrinth of rooms, coffee bars and intimate nooks serving as the deal-making dens of generations of parliamentarians escaping from the constraining atmosphere of the parliament building next door. There were many in Ottawa, most of them civil servants of one kind or another—Canada's capital is a resolutely government town—for whom the Laurier symbolised the city's solid, bureaucratic soul, but others, noting the building's mixed parentage and its jumble of cultural references, for whom the Château represented something more subtle about what it might mean to be Canadian.

The hotel staff were well accustomed to cameras. Every head of state, pop star or Hollywood face who visited Ottawa stayed there, now and it showed in her face, in the way she carried herself, in the absolute conviction of her smile. She wanted justice, certainly, but more than that, you sensed that Martha Flaherty wanted peace. And there was only one way she knew to get it.

Rynee was smaller and quieter than her daughter, and less at ease among the huddle of buildings, the press of people and the hum of lawyers, politicians, lobbyists and hacks. Over the years she had grown used to making herself invisible but over the course of the next two days she knew it was her duty to stand out. She was tired. Her eyes, once such little jewels of jet, were matt, the crescent folds beneath them swollen with the years.

The two women walked past the cameras towards the brass revolving doors of the Laurier. They were directed to a large, soft-carpeted conference room lined with plump, upholstered chairs. A bank of cameras stood beside the back wall. The formality of the situation, its grand setting, intended to reassure both the Inuit and the TV cameras that the case was being taken seriously, served only to reinforce the sense of displacement among Inuit born under canvas and brought up in snowhouses. They lined up awkwardly, like flowers in a municipal planting. Martha took in the scene. She sensed she was in for a long day.

The press gathered on the benches to one side of the witnesses were hoping for a front-page story. There had been talk that some of the Inuit accusations might be sexual in nature, rumours fuelled by the division of the hearings into on- and off-camera sessions, the off-camera session to be held with full legal privilege. Whatever the outcome of the closed sessions, no one would be able to sue. It seemed likely that the testimony would yield plenty of stomach-punching detail and the editors of all the major Canadian papers were ready to give it space. And while it was true that the reporters were all out for headlines, they were also keen to make amends. For forty years they had printed Department and RCMP press releases about the removal of Inuit from Inukjuak more or less verbatim. Over the next couple of days, the men and women of the fourth estate were from Marlene Dietrich to Nelson Mandela, but on that day in April, there were none of the usual red carpets or edgy security detail which usually accompanied the banks of cameras. That morning the TV stations were waiting not for celebrities or politicians, but for thirty-five very ordinary men and women, inhabitants of the two most northerly permanent settlements on the North American continent, the High Arctic exiles. Among those expected were Paddy Aqiatusuk's stepson, Samwillie Elijasialuk, now fifty-seven; Anna Nungaq, who was sixty-six, her stepsister, Minnie Alakariallak, thirteen years Anna's junior; Paddy and Mary Aqiatusuk's son, Larry Audlaluk, now forty-three; Samuel Anukudluk, the Pond Inlet man who taught the Inukjuamiut at Grise Fiord how to build a *qarnaq;* Markoosie Patsauq, whose tuberculosis had remained undiagnosed during the voyage north to Resolute and who was then, at fifty-three, the first published Inuit novelist and an accomplished bush pilot, and his brother John Amagoalik, forty-five, a wiry powerhouse of a man with a reputation for being difficult, and one of the chief negotiators of the treaty to set up what became, in 1999, the new Canadian province of Nunavut.

Rynee Flaherty, sixty-six, and her daughter Martha, now forty-three and herself a mother were expected to arrive together. For Martha the mill of cameras and reporters was neither new nor particularly daunting. For half her life now, it seemed, she had been lobbying, cajoling, campaigning. She had heard her voice on a dozen radio shows, seen her image on TV, been quoted in the press. By 1993, she was not only among the more prominent campaigners for justice for the High Arctic exiles but also President of Pauktuutit, the Canadian National Inuit Women's Association. Getting that far had been a struggle for Martha, a tremendous test of her resolve. Her adult life had not been untroubled. There were allegations of problems with alcohol and of financial irregularities at Pauktuutit. At her own admission, her relationships with men had sometimes been destructive. But a tougher, more fiercely determined woman you could not meet. Martha had been through too much to give up being given the opportunity to bring a sense of objectivity to the story. For the next few days they would have the chance to set the record straight.

Rynee and Martha Flaherty settled themselves among their peers within view of the seven chairs reserved for members of the Royal Commission on Aboriginal Peoples, headed up by the eminent Quebecois judge René Dussault and the human rights campaigner Georges Erasmus.

Only about half of the eighty-seven men, women and children taken from Inukjuak and Pond Inlet and sent to the High Arctic in 1953 and 1955 were still alive to testify. Most of the dead, men like Josephie Flaherty and Paddy Aqiatusuk, had lost their lives early in accidents, through untreated illnesses or by their own hands. Of all the babies born in Resolute Bay between 1953 and 1962, boys and girls who, had they lived, would have been aged between forty and thirty-one, nearly one third were already dead. Many had committed suicide.

The fact that so many of the survivors *had* come was testament to the importance of the occasion. Despite the huge distances, the unfamiliarity of the surroundings and the relative heat, almost all but the very old or infirm among the original exiles had made the journey south to be at the hearings. After forty years of telling their stories only to have them ignored, they were looking forward, at last, to being heard.

The members of the Commission filed into the conference room and settled themselves into their chairs. The cameras clicked on. The assembled journalists readied their microphones and shorthand pads. There was a short introduction. Finally, the Inuit rose to speak.

Simeonie Amagoalik was among the first. At the time of the relocation, he was twenty and newly married, he said, living in Povungnituk, a settlement up along the coast from Inukjuak, with his eighteen-year-old wife, Sarah, who was pregnant. His father had recently died and left him his whaleboat and he was using it to earn some extra money transporting supplies from the *C. D. Howe* to

Povungnituk at ship time. He was back home in Povungnituk when Constable Ross Gibson showed up. Gibson had informed him that his brothers, Jaybeddie and Thomasie Amagoalik, had agreed to go north on condition that he, Simeonie, accompany them. He did not want to go. He was perfectly happy with his boat business and his life in general, but to have said no would have been to deny his relatives, which was something that, as an Inuk, he could not do. Later he discovered that neither Jaybeddie nor Thomasie *had* agreed to go north but by then there was no going back. On board the ship it had been decided, without the agreement of the parties involved, that the three families would be split up, with Simeonie and Jaybeddie going to Resolute Bay and Thomasie going to Grise Fiord. Thomasie Amagoalik was a fragile man, and everybody knew it. Even in Inukjuak he had been someone who needed family round to prop him up. Being separated from his brothers was the worst possible thing that could have happened to him. After the death of his boys, Salluviniq and Allie, on Ellesmere Island, he had crumbled. Eventually, Simeonie had got permission to sledge to Grise Fiord and bring Thomasie and his family back to Resolute, but by then it was really too late. Mary Amagoalik was ill with tuberculosis and Thomasie was a broken man. He died on his way to hospital not long after.

Simeonie's wife, Sarah Amagoalik, was six months pregnant when Ross Gibson came round to the camp. She was only eighteen and about to have her first baby and moving north would mean leaving her mother, Minnie, and her sisters behind but with her husband agreeing to leave, she had no choice in the matter. She gave birth to her son on the *C. D. Howe*. On Cornwallis Island her only adult company while Simeonie was away hunting was Nellie, Simeonie's elderly grandmother who was deaf and would repeat the same question all day, "When are we going home?" The old woman kept a box of small gifts, a bone comb or a plaited bracelet made of ox hair, which she was saving until she got back to Inukjuak, said Sarah, but she died not long after the move and the box of gifts was buried with her. After that and for long weeks at a time, Sarah was left with no one. She had had problems feeding the baby when her milk dried up and her uncle had been forced to raid the air-base rubbish dump for some out-of-date cans of sardines to try to boost her protein intake. Living in Resolute Bay, she had contracted tuberculosis (perhaps from Markoosie Patsauq who remained at Resolute Bay with untreated tuberculosis for so long before help finally arrived that by the end he was unable to stand) and had had to spend three years away from her baby in a sanatorium. It was many years before she was able to contact her parents or her family.

At the age of two, while she was still in Inukjuak Anna Nungaq had contracted polio, which had deprived her of the use of her legs. Her father having died young, she was brought up by her grandparents at her uncle's camp near Inukjuak while her brothers, Samwillie and Elijah, were living with their mother, Mary Aqiatusuk, and her new husband, Paddy Aqiatusuk. Since her grandparents were already elderly and did not know how much longer they would be able to look after her, Anna Nungaq had no choice but to follow her mother to Grise Fiord. Up on Ellesmere Island, she could not leave the tent even in high summer because it was too cold and she could not keep sufficiently mobile to stay warm. She found the dark period terrifying. In her mind she had the idea that she would be able to drift off to sleep and wake up when the sun returned and when it did not she felt she had fallen into some black hole from which there was no escape. The loneliness was as terrible as the cold and dark. Eventually she had married Pauloosie, Phillipoosie Novalinga's son, and for a while she was happier, but Pauloosie was killed in a hunting accident and she was left widowed and with no prospect of remarrying. By the time she did get back to Inukjuak, her beloved grandparents were long since dead. She recalled the last time she had seen her grandfather, all of forty years before. He had taken off in his *kayak* to follow the *C. D. Howe*. He was waving and shouting that he would miss her. Then he slowly slipped out of view.

The testimony continued. Parents told of the deaths of children. In 1956, four children were born in Resolute Bay, of whom one died. In 1959, five children were born there. Two died. Twenty-three per cent of all Inuit children in the High Arctic died before they reached the age of one. In southern Canada at that time, the rate was 3 per cent. One of the reasons for this would come out in later testimony, when Ross Gibson would recall helping to deliver Edith Patsauq's breech baby. He had no medical qualifications. For years, Arctic policemen had been expected to function as amateur medics and there had been a consensus on the part of the police and government officials to keep quiet about the resulting deaths. In his report after the Eastern Arctic Patrol in 1955, the same voyage that had brought Josephie Flaherty and his family up to Grise Fiord, the chief medical officer on the patrol, Dr. John Willis, had written of two Inuit children he had been asked to inspect: "[they] are in such a state that they could be made into newspaper dynamite. We must pray that our friend at the *Vancouver Sun* doesn't hear about them or cannot get to them with a camera." But there was little chance of that. The *Vancouver Sun*, along with most of the rest of Canada's newspapers, was busy producing reports taken more or less verbatim from RCMP and Department press releases. Children continued to die, and the deaths went largely unreported.

Jaybeddie Amagoalik of Pond Inlet had lost his two-year-old daughter, Merrari, not long after the family's arrival at Resolute Bay. Unrelated to the Inukjuak Amagoaliks, Jaybeddie and his family had been brought up to Resolute Bay from Pond Inlet, supposedly to help the Inukjuak migrants settle. In the spring of 1954, only six months after their arrival in the High Arctic, Jaybeddie had been given the job of driving a dog team for two white men, a geologist and a naturalist, who wanted to be taken to Mould Bay to the north of Cornwallis. Jaybeddie had not wanted to take the job, he said, because it meant having to bring his family along, and he did not want to expose them to the kind of danger a long trip in hazardous conditions across unfamiliar terrain would inevitably bring. Still, he felt unable to say no to Constable Gibson, so he set off with his wife, Kanoinoo, son, Ekaksak, and daughter, Merrari and the two white men. The moment they reached Mould Bay, two-year-old Merrari fell seriously ill. After several days during which Merrari's condition deteriorated, a plane was scrambled from Resolute Bay—an airstrip had been built at Mould a few years before—but the aircraft got caught in thick fog and was unable to land. A doctor had been summoned on the radio to offer advice but, after her parents' frantic efforts to save the girl, she died and her parents were forced to bury their daughter under rocks, knowing there would be no prospect of visiting her grave in future. After that, Jaybeddie and Kanoinoo desperately wanted to get back to Resolute Bay in case their son Ekaksak fell ill too, but the scientists insisted on staying to complete their work, so the family were forced to remain at Mould Bay for another three months. Soon after they returned to Resolute Bay though, Kanoinoo fell ill and was sent south for treatment, leaving Ekaksak in the care of Jaybeddie. Having no family at Resolute Bay, Jaybeddie had to care for the boy himself, which made it impossible to go hunting. During those long months, he kept himself, his boy and his dogs alive by setting seal nets under the ice, but they were all hungry most of the time. Every so often, the two scientists would come along and borrow his dogs to go out on the land prospecting for oil and minerals, but they never thought to pay him.

During the course of the morning, witness after witness testified before the Commission that they had been trapped in the High Arctic with no way of getting home. Once the true conditions in Resolute Bay and Grise Fiord had become clear, they had begged to return to Inukjuak. Their verbal requests were brushed off. Those who could wrote letters to relatives and to the Department, even to the RCMP, but most were unable even to do this much. In the 1950s only 8 per cent of Canadian Inuit were literate. (At the same time, the literacy rate of Inuit living in Danish-controlled Greenland was almost 100 per cent.) The letters were moderate, in retrospect too moderate, but it was part of the Inuit tradition to underplay misfortune. Officials, perhaps unconsciously, took advantage of this natural restraint because it provided the perfect excuse for Inuit views and wishes to be disregarded. The Inuit looked for other outlets, but they were kept from talking to their relatives by radio and, although they were full Canadian citizens and had the legal right to vote, they had no representative in parliament because there was no constituency in the eastern Arctic. Most of their letters were not taken seriously and went unanswered. Others never made it to their intended targets; pieces of them turned up in the police rubbish dumps. Pretty soon, they had exhausted all the options and there was no one left to turn to. There was no escape. They were living in an accidental gulag.

It was in this wide, icy prison that Martha Flaherty had passed her childhood. Standing to give evidence she recalled the journey north with horror; the shrieking of the *C. D. Howe* as it ground against ice, the pitching of the fore section in stormy swells, the fierce, malevolent mountains and spiny foreshore of Ellesmere Island. But what really stood out in her mind was the grim discovery, made at such a tender age, that her parents were powerless to protect her. It began on the boat, when Dr. Willis had tried to cut off her hair and it had been powerfully reinforced when Mary had been taken from them. She felt exposed and vulnerable, her mind full of the dread possibility, which never entirely left her, that she might be next to disappear.

The family's years at Ellesmere Island had been a long descent into darkness. Martha recalled rising to a breakfast of lukewarm water and heading out with her father across the endless miles of unoccupied ice, looking for polar bear and fox and seal, anything that might fill the pot, overwhelmed by the knowledge that her father was as helpless as she was herself. Over those hard, terrible years on Ellesmere Island, Martha had come to look on her father as her burden. It sometimes seemed that she would never be free of him. During his final illness, when he knew he was dying, he had asked to see her but she had refused to come, telling him only that she would be better off when he was dead. Now, of course, she regretted that. After Josephie's death, the family had been flung in all directions, like drops of water from a blowhole. It had taken them many years to come together again.

This estrangement was replicated in families all across the High Arctic. Martha was witness to some of it. Twice a year she would pass through Resolute Bay on her way to and from school in Churchill. There was usually a bit of time to wait before the onward journey to Grise Fiord and it was during that time that Martha Flaherty witnessed the almost complete collapse of the Resolute Bay settlement. The prospects of living a traditional life in Resolute Bay, which is what the Inuit had been brought there to do, were dismal. Fighter jets and spy planes screamed overhead, scattering what little game there was and making hunting there more or less impossible. By the late fifties, just after Ross Gibson left to return to Inukjuak, most of the men were already working day rate at the air base as janitors and porters, just as Henry Larsen had dreaded and predicted.

During July and August and part of September, when activity at the base was at its height, a fleet of jeeps would arrive at the Inuit camp at six every morning to pick up the Inuit men and take them to the base. They would work a twelve-hour day cleaning the mess rooms and the barracks, sweeping out the stores, setting traps to catch the foxes which frequented the dump, mending the bear-proof fences, hauling coal and equipment and keeping things painted and greased. In return, they would receive the equivalent of a third of the average white man's pay. This they were free to spend at the base's Arctic Circle bar. And spend it they did.

By the mid-sixties, when Martha was passing through Resolute, unscrupulous airmen had set up gaming books and were regularly persuading drunk Inuit to lay down their day's pay on hockey games in Ottawa and Edmonton, the outcome of which the airmen already knew. Others had joined in, with card scams and dice cons. Inuit women began to appear at the Arctic Circle bar to reclaim their men, and soon enough, they also began to drink. The airmen quickly discovered these women could be bought for booze, cash or promises and the women were often too drunk to say no, or did not know how to say no to white men. When the first group of women had been used up, there were plenty more, and younger, down in the camp. And so it went on. A great many half-breed babies were born during that time, a good number of them with the tiny, shrivelled bodies indicative of foetal alcohol syndrome.

Fights broke out between jealous men and their wives, between husbands and between older and younger women. Inuit stumbled out of their huts into freezing nights high on rage and booze and too drunk to be able to feel frostbite setting in. There were a lot of amputations in those years.

By the mid-sixties almost every Inuit family in Resolute Bay had been affected by alcoholism. Things got so bad at the Inuit settlement that in some homes there was nothing to eat for days except the chewing gum the airmen handed out to the children to keep them quiet while they had sex with their mothers. A whole generation of Inuit children were left to bring up themselves while their fathers and mothers descended into squalor and depression. In the absence of any help, the children dealt with all this in the only way they knew how. Some learned to dissemble and lie, others sunk into states of apathy and denial. In the nine years from 1953 to 1962, fifty Inuit girls and boys were born in Resolute Bay. Thirty years later, nearly a third of them were already dead. Remembering it all brought Martha to tears. It gave her no comfort at all to know that, when it came to raw despair during those years, Resolute Bay had probably had the edge on Grise Fiord.

The testimony continued, and when the Commission broke for lunch, many of those who had heard the morning's witness simply sat in their seats, no longer able to trust their legs to carry them anywhere, while men and women of the press raced back to their downtown offices to file their copy. The off-camera session which followed did nothing to lift the mood. The accusations were widespread and devastating. Airmen were accused of assault, teachers of paedophilia. Ross Gibson, it was said, had sexually exploited women at the Resolute Bay camp and threatened them when they protested. There were allegations that Bob Pilot had paid for sex with, among others, Rynee Flaherty, with promises of extra food. While Pilot admitted to having consensual sex with Inuit women, he laughed off the allegation that he paid for the sex.

A subdued crowd left the Château Laurier that evening. At home in the smarter Ottawa suburbs, those officials who had been directly involved in the relocation sat watching the on-camera proceedings on television. Of the principal actors, only Ben Sivertz of the Department, Gordon Robertson, the former Commissioner of the Northwest Territories, Rueben Ploughman, the old Hudson Bay factor and the former Mounties Clay Fryer, Bob Pilot and Ross Gibson, were still alive. They were floored by what they heard. These men had always seen themselves as friends of the Inuit, and it seemed to them now that their former friends were turning on them. It was bad enough that, forty years on, their decisions were suddenly being brought into question, but it now looked as if their reputations as men of honour were under review too. Few slept soundly that night.

Everyone woke the following morning to a series of shrill newspaper headlines. The *Ottawa Citizen* printed a quotation from the co-chair of the Commission, René Dussault, calling the High Arctic relocation "one of the worst human rights violations in the history of Canada." The paper went on to quote Dussault's colleague, Bertha Wilson, telling the exiles that no one could "fail to be outraged by the injustice [or] not be grieved by the pain and suffering that you and your relatives have been exposed to" and that there could have been no justification for the "cruel and inhumane" government policy of moving them. The officials and bureaucrats involved in the relocation got the brunt of it. Sivertz, Gibson, Larsen and Cantley were all mentioned, in scathing terms. Comparisons were made to the notorious internment of Canadian Japanese during the Second World War. "What had it all been for?" the *Ottawa Citizen* quoted Bertha Wilson as asking. "This is the question only the government can answer."

Over the weeks that followed, gossip spread and rumour countered rumour about what exactly had been said in the off-camera session. Snippets of information began to leak out from informants and others claiming to be in the know. They did not make the headlines, but Ottawa is a small town and people talk. Of all the officials accused of sexual misconduct, ex-constable Ross Gibson was the most vulnerable to attack. After years of exposure to the pitiless Arctic sun, the freezing wind and constant brushes with frostbite, the man who had set so much store on being a credit to the force had developed melanoma and the cancer had spread to the rest of his body. He knew he did not have long to live, and he was desperate to die with his reputation intact. By the time of the hearings, he was in a good deal of physical pain but this was nothing compared with the psychological anguish visited upon him by the rumours. But by denying them, Ross Gibson knew he would only be serving to stoke press interest in the case. His one option was to wait out the months until the end of June, when the Commission would take testimony from the officials involved in the case. He had to hope that his sense of outrage would keep him alive till then.

The weather in downtown Ottawa on Monday, 28 June 1993, was hot and muggy. Outside the Citadel Hotel, a bland block in the commercial district, a group of officials gathered for the second sitting of the Royal Commission. There were no camera crews waiting for the parade of white-haired old white men, nor had many print reporters gathered. The location was drab and the lack of press interest indicative, so many of the officials said, of a conspiracy to discredit them. Bitterness, recrimination and paranoia were in the air.

The first to take the stand for the officials was Gordon Robertson. In the 1950s, Robertson had been Commissioner of the North-west Territories, of which eastern Arctic Canada was then a part, and had gone on to become the Clerk of the Privy Council in the national parliament. He had a reputation as a man of fierce intellect and moderate expression, but today he felt no compunction to moderate his language. The Royal Commission hearings, he said, were a "travesty of justice" which had "wantonly destroyed" the reputations of the civil servants involved. It was an inauspicious start.

Gordon Larsen, Henry Larsen's son, appeared dazed by the turn-around in his father's posthumous fortunes. Henry had died a hero but after the Inuit testimony in April he was looking more like a fool. Larsen spoke for a long time of his father's affection for the Inuit people, an affection so deep that Larsen had frequently kept his wife short of her housekeeping allowance while he bought bolts of cloth to give to the Inuit to make their clothes. Henry knew how difficult Inuit lives had become by the middle of the twentieth century and was conscious of the degree to which that had resulted from their contact with whites. Only a year after he had taken office as the superintendent in charge of the Arctic Division of the RCMP, he had advocated a Royal Commission on Inuit affairs, but his request had been turned down. After the decision had been taken to move the Inuit from Inukjuak, Larsen thought it best to send them somewhere where they would be able to live their lives away from *qalunaat* influence and at the same time benefit Canada. It was the Department *officials* who were guilty of rushed decisions and poor planning, Gordon Larsen hinted, but an unfair portion of the blame had landed at Henry Larsen's door. He had seen this coming, in the Department's subtle manoeuvres to shift the blame to the RCMP, and it had hurt him deeply. Shortly before he died in 1964, Larsen had said, "I shudder to think of the criticism which will be levelled at us in another fifty years' time." It appeared that time had now come.

Ross Gibson testified by phone from his hospital bed in British Columbia. The ex-Mountie was not the same defiant, bullish man who had read the reports of the April hearings in the newspaper. This bitter finale to his last months had left him too crushed to be angry. His voice sounded shaky with sickness or misery or a combination of the two. He was not a bad man, nor a dishonest one, but from the start he had betrayed his ignorance of the people whose lives he had for so long and so dictatorially managed. "From my world travels," he began, "I found the native people always gave me the impression of being happy regardless of the circumstances under which they were living. The Eskimo always greeted you with warm handshakes and a smile. I never had so many handshakes. It's like . . . it's like royalty." Gibson relived the dismal forays he'd made to the camps in rotting snow in his attempts to persuade the Inuit to move north, without comprehending that his descriptions might condemn him. "I just sold them a bill of goods," he said. "I was a salesman or a real estate man whatever you want to call it, and it was my responsibility to get across to these people the advantages." He admitted that the planning for the move had seemed deficient even at the time. "I always suspected a pipeline to the Department of Northern Affairs of which I knew nothing. They never told me what was what or what was going on. I was a low man on the totem pole. Commissioner Nicholson said, 'You must make this a success,'" Gibson continued. "'You must keep these people out on the land. This is what they are. This is what we want.'" In Gibson's mind, clouded by time and illness, he and the Inuit had been fellow travellers who had quite literally found themselves in the same boat. The control he had exercised over the lives of the Inuit in Resolute Bay seemed to suggest to him no contradiction. "They didn't know what I was really up to and I wanted to keep it that way. I had things under control." The Inuit had never been abandoned, he said, because "I was always present. The white man would be there to help them to better their way of life." He had never doubted that as one of those white men, he, Ross Gibson, knew best, and he did not doubt it now. "I never felt . . . in my culture, my upbringing, could never bring myself to their level—and I don't like to use that word level, but it is the only way I can explain it," he said. He was proud of his achievements. "[Henry Larsen] patted me on the back and he said, 'Commissioner Nicholson and I think we picked the right man' . . . I will never forget that." Looking back, he realised that it was he, Ross Gibson, who had truly been left alone. Throughout the previous few months, during the terrible accusations against him, and through his final illness, the Royal Canadian Mounted Police, to which he had given the best years of his life, had turned its back on him.

Of all the testimony given on that day, Ben Sivertz's made what few headlines appeared the following morning. A civil servant of Icelandic extraction, Sivertz had been working at the Department during the 1950s. The intervening years had hung heavy on him. He now walked on sticks and his face was in parts both bloated and hollow. Back at the beginning of the fifties, Sivertz had discussed the relocations with James Cantley, Alex Stevenson and Henry Larsen, and it was he who had suggested that his superior, the deputy minister of the Department, General Young, meet to discuss the idea with Commissioner Nicholson of the RCMP. Like Cantley and Larsen, Sivertz was an incomer into Canada and it had shocked him a little to see how few southern Canadians were living or working in the Arctic or knew much about it. The Barrenlands appeared to be overrun with Americans. In Sivertz's view, it made perfect sense to ship Inuit up to the High Arctic since they were the only Canadians likely to be able to survive there. At the time he had every faith in the programme, and he defended it now. Well into the 1960s, when Resolute Bay was being ravaged by alcohol and children were dying at Grise Fiord for lack of medicines, Ben Sivertz was planning new colonies, as he called them, at Mould Bay, Isachsen, Eureka and Alert, and he regretted that those colonies had never come into being. He dismissed out of hand the notion that any Inuk had suffered any misfortune as a result of being moved. On the contrary, he said, the Inuit believed they were a superior race and that *qalunaat* were an "astonishingly ignorant people." When Commissioner Mary Sillett pressed him on the point, he insisted, "There was no hardship, madam, in 1953, 1954, 1955, 1956, 1957, 1958. There was only great satisfaction by all Inuit people at Resolute Bay and Grise Fiord." It was a comment Ben Sivertz would live to regret.

The following morning every newspaper carried the headline, "There was no hardship." More than anything else said or done, this one remark swung public opinion resolutely to the side of the Inuit. It made the officials sound like a bunch of bitter old men clinging desperately to the past. Over the next few weeks, the unthinkable happened, and the bureaucrats, all men accustomed to the quiet regard of their peers, found themselves rising in the mornings to hate mail and death threats. In Ben Sivertz's outburst a generation of civil servants, most of them fiercely bright, committed and well-intentioned men, had been discredited. Few ever regained their pre-hearing reputations. Some, among them Ross Gibson, went to their deaths in disgrace. The hearings shook Canada's bureaucracy to its foundations. They put into question, perhaps for the first time in Canada's history, the idea that, when it came to government ordinary Canadians were prepared to believe that good intentions necessarily produced good effects. A powerful principle had been evoked. The hearings capitalised the idea that in the free world, people had an absolute right to determine their own futures. This was democracy. Anything else, however well meaning, was despotism.

If this seems obvious now, in 1993 it was quite fresh and timely. In 1993, negotiations on the establishment of the Inuit territory of Nunavut were just entering their final phase. The Nunavut Land Claims Agreement, which was signed in May, a month after the Inuit hearings, gave the Inuit title to 137,355 square miles of territory, an area nearly as large as the state of California, along with a share of federal government royalties from oil and mineral development on federal lands and the right to harvest and manage wildlife in the territory. The Agreement put the future of the Inuit people in their own hands for the first time since the Vikings had arrived in the Arctic a thousand years ago. It also made Inuit the largest private landowners in North America. One of the chief negotiators for the Inuit, and the man they now call the Father of Nunavut, was John Amagoalik, who had been taken as a child with his family from Inukjuak and brought to live in Resolute Bay.

The April hearings were nothing short of the rebirth of a people. At the time of the relocations, forty years before, the Inuit had been broken and demoralised. Inuit voices had been voices in the wilderness, they went unheard, often they went unsaid. Years of quiet and sometimes unintentional but nonetheless ruthless disregard had colonised their hearts, and had made them, on the surface at least, the smiling inscrutable happy-go-lucky Eskimos of Robert Flaherty's *Nanook of the North*. After hundreds of years of patronage and domination, they had finally shrugged off that legacy. It had taken forty years, but the dignified, insistent voices of the Barrenlanders had won through. At last their truth had been accepted as a matter of public record, and no credible history book would ever dare deny it. Those thirty-five men and women who turned up at the Château Laurier, and the others who had, over their long exile, stood up and spoken out, had put the Arctic on the map in a way hundreds of years of European exploration had never been able to do. They had given the Arctic back its authentic voice, which was not the voice of the great white explorers or the drama of expeditions and heroism and derring-do, but the quiet, still voice of the men and women whose antecedents had meandered across the Arctic from Asia and who had loved it enough to make it their home. The history of the Arctic had been given back to the people it belonged to. In the most profound sense, the people of the Arctic had, finally, come home.

The Royal Commission helped change Lower Canada's perspective on its upper reaches. Many southern Canadians now embraced the idea that the Barrenlands were just that, lands, as diverse and various as those to the south. They came to understand that the world which lay beyond the 60th parallel was not the great white wasteland of movies and explorers' tales, but rather a series of distinct and dynamic regions which were highly interdependent and also vulnerable. It was an insight that served only to make the Arctic seem more extraordinary, more worth protecting.

For the Flahertys, the Royal Commission signalled the end to a long, exhausting exile. In one sense it was a banishment which had begun a century and a half before when Robert Flaherty's ancestors had left Ireland. It was a journey that had taken them to the northern-most reaches of the world. Who could have predicted that its final phase, that terrible voyage to Ellesmere Island, would, in its turn, have led to quite another, greater kind of journey.

Martha Flaherty saw her mother off on the flight back to Grise Fiord and returned to her own home outside Ottawa. Maggie Nujarluktuk and Robert Flaherty's granddaughter is there now, smiling her grandmother's smile.

EPILOGUE

In July 1994, over a year after the first Inuit depositions, The Royal Commission on Aboriginal Peoples reported its findings.

The relocation was not aimed at relieving population pressure on limited game resources. There was no population growth in the Inukjuak area in the early 1950s and the game situation had not changed in thirty to forty years. The concern was with the ability of the fur trade to sustain the income levels to which Inukjuak Inuit had become accustomed . . . Greater reliance on hunting would substitute for the income that fur trading would, in the long term, be unable to provide.

Everywhere in the Arctic, hunting was cyclical in nature, even in areas of relative abundance. The relocation would not alter these cycles and would not alter the hardship experienced by people who lived by hunting during adverse game cycles or weather conditions. It was recognized in the Department that the cyclical nature of hunting could and did lead to periodic famine and starvation. This was considered to be the natural state for the Inuit. The goal of the relocation was to restore the Inuit to what was considered to be their proper state.

The Department proceeded with the High Arctic relocation without proper authority. The relocation was not voluntary. It proceeded without free and informed consent. There were material representations, and material information was not dis-closed. The true nature of the relocation . . . and the inherent risks were not disclosed. Nor can it be said, given the cultural factors affecting the giving of consent, that consent was given freely. Moreover, many Inuit were kept in the High Arctic for many years against their will when the government refused to respond to their requests to return.

The relocation was an ill-conceived solution that was inhu-man in its design and its effects. The conception, planning, exe-cution and continuing supervision of the relocation did not accord with Canada's then prevailing international human rights commitments.

Great wrongs have been done to the relocatees, and it is incumbent on the government to accept the fundamental merit of the relocatees' complaints. This acceptance is the only basis upon which reconciliation between the Inuit and the govern-ment is possible.

The Canadian government did accept the findings and in 1995 it set up a Heritage Fund of ten million Canadian dollars to provide housing, travel, pensions and compensation for the sixteen families who were relocated to the High Arctic in 1953 and 1955 and their descendants. In spite of many calls on the government from politi-cians, statesmen, human rights groups and from the Inuit them-selves to apologise for the High Arctic relocations, the government of Canada has never done so.

On 1 April 1999, the territory of Nunavut came into being, with its own parliament and legislative process. Nunavut comprises one-fifth of Canada's land mass and is eight times the size of the UK. Its population of 27,000, 95 per cent of whom are Inuit, would fill barely half the seats in a modern baseball or soccer stadium. Nunavut remains the only self-governing state in the world to be established for the benefit of indigenous people.

Many Arctic watchers now believe that global warming will for the first time open up the Northwest Passage to commercial shipping. The U.S.A. indicated that it regards the passage as existing in international, not Canadian, waters. Russia, Norway and Denmark all have competing claims to the natural resources that may lie beneath the High Arctic seabed. In August 2005, the Canadian government announced that it was sending its navy back to Churchill following a disagreement between Canada and Denmark over Hans Island in the eastern Arctic archipelago. It seems the issue of sovereignty remains unresolved.

The communities of Resolute Bay and Grise Fiord still exist. Resolute Bay is a tiny but bustling settlement, which makes some of its income from guiding and kitting out sport hunters, some from traditional hunting and trapping and an increasing amount from hosting polar expeditions, which most often begin from there. The devastation wrought by drink is by and large a memory, though the place still feels both fragile and somewhat anarchic. Grise Fiord remains cut off, though it is now serviced by a Twin Otter twice a week. The settlement escaped many of the privations found throughout the Arctic settlements caused by disillusionment, unemployment, social fragmentation and alcoholism and is now seen as one of the more successful hamlets in the Canadian Arctic. When I was there, it seemed a charming if eccentric place, at once part of the world and very much cut off from it. Television had arrived only three years before, and a generation was growing up with the usual fare of cop shows and soaps, but without ever themselves having seen a motorway or a skyscraper or a branch of McDonald's. In the school, posters showed pupils how to spell common words. One of these, I noticed, was "baleen."

After the Royal Commission hearings, Rynee Flaherty returned to Grise Fiord while Martha Flaherty stayed in the Ottawa area. The remaining Inuit members of the Flaherty family divided themselves between Grise Fiord and Iqaluit, where Rynee eventually moved to be with her daughter Mary. Martha Flaherty continued her work as President of Pauktuutit, the Canadian National Inuit Women's

Association. She moved on from there to the Aboriginal Healing Foundation. She has been a member of the Canadian Panel on Violence Against Women and the Panel on Economic Development for Canadian Aboriginal Women. She is listed in the *Who's Who of Canadian Women* and is now a prominent lobbyist and broadcaster on Inuit issues.

The two sides of the Flaherty family, white and Inuit, are reconciled and on good terms. Robert Flaherty's papers are archived at Columbia University in New York and the Flaherty Foundation, which is also based in the city, is active in promoting and training promising documentary film-makers. In the UK, Robert Flaherty has lent his name to the British Academy of Film and Television's most prestigious annual documentary award. In polls from the U.S.A. to Russia, *Nanook of the North* is consistently voted the greatest documentary of all time.

"In the end," Robert Flaherty said, "it is all just a question of human relationships."

SELECTED BIBLIOGRAPHY

Brody, Hugh. *Living Arctic: Hunters of the Canadian North.* London: Faber, 1987.

———. *The Other Side of Eden: Hunter-Gatherers, Farmers, and the Shaping of the World.* London: Faber, 2001.

———. *Maps and Dreams.* London: Faber, 2002.

Dick, Lyle. *Muskox Land: Ellesmere Island in the Age of Contact.* Calgary: University of Calgary Press, 2001.

Fossett, Renée. *In Order to Live Untroubled: Inuit of the Central Arctic 1550 to 1940.* Winnipeg: University of Manitoba Press, 2001.

Lopez, Barry. *Arctic Dreams: Imagination and Desire in a Northern Landscape.* London: Harvill, 1999.

McNaught, Kenneth. *The Penguin History of Canada.* London: Penguin, 1998.

Marcus, Alan R. *Relocating Eden: The Image and Politics of Inuit Exile in the Canadian Arctic.* Hanover: University Press of New England, 1995.

Mowat, Farley. *People of the Deer: The Vanishing Eskimo—A Valiant People's Fight for Survival.* London: Michael Joseph, 1952.

Newman, Peter. *Empire of the Bay: The Company of Adventurers That Seized a Continent.* London: Penguin, 1998.

Petrone, Penny, ed. *Northern Voices: Inuit Writing in English.* Toronto: University of Toronto Press, 1988.

Pielou, E. C. *A Naturalist's Guide to the Arctic.* Chicago: University of Chicago Press, 1994.

Royal Commission on Aboriginal Peoples. *The High Arctic Relocation: A*

Report on the 1953–1955 Relocation. Ottawa: Canada Communication Group Publishing, 1994.

Spufford, Francis. *I May Be Some Time: Ice and the English Imagination.* London: Faber, 1997.

Tester, Frank James and Kulchyski, Peter. *Tammarniit (Mistakes): Inuit Relocation in the Eastern Arctic 1939–1963.* Vancouver: University of British Columbia Press, 1994.

Wilkinson, Douglas. *Arctic Fever: The Search for the Northwest Passage.* Toronto: Clarke, Irwin, 1971.

ACKNOWLEDGEMENTS

In writing this book I have relied on the work of many people, though any mistakes are entirely my own. I am grateful in particular to Pita Aatami and Lisa Koperqualuk of the Makivik Corporation, Dr. Frances Abele, to my hosts in Grise Fiord, Ken Powder and their family, John Ashton who first steered me in the direction of Arctic exiles, Jack Aubrey of the *Ottawa Citizen*, Mary Audlaluk, Dr. Bernard Crystal at the Rare Books Library at Columbia University, Margarita De la Vega-Hurtado at International Film Seminars, Rachel Engmann, Professor Shelagh Grant, Jack Hicks my host in Iqaluit, Saomik Inukpuk who hosted me in Inukjuak, Tom Kiguktok, Alan Marcus who generously provided some useful contacts, Gilly Mathieson, Bob Pilot, Christopher Potter, Elizabeth Roberts, Diana and the late Graham Rowley, Dr. Rigo Sampson, Shirley Sawtell at the Scott Polar Institute at Cambridge University, Mary Simon, Thea Udd, Johnny and Elizapee Williams. The staff of the National Library and Archives of Canada were unfailingly helpful. The pupils of Grise Fiord school taught me a thing or two. Kenn Borek Air and South Camp Inn offered me invaluable assistance in Resolute.

Thank you to Nicholas Pearson, Sonny Mehta and Ed Kastenmeier, Jack Fogg, Jessica Axe and to the staff at Fourth Estate and Knopf for believing in the project and to David Godwin for supporting me through the long process of writing it. Carol Anderson meticulously copy-edited my inconsistencies and went beyond the call. As ever, Dr. Tai Bridgeman provided unfailing support and invaluable advice.

Finally, I am indebted to the High Arctic exiles of Grise Fiord, Resolute Bay and Inukjuak, especially to Madeleine Alakariallak, John Amagoalik, Larry Audlaluk and Martha Flaherty, Gailey and Geela Iqaluk, Anna Nungaq, Markoosie Patsauq, who submitted themselves to long interviews on what was for most a painful subject. Thank you.

A NOTE ABOUT THE AUTHOR

Melanie McGrath's first book, *Motel Nirvana,* won the John Llewellyn Rhys Prize. Her third book, *Silvertown,* was shortlisted for the James Tait Black Memorial Prize for Biography. She is a regular contributor to *The Guardian, The Times, The Telegraph,* and the *Evening Standard* and has produced and presented shows for the Discovery Channel and Great Britain's Channel 4. She lives and works in London.

A NOTE ON THE TYPE

This book was set in Minion, a typeface produced by the Adobe
Corporation specifically for the Macintosh personal computer,
and released in 1990. Designed by Robert Slimbach, Minion
combines the classic characteristics of old style faces with the
full compliment of weights required for modern typesetting.

Composed by Creative Graphics, Allentown, Pennsylvania

Printed and bound by R. R. Donnelly,

Harrisonburg, Virginia

Book design by Robert C. Olsson